BECOMING AN AUTHOR

BECOMING AN AUTHOR

Advice for academics and other professionals

David Canter and
Gavin Fairbairn

OPEN UNIVERSITY PRESS

Open University Press
McGraw-Hill Education
McGraw-Hill House
Shoppenhangers Road
Maidenhead
Berkshire
England
SL6 2QL

email: enquiries@openup.co.uk
world wide web: www.openup.co.uk

and Two Penn Plaza, New York, NY 10121-2289, USA

First published 2006

A catalogue record of this book is available from the British Library.

ISBN-10: 0335 20275 6 (pb) 0335 20276 4 (hb)
ISBN-13: 978 0335 20275 1 (pb) 978 0335 20276 8 (hb)

Library of Congress Cataloging-in-Publication Data
CIP data applied for

Typeset by RefineCatch Ltd, Bungay, Suffolk
Printed in Poland by OZ Graf. S.A.
www.polskabook.pl

Contents

Preface

As friends for many years, who met each other at various family and social gatherings, we have often compared notes on the parallels between our rather different academic experiences. Gavin is a jobbing philosopher, whose published output spans applied ethics, higher education, special education, nursing and social care. After a career in special education and social work he taught in teacher education for many years, and has also made significant contributions to education and professional development in both nursing and social care. These activities contrast with the data collection and statistical analysis around which much of David's teaching and research have evolved, and the more popular writing he has done for newspapers and general audiences, including his award-winning book *Criminal Shadows*. Furthermore, his professional career has focused on supervising postgraduate students in psychology, architecture and, more recently, criminology, working in an environment in which publication is expected to be commonplace.

Between us we have worked with the full gamut of people starting out on academic and professional lives in which publishing might, and often would, play a part. Some of them, it has to be admitted, have been on the cusp of illiteracy when they first sought to become authors. Others have been more fluent than was necessarily good for them – pouring out their thoughts in uncontrolled torrents, with never a sideward glance at those who might consider reading what they wrote, or perhaps more importantly, at those who might consider publishing it. Some have had a clear mission from the start and knew what they wanted to contribute, though not necessarily how; even more common have been people with a desire to break into print but little confidence that they could do it.

In conversation about our students and junior colleagues and the increasing pressures for them to become authors, we found that even across the very different contexts in which we operated there were remarkable similarities in our experiences of the struggles many people have to go through in order to publish. For example, we both know of the personal pain suffered by many people who aspire to become academic authors, which often arises not only from the lack of timetabled opportunities for writing, but also from the lack of detailed training or even any real guidance to help them acquire the appropriate skills and attitudes. These factors often combine with self-doubt of a kind that makes a surprising number of young academics think they have neither the authority nor the knowledge to write anything worth publishing (even when it is clear that they have). But most of all, in our conversations over many years, we found that we could both think of lots of excellent work we had come across, including coursework, dissertations, seminar presentations and even conference papers, that just never got published.

For a small number of people in academic and professional life, writing for publication comes very naturally, apparently without effort, just like a tight-rope-walker who looks as if she was born on the high wire. The vast majority, however, need help to get started and are surprised when they are shown that, with perseverance and a steady will, they can succeed. They may never become virtuosos, but we have found over and over again that even those who are most scared about whether they have what it takes, can achieve admirable, competent results that make a real contribution to knowledge, if only they are shown how, and given some encouragement and support.

During our discussions about working with inexperienced authors – both students and colleagues – we began to share approaches we had each developed to help others to improve their writing skills and to develop their knowledge of and attitudes towards academic publishing. It emerged that we both firmly believed that the necessary skills could be taught and, what was more, we found that the teaching packages we had created, and the associated notes we had prepared, overlapped to a remarkable degree. We became aware that there seemed to be common principles that were relevant to all academics who want to become authors. Not only that, but we found ourselves agreeing that there were approaches and procedures that could get most people beyond the blank page and into print. Even where we had differences of opinion we could see the value in articulating them so that others could make their own decisions informed by a variety of views. Out of our excitement at discovering that we agreed on common principles and had independently discovered complementary procedures for getting aspiring authors to put those principles into practice, the present book was born.

Gavin had already published a successful study guide with Open University Press and was planning another, so they were the natural choice for this book. The pressures of continuing to publish in various academic genres ourselves (and, for David, of making a television documentary series) somewhat slowed down the production of this book, so that it has been rather more years in the making than either we or, we suspect, our publisher would care to admit. However, we hope it has benefited from the long, slow cooking by which it has been prepared; certainly it could not have been more timely as the pressure and possibilities for publishing have never been greater for academics and other professionals than they are today.

As with all writing, this book has been a journey of discovery, but possibly more so for a philosopher and an empirical scientist who found so many areas of agreement that we began to think that if these tenets were not established truths, then they at least had the feel of well-established facts. Central to these discoveries is our shared recognition that all writing is fundamentally a form of storytelling. This idea has tended to be ignored in academic writing but it is very helpful in thinking about even the most arcane disquisition. There is always a narrative, whether it is shaped by the search to make sense of complex issues or by the need to find evidence for or against particular hypotheses. Academic stories are always enacted or retold in relation to particular settings, which may, for example, be the context in which a discourse unfolds, or the apparatus used for an experiment. Episodes exist in the story too: the laying out of the quest – the questions that instigate the work to be discussed – the search for enlightenment or resolution, and the dénouement when all the strands come together to make sense. And, of course, there are central characters, often ideas or concepts that change and develop through their interactions with each other, and the setting. This perspective on academic writing is a central thesis, or sub-plot, to the book we have written, which we develop as our own narrative unfolds.

Another central focus in the ways we think about academic writing and publishing relates to our awareness that any piece of writing has a life cycle. It does not come fully mature into the world, but usually emerges in a stumbling, often confused, and invariably undeveloped, state. Through contact with its author as she drafts and redrafts, and its first steps out into the world, as it is shared with others whose comments the author invites, the embryonic text develops, through a number of stages, towards maturity. Some texts will change radically when, having reached adolescence, they first try to exist independently from their author, and are subjected to the critical comments of editors and reviewers. This can be a difficult time for authors, who may feel duty bound to protect their literary offspring from the ravages of the editorial and review process (sometimes, it has to be said, they are right to do so). However, it is through this developmental process that new text, whether for a book or for an article, eventually comes to have its own independent existence, in a published form. The author's task is to help it on its way, not to assume that it will have all the properties it needs to survive from the moment of conception.

A third important focus in our views of academic writing is our belief in the power of structure. We believe quite firmly that the way to develop good writing skills is to work from the general to the particular, being aware of where the written material fits into the general picture. Many noviciate authors make the mistake of focusing on getting the words and the sentences correct (or even the typeface and font size) rather than developing a clear picture of what the overall shape of the work is, whether it is a book, a chapter, a journal article or a section of any larger work. Much of the breakthrough from the blank page can be achieved by giving overall shape to the material. This may need to be a form of collage from bits and pieces already written, or it may be a deliberate mapping out, but the work takes life from its overall structure and how the components of that fit together. Of course, as an author works on a piece of writing, it will often metamorphose so that its final shape may be very different from the one with which it began, or the one that the author carried in her mind as she imagined her text into being.

From all this comes the central belief on which this book is founded. Writing is a process, based in skill that develops with experience and feedback. This developmental process can be enhanced by understanding the principles and processes described in the following pages. But in the end, writing can no more be mastered by reading a book about becoming an author than riding a horse can be mastered from reading a book on equitation. We therefore hope that, above all, this book will encourage you to get on with the process of putting pen to paper (in whatever medium you choose) and we look forward to seeing you in print.

David Canter
Gavin Fairbairn

About the authors

David **Canter** is Professor of Psychology at the University of Liverpool and was formerly Professor of Psychology at the University of Surrey. He has published extensively in many areas of applied and social psychology, including work on the psychology of the built environment, human behaviour in fires and emergencies, alternative medicine, and criminal behaviour. He acts on the editorial board and as a reviewer for many journals across a number of social and behavioural science disciplines. Twenty years ago he established the *Journal of Environmental Psychology*, and more recently the *Journal of Investigative Psychology and Offender Profiling*, of which he is managing editor. He has published over twenty single-authored and edited books and contributed to many books of readings in the UK and the USA. As an adviser to publishers he has reviewed many book proposals for many different publishers and has edited three series of volumes, one in the environmental social sciences, one in forensic behavioural science and one in general psychology. His work in helping the police with their enquiries and in particular in the development of psychological profiling has led both to his coming to the attention of the general public in many television programmes and to his book *Criminal Shadows*, which has won the Golden Dagger award and the USA's Anthony award for Best True Crime. His most recent book, *Mapping Murder*, developed from the six-part television documentary series that he wrote and presented.

Gavin Fairbairn is Professor of Ethics and Language at Leeds Metropolitan University and was formerly Professor of Education at Liverpool Hope University College, to which he moved from a Chair of Professional Development in Nursing and Midwifery at the University of Glamorgan. Prior to that he worked for many years in teacher education in Wales, following a career in social work and special education. He has published extensively in education, and in applied philosophy and ethics, where he has a special interest in the ethical issues that arise in the caring professions. He has acted as a reviewer for a number of journals for many years and, as an adviser to publishers, he has reviewed numerous book proposals on both educational and ethical topics. His books include (with Chris Winch) *Reading, Writing and Reasoning: A guide for students*, and (with Susan Fairbairn) *Reading at University: A guide for students*. He has also written extensively on applied ethics and philosophy, including *Contemplating Suicide: The language and ethics of self harm*. His most recent book with Susan Fairbairn, *Writing your Abstract: A guide for would-be conference presenters*, was published in 2005.

1   Publishing without perishing

Learning to write for publication • Wanting or needing to publish? • Becoming an author: the need for resilience • Knowing the rules of the game • The way ahead: finding your way in *Becoming an Author*

Learning to write for publication

Many successful research students in the sciences and social sciences, capable of research of the first order – creative and scientifically sound – have something to say but never make the transition from writing a thesis to being the author of published academic work. Others will publish a few joint papers with their supervisor, but never publish independently. Indeed, a surprisingly small number of those who undertake postgraduate research ever get round to publishing anything that draws on that research. Many never publish anything at all. Something similar is true of research students in arts subjects, whose background ought to have prepared them to communicate in writing, but often does not.

Writing and communicating about their ideas and findings takes up a significant portion of the time of most postgraduate researchers. Indeed, uppermost in their minds throughout much of their period of study is the fact that, in the end, the work they are doing must underpin a significant piece of writing, in relation to which the contribution of their work will be assessed. Of course, there are differences in the way the reports of their work are produced. For those undertaking conceptual or literary research in arts subjects, the written account, in the form of a thesis, is central, and its creation will occupy them throughout their studies. In the sciences and social sciences, on the other hand, the bulk of the writing will often be undertaken after the empirical study on which it is based has been completed, and the writing itself is thus usually given a less central role in the course of study.

Many capable postgraduates, other researchers and professionals fail to move into professional academic writing because their university experience has not helped them to develop the literary skills that they need in order to do so. Few students on either undergraduate or postgraduate courses are given any help in developing as writers, other than through the sometimes cynical comments that appear on marked assignments, often from lecturers whose own writing leaves much to be desired. Typically this absence of guidance about writing will carry on into the research supervision that they receive as postgraduates, or as researchers on various projects, where most are even less likely to receive help about the nitty-gritty of actually communicating in writing. 'After all,' the reasoning may go, 'they've got this far, so they should be able to put a sentence or two together.' It is almost as if there is an expectation that skill in academic writing will somehow 'rub off' on anyone who enters a university library or accesses academic material via the internet.

Another reason that many people fail to develop careers as professional academic authors, even if they have received help in developing their writing skills, is that they will probably have travelled through the higher education system without being told anything about the practicalities of getting into print. For example, it is unlikely that anyone will ever have told them how to submit an article to a journal, or about the ways in which the peer review process works. Nor will they have been taught what they need to do if they want to publish a book. For instance, many people do not realize that agreements to publish academic books are, by and large, reached after consideration of a proposal that includes an outline of the content, rather than after consideration of a finished manuscript. What tends to happen is that those who, for whatever reason, are highly motivated towards publication will work out what to do for themselves; and those who are not will simply be filtered out of becoming authors.

In *Becoming an Author* we therefore aim to help researchers and other professionals, postgraduates and even some outstanding undergraduates to develop the knowledge and skills that are necessary if they are to become successful academic authors.

This book will therefore be useful for:

- Individuals who have recently completed higher degrees and want to rewrite their work or draw on it in order to publish, but are unsure how to do so.
- Lecturers for whom academic writing has not hitherto been a priority, but whose career development and feelings of self-worth now depend upon 'getting published'
- Professionals, such as nurses, psychologists, schoolteachers and medical practitioners, for whom publication, whether about research, or about knowledge gained through professional practice, can be satisfying as well as bringing career advantages, including promotion.
- Researchers involved in funded or sponsored projects who want to move beyond internal reports to a wider realm of publication.
- The many other people whose job or interests imply that they will publish but who have not developed the knowledge or skills to become an author.

Becoming an Author is thus aimed at anyone whose personal or career development will benefit from getting published.

Wanting or needing to publish?

In the UK, as in many other countries, it is nowadays very difficult to obtain an academic post unless you are not only well qualified, but also have a record of research and publication. This is not to say that all academics in full-time 'permanent' posts have such a record. Many lecturers in the UK do not, especially in the newer universities and the non-university higher education sector, where they have commonly had, and still have, higher teaching loads than their counterparts in the older universities. But even such institutions tend nowadays to expect new staff to demonstrate some commitment to publication. Thus, one reason for your interest in a book about becoming an academic author might be that you have not yet secured a university post that you can hope to occupy for the foreseeable future. Another is that if you achieved a permanent teaching post in the days when this was still possible without having published, it is increasingly unlikely that you will gain promotion, or be able to move between academic posts, unless you begin to do so.

Even highly experienced university and college lecturers may be relatively inexperienced in writing for publication, because for one reason or another, their careers so far have been entirely focused on teaching and administration, rather than on research and writing for publication. Such individuals often experience the same anxieties about writing for publication as recent postgraduates. It is increasingly common for British institutions of higher education – especially the newer universities and colleges in which research has not in the past been a high priority – to provide support for staff who are at the early stage of their research careers, in developing as researchers and authors. Indeed, much of Gavin's time for some years has been given over to helping lecturing staff gain confidence in professional writing.

Whatever your reason for opening a book about getting published, we suggest that you take some time to reflect on your reasons for wanting to get into print, because they will make a difference both to what you write and to the genres in which you attempt to publish. Do you want to increase your chances of landing a post in a well-respected university? Do you perhaps feel the need to publish in order to justify your salary or to gain promotion? Do you want to find ways of sharing your ideas with others? If you are a professional outside academia, say in medicine, or in some area of business and management, are you hoping to improve your chances of promotion, or to attract new clients for your business and management consultancy? Or do you just have a burning desire to get your ideas and the results of your studies out to a wider audience?

The academic community within which you will publish will influence not only what you write about but also the academic genre in which you do so. Different disciplines, and even different subgroups within disciplines, have contrasting views about the most significant form of publication. For example, whereas in the sciences and social sciences it is unusual for books to be the preferred route for presenting original material, in subjects such as philosophy and theology this is much more common. Whatever you decide you want to publish – and like both of us you may develop a mixed portfolio of published work – your choice of place and of medium will have an influence over the style in which you write.

Becoming an author: the need for resilience

Writing for publication is demanding, particularly when you have to fit it among the many other burdens that go hand in hand with academic life. And so, if you are going to put the effort into pondering, preparing and polishing text that will be necessary if you aspire to becoming a successful academic author, you will need to be very clear about why you want to do so. Holding this motivation strongly in your thoughts will, hopefully, help to sustain you whenever it looks as if you might stumble at the many hurdles ahead. Though the adventure that is academic publishing will bring you the excitement that comes from seeing your name and what you have written in print, it will also involve exposing yourself to the upset and hurt that can come from offering your work for publication and having it rejected or criticized, even if it is not rejected outright. Doubtless your work will often be both criticized and rejected, because this happens to virtually all academic authors – both the best of them, and the worst.

If you are to be successful as an academic author you will have to develop positive ways of dealing with criticism and rejection. You need not become thick skinned, but you will certainly have to become resilient so that you can bounce back ready to do whatever is necessary to be able to resubmit work to an editor after amending, or to pursue publication in some other arena. Otherwise you are likely either to give up, or to end up with a huge pile of unpublished material clogging your desk, the hard disk of your computer, or worse still, your head. In time you find it difficult to motivate yourself to revise material that seemed perfectly satisfactory to you, but which some journal referee has advised should not be accepted for publication without substantial (or even slight) changes. Even worse, will be the occasions when an article that draws on work that was the basis of your postgraduate thesis and readily accepted by examiners, and has gone down well at several conferences, is rejected outright by the journal of your choice. It can be particularly galling to have an article rejected on the basis of a review in which the referee suggests that you have nothing new or interesting to say, especially if they try to justify their decision by offering a detailed critique of your views, almost as if they really believe that you do have something to say but merely disagree with it. The frustration is even worse if, as a result of their own lack of knowledge or expertise, you know that they have simply misunderstood what you are saying.

None of us are immune to the fear of failure, and rejection can be difficult to overcome. Elsewhere in this book we discuss in some detail the need to take care in deciding the journals to which you should submit articles, and which publishers would be most appropriate to approach with a proposal for a book, if you want to maximize your chances of success. At this point we want merely to draw attention to the fact that everyone shares in anxiety about rejection – both fledgling and experienced academics. The fear of failure is probably the biggest hurdle to publishing, no matter who you are or what stage of your career as an author you have reached. We all hate being told, however politely, that our book proposal, though interesting, is not interesting enough for our publisher of choice to want to pursue it further. And we all hate receiving rejection letters from editors of journals, whether they are polite and encouraging:

> Though we did not feel that this article was suited for our journal we wish you luck in placing it elsewhere, and hope that in the future you will consider offering other articles to us for consideration.

or brutal and disheartening:

> We do not consider that this article is sufficiently academically rigorous or provides anything new or interesting to warrant serious consideration.

In later chapters we will help you to understand the process that generates such letters so that you can reduce the chances of getting them. We also discuss the many ways of taking advantage of thoughtful criticism to improve your chances of success.

Knowing the rules of the game

Whatever medium for publication you choose, if you want to maximize your chances of getting into print, it is important that you adopt a style that will be acceptable for that medium. For example, there is no point in writing in a very abstruse and scholarly way for a professional magazine or journal aimed at practitioners for whom practical advice is more important than hearing how that advice arose from a research project. Equally, there is no point in writing a first-person narrative account of an experience from professional practice for a journal whose readers are more interested in reading discussions of theory or reports of empirical research. You may get text written in one style accepted for publication in one forum but not in another, and it is as well to be aware that what suits one outlet may not suit others. That is why it is important to develop both an eye for the predominant styles adopted by authors in your field, and the ability to write in a number of different voices about the things that matter to you, thus allowing you to speak about the same things to different audiences in ways that they will understand.

We have colleagues who have struggled for years to get their work published but have steadfastly refused to shape their writing to the outlets in which they want it to appear: a foolish move for anyone who wants to get their work into print. Some of them have submitted engaging personal accounts to academic journals that only publish rigorously objective descriptions of empirical studies; they have been disappointed. Others have tried to get difficult and abstract ideas published for a mass readership. If you aspire to do the same, try to learn something from their lack of success; then try to temper your enthusiasm with the thought that just because you believe that what you have to say is important for everyone on the planet, this does not mean that everyone on the planet (or even a few thousands of them) will want to read it. Finally, other people we have known have submitted to publishers of scholarly texts, work that draws on a deep well of personal insight and owes more to poetry than to science. Oddly, from our point of view, they have been surprised by the puzzled rejection they have received. Of course, these three examples are extreme cases. We use them only to emphasize the general rule that you should make sure that both the content of what you are writing about and the style in which you are writing are likely to appeal to those who you hope will publish it; otherwise there is little point in offering it to them.

It is worth bearing in mind that in many disciplines a small number of publications in prestigious refereed journals is likely to be viewed as more important than a larger number of publications in lower ranked refereed journals or professional periodicals. Thus, if your sole aim is to forge a glittering academic career, you may decide to stick to publishing in the most important journals in your specialist area. Often these will have an international readership and an editorial committee drawn from different countries. However, even though publishing articles in weighty academic journals will help you to make your mark academically, it is never a good idea to dismiss the possibility of writing for less prestigious outlets, which can offer an easier route to developing a portfolio of published work. For one thing, it may be easier to get material accepted by them. The old adage about success breeding success is worth remembering. Indeed, in some disciplines, it might even be the case that developing a reputation as an author of serious articles in lower ranked journals is a positive benefit, provided that you do publish at least some work in the more highly ranked outlets. This might be the case in, for example, nursing, where reputations at national, if not international level, can be built at least partly on the basis of work in professional, rather than refereed academic journals.

An advantage of publishing in less prestigious outlets is that they tend to move much more quickly in getting material into print, especially if they do not have refereeing processes, because in general they appear more frequently – perhaps monthly or even weekly, rather than perhaps three, four or six times a year, which is common among more academic journals. This makes them an ideal outlet for ideas you might have that are very topical, because publishing in them offers the opportunity to 'strike while the iron is hot'. It is important to bear in mind that just because an outlet for published work is less prestigious, this does not necessarily mean that the standards of writing it publishes are any lower. A recent widely quoted comment from Lord May, president of the Royal Society is worth repeating. He declared that publication in prestige journals such as *Nature* and *Science* was becoming too important in the rating of scientists and departments. 'We need a fundamental review,' he said. 'There is a very damaging change in the culture. Our focus should be on the ideas, and their merit, not on where they were published' (Curtis 2004).

Another advantage of publishing in periodicals and professional magazines is that they tend to be read by many more people than refereed academic journals. And so, if you are motivated to influence the development of professional practice in an area in which you have an interest, you might decide that your time is better spent writing for such outlets. Doing so will gain you fewer academic brownie points, but more readers; often the difference will be between some tens or even just a handful of readers for a prestigious academic journal, and tens of thousands for a professional periodical or magazine. This might, for example, be the case if you work in a professional area such as education, social work or nursing, where reports of experience can at times be as influential in changing what people do as reports of empirical research. We have therefore included a chapter dealing with authorship in newspapers and magazines.

The way ahead: finding your way in Becoming an Author

Our intention in writing this book was to speak to authors who need help with getting published. By pooling our experience of academic publishing and of supporting others in developing careers as published authors we aimed to draw aside the veils of confusion that surround the practicalities of publishing in a range of academic genres, but particularly in books and journals, which is why, in Chapters 9, 10 and 12, we offer detailed guidance about the processes that are involved in publishing journal articles and books. In doing so we explore some of the difficulties that confront those who wish to publish but are inexperienced in doing so, and offer advice about turning an initial idea or series of ideas into a text worth publishing. Though we are primarily concerned with the nuts and bolts of writing and publishing, in Chapters 2, 3, 9 and 11 we also consider, especially in Chapter 2, some of the reasons why anyone would want to set out on a career as an author, and the merits of the various genres in which they might aim to publish.

Getting published involves not only having something to say, but also finding a way to say it and selecting the form in which to do so – whether, for example, you want to write a journal article or a book. No one finds writing particularly easy. Indeed, most of us find it rather hard, even if we know what we want to say – perhaps especially if we know what we want to say and are discerning enough to spot whether we have said it. That is why, in Chapter 4, we offer advice about getting started and about keeping going when it gets difficult, including ways of overcoming some of the psychological and emotional barriers that can interfere with the writing process. We also discuss, in considerable detail, the processes of writing, whatever species of academic writing you find yourself engaging in. For example, in a number of places, but especially in Chapter 4, we offer detailed advice about the development and management of text, gradually crafting it into a form that is suitable for the particular species of academic writing you choose to aim for. Our focus is on the importance of drafting and revising text, of learning to read your own work better.

To get your work into print you will have to develop a writing style that is suitable both for the audience you want to address and for the material about which you want to write. More than that, however, you will also have to learn to adapt your style to suit the particular outlets that you hope will publish your work. That is why, at various points, but particularly in Chapters 5 and 6, we discuss academic style, including the importance of structure. In doing so, we talk about our keenly held view that academic writing can usefully be viewed as a form of storytelling. Indeed, our belief in the importance of story-telling as a model for academic writing is a continuing theme throughout the book. In Chapter 7 we talk about the use of illustrations of various kinds, and in Chapter 8 we draw attention to some of the thorny issues that can arise in publishing, including some matters of ethics and law. Finally, in Chapter 14, we discuss the shape of things to come, and the future of academic publishing as we know it, in the age of electronic publishing via, for example, the World Wide Web. The book ends with a postscript in which, among other things, we attempt to sum up some of the main advice we have offered in 'Ten Commandments' for academic authors.

Becoming an Author is intended as a survival guide both for fledgling and other inexperienced academic and professional writers, and for more experienced authors who want to improve their effectiveness and enrich their knowledge of a range of genres of academic publishing. In producing such a guide we have drawn heavily on the strategies we have developed for coping with the demands of authorship. We have drawn extensively on our experience of academic publishing – as authors, editors and reviewers – in order to illustrate and support our views. And so, in a sense, the book can be seen as the product of an extensive anthropological study in which we have acted as participant observers (between us for over sixty years) in a number of fields, among them environmental and social psychology, architecture, applied philosophy, professional ethics, higher education and criminology. Our experience in and reflection on a range of roles – including author, book editor, journal reviewer and journal editor – have, we hope, allowed us to reveal something about the world of scholarly authorship at the beginning of the twenty-first century.

2 The author's journey

Writing 'for me' or 'for them'? • Career imperatives
• Quality control • Duties to yourself • Wealth • What
gets in the way? • Developing a portfolio • Building a
publishing history

Writing 'for me' or 'for them'?

There are many reasons for people wanting to get into print, each of which implies a different approach to, and a different form of, publication. Instrumental reasons for writing, such as the desire to gain promotion, that relate to what others ask of you, may lead you to publish in outlets other than those in which you might publish because of your own commitments, personal interests, mission to inform or other ideals. In the end, what is probably needed if you are to maintain sanity and genuine interest in the topics you research and write about, is a balance between 'publishing for me' and 'publishing for them'.

In the best of all possible worlds, authors would write for publication only when they had something worthwhile to say. However, in the modern academic and professional world, where promotion, and even obtaining a full-time permanent post, can hinge on the strength of your publishing record, other threads of motivation come into play. Each author will have her own mix of reasons and purposes in writing, and you should try to clarify what your own blend is, because it could influence your decisions about what and where you should publish at different points. For example, early in her career an academic nurse researching in wound healing might aim to publish mainly in peer reviewed journals, because she realizes that doing so is likely to be helpful in seeking promotion. Later she might cast her net a little wider when she realizes that she can have more influence over the ways in which wounds are treated in primary care settings by writing for professional journals and magazines.

Career imperatives

Some academics and other professionals only seek to become authors because they believe that establishing a publication portfolio will help them to gain promotion. It may; but it may not. Whether it does may depend on other factors, including the publishing record of those who interview you, as well as on the prestige of the publication in which your work appears, for example whether it is a refereed journal or a professional magazine. Nonetheless, it is increasingly the case both in universities around the world and in other professions, that a significant criterion for selection is the quality of the applicant's publications. The amount they have published will also have some relevance. However, it is important to note that other relevant matters may not, in general, count in their favour, including having a broad range of academic interests. In a world in which narrow specialism is lauded above most other things, promiscuity in the range of interests you develop can be an impediment to advancement. It is probably because of this that Gavin was once asked during an interview, to say which of a number of publications was the 'real' him, on the grounds that no one could have expertise in such a diverse range of areas. The publications in question were his books: *Contemplating Suicide: The language and ethics of self harm; Sexuality: Learning difficulties and doing what's right* and *Reading, Writing and Reasoning: A guide for students.* His interlocutor was a professor of obstetrics and gynaecology. It has to be said, though, that David has never had that problem, but then his publications on the psychological impact of open plan offices, the evaluation of complementary medical treatment, behaviour in emergencies, and the actions of serial killers, clearly have a coherence to them that is much more obvious than Gavin's.

In the curious world of British higher education there has for some years been what is known as the Research Assessment Exercise (RAE). In essence this is a process whereby every academic who is supposedly identified as 'research active' has the quality of their publications in the previous half dozen or so years assessed by a panel of people in their discipline, or rather, a panel of people whose academic experience and expertise is more or less fitted to a broad swathe of research interests that more or less match up to one of the 'units of assessment' that have been decided upon. Ratings are then given to departments on the basis of the overall assessment of their staff. The assessment a department receives in the RAE is put into the pot with those of all other departments in the university. This bundle of ratings then is fed into a formula that influences how much money the university gets from central government, as well as how the senior levels of the university hierarchy portray themselves and their institution to their counterparts in other universities. In coming to conclusions about the nature, extent and quality of a group that have submitted their work for scrutiny, other matters such as research income, numbers of research students and 'indicators of esteem', are also given some weight.

The RAE has probably gone further than the established tradition in US universities, which is captured in the phrase 'publish or perish'. Certainly, tenure and acceptance into various posts in the USA has long been influenced by an academic's publication history. However, teaching ability and administrative capabilities, as well as other strengths of relevance to the job, notably areas of expertise that fill gaps in the department's portfolio, are all regularly taken into account in hiring people or giving them tenure. However, in many UK universities such strengths are given minimal weight compared with the contribution to research as revealed through publication.

It would be foolish, though, to think of the RAE as the only reason to publish. To quote from Donald MacLeod's article in the *Guardian* (9 November 2004): 'Pressure is growing for the research assessment exercise to be axed – once universities have spent four years fighting themselves to a standstill in the battle for the best academics.' This peculiarly draconian and distorting form of evaluation of academics may (hopefully) fade into history.

The reason that universities emphasize publication as a criterion in the appointment and advancement of staff is not merely that they have a cynical desire to control academics who might otherwise waste their time reading books and chatting to students. Rather it is a reflection of the belief that anyone who is a professional should be making some contribution to the growth and development of their professional discipline. Even outside the academic realm, in situations where contributing to knowledge is not a primary objective, there is a growing belief that professionals in many areas of life should, from time to time, be contemplating their discipline and extending its value and contribution. Since this implies finding a way of sharing such reflections with the professional community, there is a real sense in which being a committed professional implies writing for publication.

Over thirty years ago, Bender wrote a fascinating paper arguing that psychology can be constructively construed as an industry, '. . . a collection of producers sharing common organizational and/or technical problems and operating in a market which subjects them to similar or equivalent commercial pressures' (Bender 1974: 107). We believe that this is a fruitful way of considering any academic discipline. The products are the ideas, theories, methodologies and processes that the members of the discipline make their own. The consumers are, as Bender makes clear, students, people who fund and support research, and other members of the discipline. Although this is a rather subversive notion, challenging the idea of neutral, objective, virtually altruistic scholarship, it does make clear that publication is an important showcase for what it is you have on offer, as well as being in many cases the front to the shop from which the products are acquired.

We still have memories of our earliest days as academics in which publication, in what we thought were obscure places, quite unexpectedly opened doors to collaboration and support for other activities. For example, David once published a paper in what he thought was the house journal of a London college only to find that senior professionals in Japan had read it, so that when he later arrived there wishing to carry out research, the publication had acted like advanced marketing and the senior professionals were more than ready to help.

It is worth emphasizing that this focused career imperative can carry with it very particular assumptions about the *form* of publication. A CV that lists all the times you have been interviewed in newspapers (which we have seen in job applications), or even all the articles you have written for the popular press, will carry little weight in most universities unless you happen to be applying for a job teaching journalism. Sociologists often publish in books of readings rather than journals, without attracting the disdain that may be wished on colleagues who do the same thing across the corridor in psychology. In psychology, curiously, books – especially widely read books – can carry far less significance in selecting people for jobs than articles in obscure but highly regarded journals, whereas a philosopher without a book to her name may be taken less seriously by colleagues. Of course, these are generalizations bordering on caricature. We make them to alert you from the start to the need to understand forms of publication and how these forms relate to your personal objectives.

Quality control

One step away from the purely instrumental objective of publishing is the recognition of the personal benefits to be gained from having others see your ideas and results in order to respond to them and comment on them. This emphasizes the link between research and publication. Secret study is almost invariably of poor quality, unless you are a genius. You need feedback from others in your area to identify obvious and not so obvious mistakes. You benefit from the challenge to what you take for granted and from the broader perspective on your work that comes from others reading it and commenting upon it.

When you submit your work to refereed journals, the feedback is direct. The more critical it is, the more it helps you to understand what the 'competition' is in the marketplace and what it is your 'customers' are looking for. But even comments from an editor or a colleague who has read your work can open your eyes to ways of thinking that are as productive as they are disconcerting.

Duties to yourself

At a more personal level, the urge to publish can arise because you feel you have something to say. For some people, preparing an article for publication can be a useful way of finding out whether what they have to say is worth saying. The discipline involved in attempting to say what you want to say clearly enough for other people to understand, can help to clarify whether your ideas are worth sharing. The only way in which anyone knows that a piece of research, or scholarship in a broad sense, has been carried out is by some public – that is, published – account of it. By carrying out a study with the intention of benefiting someone other than yourself, you are undertaking a task that requires publication for its completion.

Excitement and immortality

Many academics publish because it gives them a sense of achievement to do so. One of the joys of academic life, and learning in general, is the sensation of being part of an unfolding tradition, the pleasure of passing on knowledge and being part of the chain of scholarship. In this sense, there is for some people a feeling that publishing presents them with a slight chance of immortality – certainly much of what any of us write will be around long after us. There is no doubt that getting through the hurdles of publication and seeing the finished product is very satisfying. It brings a clear conclusion to what often feels like a messy exploration of possibilities. The published work, no matter how humble, goes on to an existence of it's own that is an aspect of you that can reach out into the most unexpected places (and which, on occasion, may come back to haunt you). Publishing puts the present into the future, drawing on the past. It is what extends human memory.

Addiction

Having realized the feelings of excitement that can come from getting into print, many people carry on writing because, having been bitten by the bug, they are for ever after driven to do so. However, they may be driven in different ways. In contrast to the external pressures of a rod-bearing head of department with an eye on research ratings, some may be driven by ambition for whatever glory or immortality they see in having their name in print. But perhaps even more are simply driven by a compulsion to write; they are addicted to the process and perhaps to the excitement that accompanies finding solutions to the problem of how best to communicate. Such people are incapable of not writing – they cannot not write. It is what they do; just as being funny is what some comedians are. If you ask most committed authors why they write, their honest answer will be 'because I must'. It becomes a form of addiction, an itch that has to be scratched. They feel uncomfortable when they have not written for a while and distracted when they are in the process of writing, as their partners will readily tell you.

These addicts sometimes talk about having a book or article 'inside' them waiting to be written. We have both had this experience, on several occasions. This is not to say that giving birth to a book is a simple process. Even if it is genuinely the case that it has been waiting around in your mind in embryonic form, struggling to attract your attention for some time, the business of writing a text and bringing it to fruition still requires physical and intellectual effort in drafting, organizing, planning, revising and so on. Turning the ghost of an idea into something tangible and then refining that into a form that others can understand and enjoy, is hard work.

Moral duty

There is another, slightly more community minded reason for publication. Most scholars and academics are in relatively privileged positions. We are given at least some time to think – something that is a luxury in the modern world. This is true even for those who have enormously high teaching hours, of the kind that is typical in many of the UK's non-university institutions of higher education, who often plead lack of time as an excuse for lack of research activity. Often, also, we are involved in studies that require the co-operation of others, as sources of information or as subjects in our experiments. These people typically offer their help, usually with goodwill, because they believe their help will contribute to knowledge and the greater good. There is therefore a moral obligation to contribute back to the society that nurtures science and scholarship. One direct way of doing this is by publication.

Wealth

Some inexperienced academic authors naively believe that publication is the royal road to wealth and glory. While some of the time there may be some small fame in being published, wealth is far less likely. As Charles Jenks (who probably made more money as an architect than as an author) put it, paraphrasing Karl Marx's view on property, 'publishing is theft'. Academic publishing relies on the assumption that the author already has a paid job. Even though the major academic journals are usually published by publishers whose objectives are not entirely philanthropic, but are rather to make a profit, most scholarly journals do not pay their contributors, and some may in effect require contributors to pay to be published, by expecting them to purchase a certain number of reprints of their article as part of the agreement to publish. An exception to this is that some refereed periodicals and journals do pay a small fee for articles on publication. This is the case, for example, with a number of journals published by the Royal College of Nursing in the UK, though the amounts paid in no way properly pay for the time and effort involved in writing even the briefest of articles.

Even the royalties from books rarely add up to anything close to a minimum wage. You can easily do the calculations. In very round figures, an author may get somewhat less than 10 per cent of the price that their publisher receives for the book, which is perhaps half of the book's price in the shops. So if their book is being sold for £30.00, an academic author will typically earn £1.50 for each copy sold. The average scholarly book sells about 1,000 copies, but let us assume that over a number of years this book does especially well and sells 5,000 copies. That is still only £7,500 for what will usually have been a year's work at the very least.

Though the chances are slight, some academics do actually manage to make significant income through publication. Usually if they do so they will do it by publishing a popular text, whether an original academic work that can be marketed through the 'trade' lists – the kind of book that you might find on railway station bookstalls – or a textbook aimed at the student market, which finds a niche as a recommended text on courses in many institutions. Much more likely is that they will make a more modest, but regular income over a number of years by publishing a textbook aimed at meeting the needs of a particular course or courses, or a book that presents original ideas in their field, or an original way of thinking about established ideas, that has the potential to be used as a textbook. Such books could manage reasonable sales for a sustained period – perhaps selling 20,000 copies or more, over ten years, in which case the income it produces starts to look more healthy. Just in case you are beginning to see pound signs, because you are the director of a programme that recruits a thousand students a year, each of whom you can issue with a copy of your text as they register, and you have several friends who are willing to tout it to their students, you should bear in mind that you will have to declare whatever you earn in royalties to the Inland Revenue who will feel duty bound to take a good chunk of them away from you.

The other main avenue to significant earnings drawing on academic work is to write regularly for newspapers or magazines, which a few academics manage to do. However, doing so has drawbacks. For one thing, it is very likely that editors will take liberties with the text you submit – usually by cutting it down, so that you find that what your article says is not quite what you intended, and perhaps is less elegant or witty than you wanted. In any case, although writing for newspapers and magazines is much more lucrative per word written than writing for academic journals for example, there is always the risk that you will get nothing for your trouble. Though you might get as much as £300 for a newspaper article, there is always the risk that the article, even though commissioned, will not be published because of some other demand on the space, in which case you may not get paid unless you had agreed that first. Also you need to have a well-organized bookkeeping arrangement. Newspapers may forget about you the minute your article is printed, and will not pay anything unless you send them an invoice promptly. To make such an enterprise a real income generator you will have to treat it as a business, not as a casual hobby, and doing this alongside a regular day job is probably beyond all but those who are really fluent on the printed page. We discuss all this further in Chapter 11.

What gets in the way?

Blocks and dampeners

Having got some idea of why you want to publish and the implications that has for the outlet you will aim for, and assuming your ideas or findings can contribute something new to the literature, what could possibly stop you getting the nascent material into a published form? What will dampen your enthusiasm or block your way to success, either in finishing your text or in getting it into print? And what will most encourage you to get going, and sustain you through the trials and tribulations that lie ahead?

One essential requirement for getting into print is a desire to say something, combined with the courage to say it in a way that is readily accessible to others who may wish to criticize what you have had to say. In some ways, getting published involves having a bit of a brass neck – the brass neck to believe that you have something fresh and important to contribute to your academic discipline, or to your professional area. It also involves having the ability to decide when what you have written is good enough to submit for publication.

The fear of criticism from others, or a personal desire to offer only the best, inhibits some people from publishing; such people suffer from too strong a desire to attain an unattainable goal: perfection. A proper degree of obsessionality and the desire to get things right are good things, but need to be tempered with the ability to know where to stop and where good enough is good enough. Very little of what is and will be written is as good as it could be. Few authors will be completely happy with their work. The best we can hope for is that we can manage, in what we write, to say something that will contribute to the development of thought and knowledge in our areas of concern, in the best way that we can, given our abilities and, more importantly, given the time we have available for this aspect of our academic lives.

Some people fail to publish because, they claim, they are constrained by lack of time. They live their professional and academic lives muttering that one day they would like to get round to writing if only they had less other work – for example, less teaching and fewer administrative duties and less responsibility for the pastoral care of students. However, since most people who do get round to publishing a little (or even a lot) are also short of time, there are probably other factors that differentiate those who publish from those who do not. The simple truth is often that people who write, write because they find the time to do so, whatever their other commitments. As a result they will prioritize writing over other activities – and not necessarily professional and academic activities either. They may, for example, make writing a priority over leisure and family activities, which their non-publishing colleagues rate more highly.

Some people do not want to commit their ideas to print until they have time to do it well. Some are so inhibited by the fear of failure that they cannot get round to doing the necessary work. Some people even avoid publishing because they are afraid that other people will steal their ideas. This is a confused idea because publishing is one way in which you can actually lay claim to ideas as your property. After all, unless you share your ideas with other people, they will not know that they are your ideas. This is what spurred Charles Darwin on to publish his *On the Origin of Species*, after twenty years of prevarication. The final straw for Darwin was becoming aware that Alfred Russel Wallace was about to publish a remarkably similar theory.

Publishing is one way of letting the world know that your ideas are your creation – just as much as sharing your ideas with colleagues by speaking at conferences, or with students by discussing them in class. There are offices and filing cabinets and computer directories and minds all over the planet (and perhaps beyond) that are filled to overflowing with half-written, half-worked-out attempts at putting ideas into a literary form, suitable for publication as academic articles. Half-finished articles are good for one thing – turning into finished articles. Ideas for books will never be of any use to anyone unless they give rise to a book that is written and read.

There is one exception to the value of publishing in order to fix your claims to ownership of the intellectual property. That is when you have made a discovery that you wish to patent for commercial ends. Obtaining a patent for an idea requires that it is 'new art' and not in the public domain. This means that it should not have been published in any form (this usually includes even a PhD available on the library shelves) prior to your application for a patent.

Developing a portfolio

An evolving career

The different benefits of publication can be reaped at different stages in your publishing career. Any journey, as they say, starts with the first step. For many people setting out on the road to publishing success as an academic, this first step is to write a book review for a journal. Reviewing a book has the advantage of being a prescribed task that involves writing in a particular way, usually describing the book's aims and contents briefly, before offering an opinion of the text. Good reviewers usually manage, even in a brief review, to make one or two points that relate to their own interests, and longer reviews give much more room for this kind of thing, while providing the security of knowing that unless what is written is obviously gibberish, with no relation to the book mentioned, it will appear in print, thus putting your name in the public arena.

Conferences offer good opportunities to begin the process. Apart from the fact that many produce proceedings that include all papers, giving strong presentations at a conference might lead to invitations to submit your paper to refereed journals, or to contribute to edited books. In any case, provided that whenever you give a paper, you make a habit of preparing well, you will have gone part of the way to developing an article that will be suitable for submission to a journal. Of course, in many disciplines, especially in the sciences and social sciences, where conference slots tend to be relatively short, articles will be longer than the conference paper on which they are based, so that you will be able to include a more extended review of the context of your work and possibly more detailed analysis than you could in a conference presentation. That is why it is a good practice, whenever you are going to present at a conference, to prepare a paper that would take longer than the allotted time to read, which you then cut down to size for public presentation, knowing that afterwards you can revert to the longer version to submit for publication. Of course, not everything that you present at conferences will be suitable as an article, but it is always a good idea to bear this possibility in mind. You might write a more popular account of this work for a magazine and then begin to submit fuller extensions and developments of your studies to journals that have a different audience and possibly more stringent selection criteria.

It is helpful to consider the various forms of publishing as stages in your evolution as an author. You may start writing because you feel you have to, and then get a taste for it. You may publish in peripheral professional journals first for rather cynical reasons, but when you get positive comments from colleagues (not a common experience, but not unknown either) you may decide that you really do have something to say and want to reach a wider audience. In developing a knapsack of publications, it is important to keep in mind that the journal article process can be a cumulative one. In some disciplines you may be able to start with small components of your overall argument, or distinct subsets of your analysis, publishing them in specialist journals. Once you have a few such articles they can be drawn upon to generate larger overviews and to establish the basis for a book.

In considering where you should publish you have to balance your own view of the quality and nature of your work with the outlet that you think will make best use of it, against the consideration of the audience you would like to reach. One ready way of determining the outlet is to look at the journals you find yourself reading and citing most often. The chances are that those publications will be most receptive to your work.

It is also fruitful to keep aware of new opportunities for publication in your area – what we think of as the 'new restaurant syndrome'. When a restaurant first opens it wants people to know it is there and to establish its quality clearly. But, before it has established its reputation it may be short of customers and therefore look after anyone who comes in with particular care. It is our experience that new publishing outlets, such as new journals or new publishers, are much the same. They often do not have as many submissions as they would like but they want to encourage people to send them material, so they deal with all authors with particular care. Often too they are very flexible at this stage, not having settled on a fixed range or style of content.

Another way of determining appropriate places to publish is the age-old one of asking experienced colleagues. You will be surprised at the informal knowledge there is around of what journals or publishers publish what sort of material, and under what conditions. A lot of this may be hearsay and thus lack deep validity. It may also be out of date. This might be the case, for example, if the editor has changed since your colleague had contact with the journal; the new editor might since have imposed radical changes on the publishing ethos, and hence on what gets published.

Building a publishing history

People jump into print in many different ways. Some launch their careers with a bang as authors with a book based on their postgraduate dissertation. Others gently dip their toes into the water with a brief book review, moving on from that to a short journal article, learning to paddle before they try to swim. But whichever route you take it is useful to have in mind that it is a path you are journeying along. You can build up your portfolio in many different ways, but each step along the path is both a further training in the art of becoming an author and the accumulation of experience and credibility from which you can aspire to more challenging realms.

Stages in a publishing career

- Review books for journals
- Brief commentary on aspect of a literature
- Act as journal reviewer (this may come later in some disciplines)
- Short original journal article
- Article for practitioners in a professional journal/magazine
- Longer journal articles
- Article for an encyclopaedia
- Review an area of work on which you have published
- Really significant journal articles in prestigious journals
- Edit book of invited contributions (readings)
- Newspaper and magazine articles (may come earlier in some disciplines)
- Monograph/book that covers your area of expertise
- Textbook that is aimed at undergraduate market (may come earlier for some)
- Edit book of invited contributions (readings)
- Further journal articles
- Further books
- Popular trade book
- Senior editor for a series of books in your discipline
- Further journal articles
- Preside over *Festschrift*

David's authoring career helps to illustrate this point. He first got into print by writing very brief conceptual overviews, while still a PhD student, of how buildings may be relevant to people's lives. These were published in the *Architects' Journal* at the invitation of his PhD supervisor who was at that time editing a section of that professional weekly magazine, devoted to more technical aspects of architecture. From this, David moved on to publish results of small studies in the *Proceedings of the Bartlett Society*, a journal with limited circulation, which in those days focused on aspects of building science. It was after these initial forays that he published more detailed research studies in major psychology journals, notably the *British Journal of Social Psychology*.

He edited a book of papers derived from a conference he organized on architectural psychology and then, having established himself as having some expertise at the interface between psychology and architecture, he wrote a general textbook entitled *Psychology for Architects*. Various academic journal articles followed, interspersed with editing specially commissioned chapters to form textbooks, notably *Environmental Interaction*. He then wrote his first singly authored text that provided a framework for thinking about *The Psychology of Place* before he eventually became the founding editor for the *Journal of Environmental Psychology*.

Gavin's first step into publishing was a review of a book by a controversial public figure, during which he took the opportunity to comment on an aspect of her presentation at a conference he had organized. Unusually, she responded by writing a letter to the editor, which attempted, quite firmly, to put him in his place. She failed. A chapter in an edited book about ethics in social work, was swiftly followed by an edited book, *Psychology, Ethics and Change*, with his longest-standing writing partner. At the same time he began to write articles about issues in applied ethics, and on educational topics for refereed journals, along with chapters in his own and other's edited books. Gavin has always been somewhat sceptical about the orthodox view that the most valuable way for academics to publish is to stick to a relatively narrow field, and to publish mainly in prestigious refereed journals. This is evident in his many publications in professional periodicals, and other non-refereed publications, as well as refereed articles in education, nursing, applied philosophy, medical ethics, and health and social care journals. His first authored book, *Reading, Writing and Reasoning: A guide for students* (with Chris Winch), was published in 1991. It has been followed by a number of books in applied ethics and on educational topics.

Our central message for this chapter is that you will have a mixture of reasons for wanting to publish. You should think carefully about those reasons and shape your publishing aspirations to reflect them, rather than just thinking without question that you should publish where your senior colleagues publish. We are also advocating the longer view in which you consider the developing range of publications in which you are likely to be involved. As an author you are embarking on a journey that can lead you in many exciting and unexpected directions. If you have a mental map of what is possible you will be in a better position to follow up those opportunities as they emerge.

3 Varieties of publication

Planning ahead • Forms of authorship • Kinds of
academic publication • Newspapers and magazines
• Beyond the book – the World Wide Web • Connecting
outlet and aspiration

Planning ahead

Before you start doing the work you should have in mind the sort of outlet that
your work will reach. If you have spent years studying a particular topic,
whether it be in the library working through earlier scholarship or on the
streets interviewing people, or even in a laboratory running experiments, and
you then decide you would like to publish the outcome of your endeavours,
you are working backwards. By thinking about publication *after* you have done
all the work you are making the task especially difficult for yourself. There is
only minimal benefit in original research if it is not published, and that benefit
is of a very egocentric and personal kind. The publication is the evidence of the
work. It is the work brought to life and to the benefit of others.

So if you plan to start on original work you are, at least implicitly, planning
to publish it – or at least you should be. Therefore, from the very beginning
you should be considering how your studies will see the light of day. This

includes some idea of where and how you will be publishing it. Are you aiming for a major journal in your discipline? If so, what are the central criteria they will use to evaluate your work? If you have carried out an empirical study in the social sciences, is it the number of respondents or subjects in your experiment or survey? Is it the way your arguments engage with current debates in your discipline? Perhaps the journal you have in mind has a particular penchant for the relevance to professional practice of anything it publishes, or perhaps it favours work that is highly mathematical or abstractly theoretical? All of these matters will influence the way you set about your studies from the outset.

But perhaps your work encompasses a broader arena than can be handled in a journal article. In that case you may be drifting towards the idea of a book. Who would the audience be for such a book: undergraduates, specialist researchers, people in professional practice? Do you know of publishers who handle that kind of material? We will discuss how you approach publishers later, but it is never too early to make some contact with them so that you can get some guidance on what they would be looking for in a book. This guidance may influence how you tackle your subject.

Whether you intend to publish an article or a book, it can be helpful to have in mind, from as early as possible, a title, or titles, for the likely published outcome or outcomes that may arise from your work. These should not be generic titles that could apply to anyone working in your area such as 'Revisiting Aristotle', 'Attitudes to religion', 'Studying memory', 'Brain mechanisms' or 'Twentieth-century art', unless, say, you are planning to produce a broad overview as a textbook. The titles should grasp your central thesis as best you can: 'The concept of infinity in the later writings of Plato', 'The influence of the railway on support for religious practice', 'The emergence of coloured sculpture after the Second World War'.

The titles you have in mind are likely to change as your ideas and discoveries unfold, but titles give focus to your work and help you to keep a grip on what you are aiming for. Indeed, maintaining a record of the changing titles by which you have referred to your work as it progresses can be a helpful guide to how your ideas are developing, as well as being useful in discussion with others of what it is you are studying. A similar point is made by Russo (1980) in the context of a book on musical composition. He insists that any musical exercise, even if it is only a few seconds long, should be given a title, because giving a title to even their earliest fumblings with musical ideas, however sketchy, will often help or even force the composer to come to terms with what their work is about. Naming their work may change their attitude towards it, leading to revisions that move it towards its final form. It does not matter what the final name is. For example, a novice composer's piece may end up entitled 'Quartet number three', even though it began as 'Mist clears over the estuary at daybreak'. However, naming it will have facilitated its growth through its various transformations. The same is true when composing writing. The title gives direction to the narrative.

Forms of authorship

Because academic publication takes many forms, the first thing to develop is an understanding of the many, subtly different forms of publication. The two extremes may be thought of as academic and trade. This is an oversimplification of a multidimensional space, but it helps to have these extreme points as markers to think around. The most austere and arcane publications at the academic extreme will be journals that send any submission out to a number of academics for comment: refereed journals. These comments are used by the editor to decide whether to reject the paper or what revisions are necessary to allow publication. The more specialist the area and the more well known the journal, the tighter will be the criteria for acceptance. These journal editors are not concerned with writing style or how engaging an article is, but how clear it is and whether it 'makes a contribution' to the literature. Typically, every last comma and apostrophe has to be approved by the author and must be clearly the author's original work.

Such journals hardly ever pay their authors for submissions and rarely invite submissions. They rely entirely on their specific community of scholars to submit and review articles. Their journal may only have a circulation to a couple of hundred specialist subscribers and a few libraries. There often will be little or no publicity surrounding the journal. People will only know about it through their colleagues and academic searches. There may be a university or charitable trust that funds the journal so that it operates almost outside of any economic considerations. More typically it will be part of a stable of journals published by a commercial academic publisher that makes its money from subscriptions and the selling of reprints of articles.

At the other extreme is the trade press. This is a strongly commercially driven publishing venture that sells, mainly books, through bookshops, book clubs and, increasingly, over the internet. The selection of material is made by commissioning editors within the publishing house, who may or may not take advice from others on what to publish and may or may not evaluate what is actually written to determine its validity. At the commercial extreme such publishers are interested only in whether they can sell the books they print. They may wish to maintain a reputation for a particular quality of book, but that will be to ensure their image in the customer's mind and continue thereby to sell books. Their main concern is often whether they can get their books into bookshops. Will the buyers at WH Smiths, Borders, Barnes & Noble, or Waterstones be prepared to put the book on their shelves? Their evaluation of a book proposal often has nothing to do with what academics would recognize as quality, or scholarly contribution, but whether people will want to read it.

Authors get paid for trade books (typically 10 per cent of the price the publisher gets paid for each copy of the book, which may be half to two-thirds of what the book costs in a bookshop). The publisher, though, has the last word on what and how the book is written, its title and cover and how much will be charged for it. There will be no compunction about ghosting work under the apparent authorship of a celebrity. Work of little or no scientific or scholarly merit that is written in a lively, plausible way will be sold with claims for the authority of the author that can make professionals in the area cringe with embarrassment.

These two extremes, which might be caricatured as an article entitled 'Room names in twelfth century Japanese poetry' published in the *Journal of the Tokyo Institute of Historical Linguistics* at one end, and 'Star Signs and Sex' published by Target Paperbacks at the other, do imply a distinction that is not as complete as might be assumed. For example, the very highly regarded journal *Science* is a commercial venture, sold on newsstands. So that when David submitted a paper on serial killers they were very interested in it, not least because it would make an inviting cover. However, they did put the paper through an exceptionally thorough review process, submitting it to more than five experts, and decided that it did not warrant publication. Similarly, Academic Press, which sounds like the epitome of scholarly publication, has published among its many excellent books plenty of volumes that are very weak, but when the commissioning editor was challenged on this, his answer was that he knew their weakness but they sold well. In contrast, when David submitted his manuscript for *Mapping Murder* to the highly commercial publisher Virgin Books, its editors went through it with a fine-toothed comb and required him to deal with any ambiguities or contradictions they had found in the material and welcomed the more abstract and academic parts of the book, which had started life as part of the prestigious Darwin Lecture Series at Cambridge University.

So, if you are thinking of writing a 'commercial' book for the book trade then you usually have to convince one key person, the commissioning editor, of one simple possibility: the publisher will sell enough copies of the book at an appropriate price to make a reasonable profit. The editor would also like to believe that there is the possibility, however small, that the book may be a bestseller. If you are well known for being well known (what passes for celebrity these days) or are writing about a topic obviously of great public interest – sex, violence, football, a celebrity (preferably all four) – then you will be listened to; otherwise you have to make your pitch very strongly with evidence of why you think the book will sell. Of course, if your aspirations are more towards the academic end of our continuum, the task is not so challenging. We will spell out how you go about that later.

Similarly, these days, most journals are published by commercial publishers. So although they are keen to maintain the standard of their journals, this is because they want academics or professionals to continue to purchase the journals. They believe, probably rightly, that if subscribers regard a journal as including high quality material, they will continue to subscribe. But do not forget that the publishers need their journals to continue. They need material to include. Journals have voracious appetites for new material. Any, even limited edition, journal will need a minimum of about twenty original papers a year. If it has a subscriber base of even 500, including libraries, and most of its contributors come from people who read the journal, then perhaps one in ten or one in twenty of the people who read the journal must be submitting to it each year for it to have enough material. But there is a lot of overlap between journals, so the number of people available to produce original work is rather less than these numbers may suggest.

The simple message, then, is that journals need your material. So why do people have papers turned down? Of course, the calculations we have gone through are for limited areas of any discipline and journals with limited circulations. A well-established journal published, say, by a large American professional society such as the American Psychological Association, may have a subscriber list of many thousands. There may be hundreds of people submitting papers throughout the year, so the journal editor has to be selective. You can often find out how selective a journal is by consulting one of the reference sources listed at the end of this book. These may tell you the proportion of papers, on average, that is rejected by the journal or at least how many subscribers the journal has. Colleagues will also tell you of their success and failures with different journals.

The selection process will relate directly to the objectives of the journal and the central criteria that are used for evaluating submissions. The more submissions they have the more stringently (some may say subjectively) they will be applied. We will come back to how you improve the chances of having your submissions accepted when we have reviewed in a little more detail the other forms of (essentially) academic publication.

Kinds of academic publication

The box on page 28 sets out a brief list of some of the major kinds of publication available. It is certainly not exhaustive and omits many important but subtle variations. For example, we have not included chapters contributed to an encyclopaedia that have a rather different feel to them from chapters in books of readings. We have not explored the contribution to those journals that take long monographs and thus demand as much, if not more, than what would be required for a book. Then there are part-works – those publications that are marketed as weekly magazines but actually are just popular books divided up and sold on a week by week basis, with titles like 'Battles of the First World War' or 'Crimes of the Century'. Compiling a dictionary or bringing together quotations or an anthology of previously published work makes other demands as well that we will not go into here. The table is really to open your eyes to the publications you see around you and to think through the opportunities they may provide for you.

Forms of publication

Forms of publication	Review process	Payment
Refereed journals	External specialists	None
Non-refereed journals	Specialist editors	None
Magazines	Subject editor	Reasonable
Newspapers	Journalist/sub-editor	Moderate
Authored trade books	Commissioning editor	Royalty (% of sale price)
Authored academic books	Commissioning editor/ specialist	Royalty (% of sale price)
Monograph	Commissioning editor/ specialist	Not usual
Chapter in book	Book editor	Varies
Editing a book of readings	Limited	Royalty (% of sale price)
Conference paper	Conference committee	None
Internal report	Unusual	Client (if there is one)
Website	None	None

We have dealt with refereed journals and single-authored books as if they were two extreme and totally distinct types of publication, but there are many other forms that can be regarded as sitting between these extremes. There are, for example, non-refereed journals, periodicals, newspapers and magazines. It is not always easy to tell exactly which sort of periodical you are dealing with. A popular magazine like *New Scientist* may employ full-time scientific journalists to edit and evaluate the work that is submitted to them. Some of its articles may be sent out for comment by specialists, and others may be treated like newspaper stories, edited and evaluated in-house. If you have any doubt about what process your material will go through before it is accepted for publication then you should certainly ask. Even established refereed journals may invite people to contribute and limit the evaluation to the main editor.

The editor's role is even more crucial in books of readings. Typically the editor will discuss with a publisher the production of a book on a given topic that will be made up of chapters, each contributed by a different authority. There is something of a chicken-and-egg problem in producing such a book in that the publisher will want to be sure that enough authors will contribute before a contract is issued to the editor, but the editor may not be able to get a final agreement from potential contributors until a publisher has agreed to publish the book. More experienced authors may also wish to know who else has agreed to contribute before they commit themselves. Thus there is often quite a lot of discussion back and forth between all concerned before the book is settled on.

In some areas of academic life the book of readings is a primary source of information. It allows a variety of perspectives and issues to be put together, each one commented on by a particular authority. It is often a good way of bringing together a set of contributions that help to define a new area of activity and to identify a community of interest that goes beyond the expertise of any one individual. The disadvantage from the reader's, and hence publisher's, point of view is that the book may be very disjointed and have a mixture of styles and content that do not hold together well. The publisher therefore looks to the editor, usually the academic who planned the book, to impose order, structure, quality and appropriate homogeneity on the material sent by the authors. (We have devoted a chapter to guidance on how to put a book together. In that chapter we also discuss the particular issues about putting a set of readings together.)

Each form of publication has something to say for it, and in deciding whether to publish one's work in journals or in books it is necessary to decide on the merits of each. For example, one merit of publication in books is that there is the possibility of making a little money (and for some people rather a lot of money) by doing so. It is also worth considering the fact that publication in less prestigious periodicals and newspapers may be a way of gaining wider publicity for your ideas, beyond the limited readership of refereed journals. Furthermore, if you write the article yourself, rather than give an interview, you can have some control over what is said and how it is expressed, as well as earn some money since most periodicals will pay for written contributions but will not pay you for an interview.

We ought to mention one other form of publication: vanity publishing. This may be less prevalent than it used to be because the internet provides a much cheaper way of doing this, but for a long time some publishers have been willing to organize the printing and publishing of work, say a book of poems or an extended monograph, provided the author is willing to cover the essential costs. In effect the author is paying for the book and taking all the commercial risk. In such cases there is likely to be next to no quality control except for superficial matters like typeface and page layout. There will be no promotion of the material other than that which the author does. Such publications can be a pleasant achievement but it is extremely difficult to get the academic community to consider them. They are typically dismissed as publications merely to satisfy the vanity of the author.

The criticism of vanity publications, or more specifically self-publication by an author, is certainly not always justified. We have highly respected colleagues who thought it was appropriate for both personal and professional reasons to publish their own work themselves, and they have made a good job of it. We have been handed novels published by friends themselves that would have stood their ground against more commercial publications. But in the world of academic evaluation such a route has to be followed with caution.

A publisher provides many services that are hidden from authors and too easily taken for granted. Besides the assessment of how worthwhile the work is (albeit strongly influenced by commercial considerations), the publisher may well have a much clearer idea of what the audience, or market, is for any given topic. The publisher will have experience in how to present material, produce it and print it, that is acceptable to that market, and how to price it. Beyond these matters of selection and production there is the matter of publicity and promotion which it is difficult for a single author to do in anything but a limited way. As we have noted, much of the success of a publisher, whether it be of books, journals or newspapers, depends on developing an audience that recognizes and welcomes the particular qualities of the publications produced. It is extremely difficult, although not impossible, for authors to develop that reputation around their own work if they publish themselves.

Newspapers and magazines

Academics, in our experience, are often reluctant to talk to journalists. The reasons are understandable. The journalist asking you now with great determination what you know about how music causes aggression (a request that came in as we were writing this section!) probably knows nothing much about music, certainly knows nothing about explanations of aggression, and anyway the last thing she worked on, a couple of hours ago, was whether the local stray dogs' home should be closed. Because they are usually working to very short deadlines or within the time constraints of a live broadcast, journalists need simple, instant answers to questions that academics would not ask. David still remembers the confusion on the face of a very experienced journalist when he asked on live radio whether he could summarize his work (ten years of it) in a sentence and David said he could not. Fortunately, however, not all journalists are given limited time to tackle important topics. Although we all love to hate 'hacks', newspapers still sell well and the news and current affairs programmes still attract huge audiences. Many journalists are highly trained and remarkably skilled. We should not be tarring them all with the same brush. Perhaps we should consider improving the output of journalism, or at least trying to adjust it more closely to what we think is a good standard, by writing directly for newspapers and other periodicals from time to time.

Writing for newspapers is an avenue for publication that many academics do not consider, probably because it is unlikely to win them brownie points in the race for promotion, new jobs and other kinds of advancement. It is easy to see why. However, it is easy to see that those academics who do engage in this means of promoting their work and their ideas are often among the most successful, or at least the most well-known people in their fields. By writing for newspapers and magazines it is possible to reach a much wider audience than would be possible by publishing in even the most successful refereed journal. Furthermore, your colleagues and other academics read newspapers too. We have often had productive contact from like-minded colleagues on the basis of newspaper articles when those colleagues had been unaware of the material we had published in learned journals.

Finally, there is the matter that many academics claim they are misquoted or that newspaper articles about their area of expertise are misinformed. One answer to this is to quit complaining and have a go at writing the material yourself. As we have noted, you may get paid if you write the piece, but if you give an interview and a journalist writes it, with all the risk of misquoting, you will not get a penny. So perhaps it is worth at least considering the possibility of writing for magazines and newspapers.

How, then, do you get to write for newspapers or magazines? You ask. A journalist may contact you for information or an opinion. You could suggest that you write a short piece for them instead. You might bump into a journalist at a conference or other gathering and propose that you had something interesting to write. We would not suggest that you send unsolicited manuscripts to editors or others that you know unless you are aware of a distinct policy to consider any such material. It is better to make contact first. Summarize as clearly and as briefly as possible what you want to write about and then ask the editor if they would like you to submit something. If you get a taste for this, you should obtain a copy of the *Writers' and Artists' Yearbook*. This lists all the possible outlets for publication with addresses and other details of relevance. We will talk about literary agents in Chapter 8.

Beyond the book – the World Wide Web

With a readily available piece of software you can publish what you like (within legal bounds) in full colour on the World Wide Web. Salaam Pax has become a celebrity from the diary he produced on the web (known as a blog – short for 'web log') documenting his experiences in Baghdad during the recent Iraq war. This has been turned into a well-received book (Pax 2004). Many other personal accounts, essays, and more formal papers and reviews are now widely published in electronic format over the internet. There can be little doubt that this is a form of publication that is growing exceedingly rapidly. It does, however, have one fundamental weakness. It easily becomes the form of vanity publication we have mentioned earlier.

What formal editing and publishing offer fundamentally is some framework for quality control. The day will doubtless come, is probably here in some cases, when you can go to a website and it will guarantee the quality of all the material you can access directly from that site. In effect it will be an online book of readings, or journal with a designated editorial policy. At present this is being achieved by putting existing paper publications directly on to the internet. Given the much greater space available on the web than on the page, these electronic publications will often contain more than their printed counterparts, but there will be an attempt to maintain the same standards of quality.

Connecting outlet and aspiration

We have argued that your reasons for publishing should influence the sort of outlet you might choose. We showed how decisions about the most appropriate way of publishing your ideas, or the results of your research, are influenced by many factors including the intended audience, your motivation in wishing to publish, the nature of the material and its relationship to previous work. In this chapter we have looked more closely at the various forms of publication and their strengths and weaknesses. Given that, for most academics, publication in scholarly journals is assigned the highest value when developing a career, we paid particular attention to the different kinds of journal and what you can do to enhance your chances of having your work accepted for publication by a journal.

To summarize the choices you can make we have created below a greatly simplified table that relates, in our understanding, the purposes you might have for publication to the different outlets available. But we recognize that within the loose framework people will be at different positions along a continuum, from those that are most determined to use the process of publication to achieve personal ends, to those that see their task as a broader social contribution. We have therefore provided columns that mark the two ends of this continuum.

Framework for considering publication outlets

	Approach to task	
Driving force	**Instrumental (Machiavellian)**	**Personal (altruistic)**
Career	High-impact journal	Relevant journal
Quality control	Narrow specialist journal	Broad specialist journal
Moral duty	Elite professional magazine	Local/professional magazine
Excitement/immortality	Popular book	Academic book
Addiction	Supportive journal	New journal
Wealth	Sex and celebrity magazine	Charity campaign

However, there is one central matter on which we have been coyly quiet: quality. Different publication outlets have different standards. These are differences of kind and quantity. Some quite academic journals, for example, despite their academic pretensions do want the work they publish to have practical relevance. Other journals may publish only material using a particular theoretical framework or drawing on a limited range of methodologies. In addition to these qualitative constraints there will be the much more difficult to specify quantitative criteria. In empirical disciplines this may be easier to establish on the basis, for instance, of the size of the sample, or the level of statistical sophistication applied to the data. More often, though, it is some less tangible assessment of the degree of significance of the contribution that the paper makes.

As you start on your career as an author you may find it difficult to judge how significant your work is. Our experience is that students underestimate the potential significance of their work and overestimate the quality of their writing and arguments. These judgements are part of what you learn by the process of submitting work to the critical evaluation of others, either colleagues prior to publication or from the review process once work had been submitted.

The crucial issue about quality, though, is that even if you have the skill to make the proverbial silk purse out of a sow's ear, it is much easier to start with silk. Committed authors do not talk about what they are researching or studying. They always think in terms of what they are writing. The authorship process starts from the minute you decide to explore a topic. If you are aiming at significant publication you have to prepare your material from the start in a way that will facilitate that aim. This is not a book on research methodology or the process of scholarship. We are assuming that you have gained that expertise in other ways, but the fact that we do not mention these matters should not be taken as implying that we think all writing is merely an issue of form and style. Content is the crucial component. We have seen badly written material published because the data source is so fundamentally fascinating, but it is rare to read a scholarly publication that is extremely well written but has no substance.

4   Beyond the blank page

Writing takes time • Approaching academic writing
• Getting down to writing • Learning to read your own
work better • Unblocking

Le genie n'est autre chose qu'une grande aptitude à la
patience.

(Buffon)

Or, as Carlyle put it:

Genius, which means the transcendent capacity of
taking trouble, first of all.

Writing takes time

One of the most important lessons you can learn as a writer is that writing
takes time. It involves creativity, but for most of us it also involves a great
deal of hard slog as we sort out what we want to say and how best to say it.
Very few authors have the ability to write well enough in one sitting to
communicate clearly what they want to say, or at any rate to communicate
it as clearly as they could. That is why writing is a slow process for most
people.

Both of us find writing fairly easy, in that words come easily to us when we
are writing. However, the process of creating text is inevitably interspersed
with periods of reading and revision as we gradually shape successive drafts
into a form that pleases us and is one that we are willing to share with others,

in the public display that is publication. This approach is rather like the work of a sculptor, working in clay, who adds a bit here, moulds and shapes a bit there, takes a bit away there, until eventually he achieves something that feels right and communicates appropriately. Gradually developing and sculpting a piece of academic writing over several days, weeks, months, or even years, is likely to produce a better product than attempting to dash it off quickly, checking only for any outlandish errors before printing and submitting the text.

Writing well is hard, even if the words come easily to you. That is why, whenever you experience difficulties with an academic writing task, you should remind yourself that most academic writers are labouring under similar problems. The difference between those who succeed as academic authors and those who do not, is that the successful ones find ways of persuading themselves to start writing, rather than thinking about it.

One reason that producing text is hard for most people is that they become hung up about getting things right before they write them down. Part of what it is to be a productive writer is learning that it is better to write something that is not good enough, than to write nothing. Sensible authors know this and act on it. It is what Lamott (1995) is talking about when she writes about 'shitty first drafts':

> All good writers write them. That is how they end up with good second drafts and terrific third drafts.
>
> (Lamott 1995: 21)

Although we think she is perhaps somewhat optimistic if she believes that all shitty first drafts will end in terrific third drafts, Lamott is absolutely right in her belief in their ubiquitousness. Don't be afraid to write them; the best authors do. The point is that at least once you have written something, you can then improve it. That is why we offer the following advice to anyone we are helping to develop as a writer:

Don't get it right; get it written.

This is such a sensible and well-stated piece of advice that it must have an author. Unfortunately we do not know who that author is. If you follow it and write things down before trying to get them right, what you get written may be poor; it may not say as much as you wanted to say, or say it as elegantly or succinctly as you had hoped to say it. But at least if it is written, you have a basis to work from.

In this chapter we pay particular attention to some ways of getting down to writing, and on developing your text once you get started. Before that, however, we will say a little about different ways of approaching academic writing, because whatever your normal approach to writing, it is worth experimenting with different ways of creating and working on text. By doing so you may discover that the approaches you have always adopted are less helpful than some you have rejected.

Approaching academic writing

Academic writers can be characterized according to the approaches they favour and the ways in which they think about their writing. It is worth taking some time to reflect both on the kind of academic writer you are and on whether there are any ways in which your approach to writing might usefully change.

Planning versus spontaneity

One division comes between those writers who plan their writing meticulously and those who approach it in a more spontaneous and organic way, seeding a few ideas and gradually working at them until they grow into something worthwhile. While we were working on this book we learned that, as authors, our favoured approaches lie towards opposite ends of this continuum. This led to some fruitful discussions as we negotiated about who was going to do what, and when they were going to do it. In reality, most writers will employ a mixed economy, adopting a range of approaches at different times during the same writing project.

Planning your writing can be useful in ensuring that you cover everything that you want to say, and work out a helpful order in which to say it. In addition, developing a plan for a piece of writing can help to build confidence that you can actually get the job done. Such plans usually involve setting out subsections and splitting the writing task into several smaller portions, which may make it seem more do-able. However, planning can be extremely unhelpful if you allow it to exercise control over what you do. For example, becoming too tied down by the plans you have laid out for a writing project could close your mind to the possibility that the material you want to write about might be more helpfully structured in a different way. In any case, no matter how hooked on planning they are, few authors never write freely – just allowing their hands to do the writing and the thinking if you like – even if they need the security provided by a plan before they can do it. For most authors the detailed plans they drew up initially, along with subsidiary plans they make along the way, will typically act like scaffolding to support their creativity, providing appropriate niches into which they can place the information, views and arguments they want to share.

No matter how committed an author is to the importance of an organic approach, in which text seems to flow spontaneously, out of the ends of their fingers, as they type, such an approach alone is unlikely to be successful because few people are able to write cogently and persuasively without some planning. Whether they plan on paper or in their head, and whether they plan before they begin, or only begin to formulate plans after a substantial chunk of text has begun to take shape, planning will come into things at some time. If it does not, success is unlikely.

'Knowing what you want to say' versus 'Writing to find out what you think'

A related, but perhaps more surprising, way of grouping academic writers, is to consider the extent to which they know (or think they know) what they want to say before they begin writing. Here again we can distinguish two main groups. Some authors cannot imagine writing without knowing pretty much what they expect to see on the page when they have finished. By contrast there are others who know what they want to write about, but are rarely sure what they want to say, when they start writing.

Perhaps you have come across people who claim that they do not know what they think until they have written it down. Actually, one of us falls into this group and is often telling the literal truth when he does so, as evidenced by the fact that he is frequently surprised to read what his fingers have typed. It is much more likely, however, that you will find it difficult even to imagine what such a person is talking about. Whether or not you can understand what they are saying, it is worth trying out the kind of approach to writing that they adopt, because you might find it useful. One way that you might do so in a fairly pain-free way (even if you are an obsessive planner), is to try writing freely for five minutes on a subject you care about, but without thinking about what you want to say beforehand, and certainly without worrying about how you might justify or support what you say. We will explore the details of this approach later in the chapter.

Getting down to writing

Getting started on a writing project can be the most exciting thing in the world, if you set out knowing pretty much where you want to begin – if, say, a first sentence has formed itself in your mind even before you switch on your computer or take up your pen, or if you have already planned the first draft in a series of bullet points. If, on the other hand, you set out with only a vague notion of what you want to write and no ideas about how to get started, things can be very different. Facing the blank page can be disheartening for novice and experienced writers alike.

It can be helpful to regard that first blank page as the start of a journey. Knowing where you want to go – what you want to write about – will be a great help, but, as is the case with all expeditions, deciding how to get to your goal may take some planning. Finding the best way to say what you want to say will probably involve a number of exploratory trips into the territory about which you want to write, during which you try out different ways of beginning your text.

Whether you lean towards the more spontaneous approach to writing, or always begin with a plan, you have to find a place to begin and a way to get started. Many people find that the easiest way to get started on a piece of writing is to begin with whatever aspect of a topic first grabbed their attention – for example, with something that someone else has written. Others find it easier to begin by drafting the main argument they wish to put forward, or by writing a description of their research methods; or they may find it helpful to begin by writing about an example that they want to use at some point in their text. None of these is any better than the others. The best place to start is with something that you feel able to write about, because having drafted that section, you will have a basis around which to begin building the rest of your text.

Finding the time

Inexperienced authors often develop the idea that it is only possible to write if they have a decent chunk of time in which to do so. Some even believe that writing is possible only when they feel inspired. Taken together, these mythical beliefs form the most common excuse for academic inactivity. They are mythical because it is possible to be a productive author even if time is short; and it is possible to write in the absence of inspiration, which rarely comes to most of us at convenient moments.

Actually, inspiration is rather overrated as a motivating factor in academic writing. This is true in areas other than academia as well, as illustrated by a wonderful television documentary many years ago in which the American singer songwriter Randy Newman talked about the fact that whenever he had a new album to cut he would rent a room, move a piano into it, and then work regular office hours until he had written sufficient songs. He did not wait until he was inspired; and neither should you. Journalists sometimes point out that only rich authors claim to have 'writer's block'. Those who earn their living by the pen cannot afford such a luxury.

Later in this chapter we will discuss some ways in which you can get started and develop your work with minimum amounts of time; but realistically, few people, if any, can produce polished pieces of work with just a few minutes here and there. If you are to be as productive as you can be, you will need to create times in which you can develop your writing. No matter how difficult, if you want to make a career as an author you should address this issue seriously. While there may be periods when your other commitments are so heavy that it really is impossible to do any writing, there will no doubt be times when you could find at least a little time to write. The trick is in finding those times, pinning them down, and then making the best possible use of them.

We can all think of occasions when we are happy to allow other activities to nudge our writing into touch. This is a recipe for disaster, because every time you leave your writing to do something else makes it more likely that you will abandon whatever you are working on. Many people find that the more clearly they can specify times for writing and stick to them, the better. Sometimes they will find that they begin such a session with a head full of new ideas just bursting to get out on to the page. But sometimes they will start off with no idea of how to begin. At times like these they have to remember that the process of writing is complex and involves many steps besides text production. Sometimes, for example, rather than producing coherent prose, all they will do is to draft some headings that they later abandon. And sometimes they will spend their writing time in carefully reading and interrogating what they have written earlier, which, as we shall argue later, is perhaps the best way of making decisions about how to develop the text further. All of these activities are essential parts of the academic writing process, every bit as much as the creation of fresh text.

Some established authors find that they do all their production of text early in the day and return to it in the late evening when they prepare notes for the following day's writing. However, you may be a night owl, feeling most able to get words down on the page when everyone else is asleep. Find out what works for you and try to organize both your professional and your personal life to allow you to make the most of the time you have available for writing, even if you cannot develop a routine that allows you to write regularly at the same time or times each day.

Always bear in mind the amount of time that you will need to write anything of any substance, so that you do not lose hope when you seem to be making painfully slow progress. When David was working on his book *Mapping Murder*, with most of the notes in place for it from the television series he had made earlier on the same topic, it took him about five months, more or less full time, from receiving the contract to submitting the final text of around 95,000 words. That is around 900 words for each working day. These calculations do not include much allowance for preparation and sorting out the material, and they relate to an experienced author who was developing the text of a book using material in which he had been immersed over a number of years and about which he had just presented a television series.

As we said at the beginning of this section, writing takes time. So if you are planning to write a journal article of, say, 5,000 words, which would be an average length for many journals, the sheer business of writing a final, full draft could easily take you around a dozen working days once you have got everything organized. Of course, people differ greatly in how quickly they write and doubtless speed up as they get more experienced. Not only that, but some topics are more difficult to write about than others. Nonetheless, the message is simple. Plan for the long haul rather than to get any writing task over in a rush.

Finding the place

Finding the right place in which to write is just as important as finding the time in which to do it. Some authors are obsessional about having to be in a particular place before they can even think of writing, whereas others can write almost anywhere provided they have a few minutes to spare. The poet drifting out of his garret to scribble his stanzas in the local bistro became a cliché for nineteenth-century Paris; in a modern-day version of the same phenomenon, we have colleagues who claim to get all their first drafts written in coffee bars. Challenged about the apparent frivolity of this claim, they draw attention to the fact that J.K. Rowling writes her *Harry Potter* bestsellers in just such a way. To some extent we can understand the attraction. Indeed, when he is having difficulty in getting to grips with sections of text, Gavin often persuades himself to undertake the rereading and interrogation of drafts that are a central plank in his writing process, by driving into town to have afternoon tea in a café, while he does it. Now of course he could have tea at home, but that wouldn't be the same, because on such occasions in order to get down to the rereading and redrafting that needs to be undertaken, he knows he has to go somewhere different, and the café in question is often just the place.

Find the place or places where you feel most comfortable writing and try to arrange that this is where you write. Be aware, however, that the best place to write may vary depending both on what you are writing and on the stage in the writing process you have reached. For example, even if you are the kind of person who in general finds that she is most productive when she is sitting at the desk in her study, with all her notes and books around her, you might find that sometimes it is helpful to do certain bits of writing somewhere else. You might even find that writing in, say, the library, or on a train during a trip, is rather liberating, because at these times you will be writing in the absence of the opportunity and perhaps the temptation to keep checking your sources.

Audition a variety of places as settings for getting down to different kinds of writing. Find what works, note it and act on what you have learned.

Writing is a job like any other

The truth is that academic writing is just a job, like any other – like washing the dishes, marking essays, fixing a bicycle or writing a song. None of these would get done if you waited until the ideal time arrived to do them; and neither will writing. It is because they fail to learn this, or at any rate because they fail to learn what to do about it, that so many students end up rushing their assignments and essays at the last minute. It is also, arguably, why so many university lecturers are much less productive as authors than they could be.

One thing is sure. If you want to write, but find that whenever you get round to trying to write you are unable to do so, drastic action is called for. Day refers to a writer who claims to be of the 'feel the fear but do it anyway school' (1996: 4) This writer, she says, claims that he will chain himself to the word-processor rather than letting the empty screen get the better of him.

It does not matter whether you are writing a book or something small like an article, conference paper, or even a conference abstract, the same problems arise and the same solutions can help to get you going. Paradoxically, one of the most helpful ways of pushing yourself into those first few steps with a new writing project, is to abandon any hope you had of completing it quickly. Then instead of chaining yourself to your computer, or locking yourself away in a room until you have finished it, try setting yourself an easily manageable task that will help you to get started.

The trick is to decide on a task that is so small that it is hardly conceivable that you could fail, however tired, depressed or overpowered by other demands you feel. You might, for example, decide to write one sentence summing up the main view that you want to communicate; or you might write some headings for the principal sections that you imagine your text will have, whether they are section headings for an article or chapter headings for a book. The point is that, even if all you decide to do is to write a list of keywords or to draft an introductory sentence, you will make some progress, so that the next time you come to this piece of writing, you will already have some text, however short, with which to work.

A warm-up sprint: five-minute writing

One very small task that you will find helpful is to write about your topic – freely and without stopping – for a very short time; we suggest five minutes, which is so short that even those with the busiest schedules should be able to find several occasions during the day when they could devote this much of their precious time to writing. Doing so is a good way of developing the stamina and discipline needed to become a writer who is able to endure the slog of producing text, even on days when she is not feeling up to it. When we first introduce novices to this idea we tell them that, at least initially, they should aim at nothing more in these five-minute writing sessions than to write as much as they can, because this is a good way of limbering up for the rather strenuous activity of academic writing on a larger scale.

Writing regularly for just five minutes a day is the best way that we have found of helping inexperienced authors, whether they are students or professional academics, to develop the attitudes towards writing that they need for success. It is because we believe it is such a good way of developing stamina and discipline as a writer that we suggest you should try to develop a routine in which you write freely for five minutes every day. It does not matter when you do so, though you may find it helpful to try to fit these sessions in at the same time each day. Undertaking five minutes of free writing a day is rather like exercising in the gym; the work you do will help you to limber up for more adventurous literary exercise, by helping you to get fit to write. More surprisingly perhaps, it will also help you to get your head in trim, to set your mind working, whatever you choose to write about.

You will probably find it helps if you write first of all about topics that have nothing to do with your academic work. Doing so will help you to throw off some of the constraints that often interfere with the ability to write freely. It is important, however, that you should decide what you are going to write about before you start writing. You might choose 'what I've read this week', or 'what I think should be done about X' (insert a contentious topic of your choice).

Five-minute writing rules

- Write for no less, and definitely no more, than five minutes. This will necessitate a clock or a watch with a second hand.
- Once you start writing you must not stop until five minutes have passed.
- Don't plan what you are going to write before doing so.
- If you run out of things to say, rewrite the last word over and over again until you come up with something else to write. (If you want, you can substitute your name, or your favourite swear word.)
- Don't allow yourself to be distracted into thinking about the words you use; just write the words that come, totally uninvited, into your head as you are writing.
- Don't stop to think about punctuation or spelling.
- Don't allow yourself to worry about whether what you are writing is making sense.
- Avoid thinking about whether what you are writing will impress your readers.
- Don't worry about how you might justify or support what you are saying, or how you might illustrate it.
- On at least the first dozen or so occasions that you undertake this activity, write by hand, rather than word-processor.

If you try out our suggestion and get into the habit of writing for five minutes a day you may well find that you are surprised to see what you have written and to discover that, even without any planning, it often has some literary merit. That is why, once you have become used to writing under the constraints imposed by these rules, you might find that such sessions can be a useful way of generating text that will contribute to the completion of published work, and especially as a way of producing first drafts. And even though the rules say that you should not plan what you are going to write before you start, you will probably find that practising writing in these short and intensive bursts will have an effect on your ability to plan in relation to other, more focused aspects of your academic writing. It will do so because the fact that you have only five minutes in which to write will sharpen your ability to access information that you have stored in the vast ideas bank that you call your memory, thus influencing your ability to decide what you want to say, and to plan how you might say it.

Five-minute drafts

You should never use these five-minute writing slots as a time for editing, or redrafting. They are intended for the production of text, not for its improvement. Practising writing in focused five-minute slots in the disciplined way we are proposing is rather like meditation, in that it is about freeing your mind up, as well as increasing your ability to get ideas down as quickly as you can think them. And so you will probably find that after you have practised the discipline of five-minute writing for a time – say for a month or two – you are able to adopt this approach as a way of exploring possible ways of expressing yourself whenever there is something you want to write about.

One page at a time

Like most tasks, part of the problem of getting started on writing is the ability we have to imagine the route to completion, and the problems that will inevitably be encountered. Often you will feel as if you have a mountain to climb, and yet be unsure whether you have the skills or energy even to get to base camp. The sheer number of words that have to be put down – perhaps 6,000 words for a lengthy article, or 60,000 for a short book – can make it feel impossible that you will ever get there. It is the daunting idea that you somehow have to think up all these words that makes the blank page such a challenge.

In order to avoid the fear that can paralyse even the most experienced writers when they set out on a new project, one approach is to try focusing on one page at a time. The idea is to try always to focus on the current page, in order to help you to feel in control. This strategy is analogous to the way in which Alcoholics Anonymous get their members not to think about staying sober for life, but just 'one day at a time'.

Once you have decided that you are going to avoid worrying about the mountain, focusing instead on one page at a time, there are many different ways in which you can get started. One approach that can be very productive is to begin by answering, briefly, some key questions about your work. For example, in writing about an empirical research project, it might be appropriate to focus first on a series of starter questions[1] such as:

---

[1] We develop these more fully on page 47.

- What was I seeking to establish?
- What did I do to try to find that out?
- How did I go about making sense of what I had done?
- What did I find out or conclude?

The answers to these questions will revolve around your data, why you collected that data and how you went about analysing and understanding it. Noting your answers on one page can provide a framework for what you are writing. Your notes do not need to be written in elegant prose – you are the only one who need ever read them – they are simply notes that give you a starting point.

If your research is of a conceptual kind, you will often be able to adopt a similar approach. Often such research will involve trying to answer questions that have arisen for you as a result of what others have written about a topic, and what you write about it may, for example, focus on the development of an argument in favour of a contrary point of view. In beginning to structure what you want to say in such a case, you might find it useful to begin with questions such as these:

- What was I interested in thinking about?
- What is my view, why do I hold it? What arguments support it?
- How can counter-arguments to my view be addressed?
- What follows if my view is justified?

Depending on the area in which you are working, you may want to develop a different set of starter questions as a way of constructing a scaffold from which to develop your text. Whatever questions you use, however, it is important, at this early stage, that you do not get sidetracked into elaborating on these matters. What you are aiming to do is to produce – on one page – a few pointers for the way ahead.

The next stage involves developing each of the answers you have given to your starter questions into a single page. At this stage, or even earlier, you should start to consider the main arguments you want to present and any examples or illustrations you might need to underpin your point of view. They will help to shape your unfolding story.

By now you will have a few pages of notes, which represent the first draft of your text, albeit in a primitive form. As you work on these notes, filling them out by clarifying and elaborating the points you have made, you will grow and develop your text; in this way you will gradually clarify what you want to say, and ensure that you say it as well as you can. One way of deciding what to write is to try imagining the questions that another person might ask about your notes, and to incorporate the answers you would give to those questions. Another would be to work methodically on each page in turn, developing each note into a paragraph or two. Gradually your text will expand towards the length that you are aiming for, and perhaps considerably beyond that. If this happens, don't worry, because as you continue to develop your text you will inevitably find that there are words and phrases, whole sentences, and perhaps even whole sections that do not earn their keep, and have to be excised. As your text grows and changes, you will increasingly become aware of the ways in which the different sections relate to one another, noticing, for example, places where the order of ideas is not as smooth as it might be.

Oddly enough, when you feel in control of what is happening with the page on which you are focusing at any given time, you will often find that ideas come to you about other parts of your text. For example, it might suddenly occur to you that some ideas, or even a particular phrase or sentence, that you recall writing in another section would actually be better placed on the page on which you are currently working, or that an idea that you are currently working on actually belongs elsewhere. At this point you might want to refer back to any plans you had originally made for this text, including a draft structure if there was one, to enable you to see the consequences for your overall framework of any move – if, for example, any headings or sub-headings you have decided on need to be revised. What is going on in such a scenario is that although you are actively focusing on a particular part of your text, other parts of your brain are at the same time remembering what you have written elsewhere and making links. As you become more experienced as a writer, you might even find that while you can only actively engage in writing one section of text at a time, you develop the ability to think about several sections at once.

Learning to read your own work better

Learning to read your own work better is probably the most important thing you can do if you want to become a better writer. You might wonder why we should assert this. After all, why would you want to read your own work, other than to give yourself the opportunity of enjoying your own beautiful, crisp, clear prose, basking in the glory of being such an accomplished writer? Well, for one thing, you will have to do so if you are to develop skill in spotting all the places where your writing is not quite as crisp and clear and accomplished as you think it is; and at least in the case of early attempts to write about things that matter to you, this will nearly always be the case. It certainly is for us. We want to encourage you to practise reading your own work critically, looking and listening for mistakes, looking out for places where you can improve it. In fact, one of the best ways that you can force yourself to read sufficiently carefully to allow you to evaluate what you have written, is to read your work out loud.

Developing your text: drafting and revising

When you are writing it is a good idea to draft and redraft your work as often as you can, adding and juggling ideas; rethinking arguments and examples, at the same time as sorting out obvious problems in punctuation, spelling, grammar and your use of citation. Some people have the idea that housekeeping of such technical details can be left to the last minute, but experience suggests that it is best to keep on top of them from the start. Your text will gradually grow and take shape as you see places where you are less clear than you might be, and ways of improving your arguments, perhaps by responding to possible counter-arguments.

In reading what you have written you should constantly be thinking both about whether you have actually managed to say what you want to say and about whether you have done so as effectively and clearly as possible. It is always a good idea to get someone you trust and for whom you have respect, to read your work over for you. If you can persuade more than one person to read your work over, so much the better, provided that they are the kind of people who will be willing to make truthful, but constructive comments aimed at helping you both to excise mistakes and to polish your text. Make sure that before asking someone to read and comment on your work, you have satisfied yourself that they (and you) are willing to take the risk that they might offend you by being truthful.

Although enlisting the help of others to comment on your text is a good idea, if you are serious about wanting to write as well as you can, you should also learn to read your own work carefully. To do so efficiently you will have to develop skill in two closely related but distinct ways of critically reading text: copy editing and proofreading.

Copy editing and proofreading

Copy editing and proofreading derive their names from the processes carried out by editors and sub-editors who work for publishers. Their roles are similar, but distinct, both from one another and from the roles that you will play in copy editing and proofreading your own work. Copy editors read and edit 'copy', that is, text that has been submitted for publication before it is prepared for printing, whereas proofreaders check the 'proofs', that is, typeset pages produced in a form that is very similar to what they will look like when they are finally printed.

Copy editing

Copy editing is like a whole-body health check to which a text is submitted to ensure that it is fit for the job it is expected to do. It involves reading the text closely in order to check that it makes sense and does not contain omissions; ambiguities; inconsistencies; mistakes in the use of words; spelling or grammatical errors; peculiarities of style, or unhelpful punctuation. It also involves spotting 'dead wood' in the form of words, phrases or even whole sentences that add nothing to the sense the author wishes to communicate, and places where clarification or further development of an idea or the introduction of new ideas may improve text.

Copy editing checklist

Copy editing involves reading the text carefully, bearing in mind questions such as:

- Does it make sense? Is its main thrust clear and succinct?
- Is it well argued, well structured and easy to follow? Are points of view and arguments presented in the best order? Are readers given enough help, in the form of effective signposting, to allow them to find their way round?
- Is it clear? Is any of what is written ambiguous?
- Does the text include any irrelevancies? Is it well focused? Does it ever wander into interesting but irrelevant side issues?
- Is the text coherent? That is, does it 'hang together'? Or does it contain inconsistencies?
- Are promises fulfilled? For example, if on page 1, it says that arguments will be offered in favour of a point of view, are arguments offered, or are the points of view merely asserted in different forms?
- Are arguments that are presented helpful to the points of view they are intended to support?
- Are examples and illustrations interesting and appropriate?
- Does any of the text serve a merely decorative function, making the text look scholarly and important, because it employs technical or intellectual sounding words and phrases?
- Is every single word essential to the sense conveyed? Do some words serve as padding, bulking up what would otherwise be rather a thin piece of work?
- Does the text make use of any annoying stylistic mannerisms, that is, words or phrases that appear over and over again, whether or not they convey meaning? If they do convey meaning, could a more apt word or phrase be substituted?
- Is there any unnecessary repetition? Is there any unnecessary repetition?

We suggest that you should think about these questions each time you read through and interrogate a draft of your work. In addition, you might care to stop at the bottom of each page and ask yourself the general question: How do this page and each paragraph on it help to convey my ideas, what I did or what I found?

Proofreading

Unlike copy editing, proofreading is not about improving text by identifying places where it could benefit from adjustments to style or content. Rather than characterizing it, as we did copy editing, as being like a full-body health check, we think of proofreading as being akin to a detailed surface scan of a body of text, aimed at identifying a limited range of problems. It is concerned with the correctness of technical aspects such as punctuation, spelling, grammar, citation and typography. That is why, in proofreading your own work, you will find it helpful to read, so far as possible, not only as if it were written by someone else (about which we say more below), but also as if it is devoid of interest or meaning. This is particularly important during the proofreading that you undertake immediately before deciding that any piece of text is ready for submission; if you do not manage to achieve such distance from the meaning of the text, you may be drawn into making changes at a textual level, and as a result might miss some technical errors.

For many people, proofreading is usually a process that takes place towards the end of a writing project. However, although careful proofreading at this stage is crucial to avoid submitting work that contains easily avoidable errors, we suggest that you should develop the habit of checking your work in a proofreading, rather than a copy editing, kind of way on several occasions during the development of your text.

Unlike copy editing, proofreading can become quite a quick process, provided that you manage to avoid allowing meaning to come between you and the mistakes you are trying to spot, though you should not aim for speed at the cost of accuracy. After a while you will probably find that you do not really have to look for mistakes. Indeed, when you have had a fair amount of practice in proofreading – perhaps especially in proofreading work by others – you may find that technical errors in a piece of text seem to jump up to meet you, so that you no longer really have to go looking for them.

Unfortunately, some people will never spot spelling mistakes, no matter how madly those spelling mistakes jump up and down and tear their hair, and shout and scream to be spotted. If you are one of these people, you should make absolutely sure that you engage a trustworthy friend as a human spell-checker, because computer spellcheckers do not spot all mistakes. Far example, although yew mite expect that it wood, a spell checker would note spot awl off the mistakes in thus paragraph. Win we invited hour spellchecker to look at this page, it did not spot that 'off' should have been spelled 'of', that 'awl' should have been spelled 'all', or that 'hour', 'yew', 'mite' and 'wood' and a number of others words were also miss-spelled.

Copy editing and proofreading: two sides of the same coin?

We have written about copy editing and proofreading as if they are two separate processes. In reality there will be a lot of overlap between them, and much of the time when you are reading your own work, you will do both things at the same time. As you read and revise successive drafts of your work, you will spot errors in spelling, punctuation and grammar, even if you are reading primarily for content and sense. It is always best to note mistakes whenever you see them, correcting them in your text as soon as possible, rather than leaving them till the last minute. You should not allow yourself to fall into the trap of thinking that you can sort out all these niggly little technical problems and mistakes at the end, just before you submit your article or other piece of writing.

Reading your work as if it was written by someone else

In copy editing your own work in successive drafts, it is easy to allow your familiarity with what you wanted to say to lead you to believe that you have said it, even when you have not. And even if you have said it, it is easy to allow your familiarity with your text to fool you into thinking that it is well written, clear and coherent, even when it is not. Not only that, but familiarity with your text can also lead you to miss linguistic mistakes. For example, it is easy to skip past repeated words and and phrases; places where words missing; places where you have used the wrong wood; misuses of words; places where you have make a mistake with tense; typoss (that is, apparemt mistakes in spelling or in the use of wards that are actuallt the reslut of mistake on typung) as well as genuine mispelings; mistakes in punctuation? and grammatical error. Modern word-processors highlight many of these as you type, but always remember computers are exceptionally fast idiots. No word-processor actually understands what you mean to say.

One way of getting past the problems that familiarity with your own text can cause, is to leave it aside for a while between drafts so that you approach it with fresh eyes. Another, even more important, way of tackling such problems is to enter into the imaginative game of reading it as if it were written by someone else. This is not easy. However, it is essential that you should practise reading your work as if you are not its parent, and are hence unfamiliar with what it says, because doing so will help you to identify not only all kinds of technical mistakes and mistakes in reasoning, but also occasions when your examples or illustrations are weak or inappropriate, however entertaining, enjoyable or interesting they may be, as well as occasions where your style is clumsy or boring.

Unblocking

One of the worst experiences writers can have is getting to a certain point in the journey they are making with a text, and then finding that they cannot do any more – that they do not know how to proceed, do not like what they have written, and perhaps cannot even see the point of what they have been writing. Such writing blocks can seem insurmountable even to the most highly motivated writers. They are particularly difficult to cope with when there is a deadline to meet.

There are a number of different ways in which you can unblock yourself. You could make use of the discipline you have developed as a writer of five-minute drafts, and set yourself the task of writing for five minutes and no more about what is blocking your progress (promise yourself a reward when you've done it – a piece of cake or a glass of wine?). Another way forward would be to try imagining the questions that an interested but uninformed reader might ask about the part of your planned text that is your current hurdle. Use your answers as the basis of the section in question. You could, of course, give yourself no more than five minutes in which to do so. Alternatively, you could use these answers as the focus of a single page of writing, which you then develop in the kind of way we have discussed earlier.

Waiting for inspiration is a bad move. Leaving your draft to one side for a while in the hope that when you come back to it the source of the blockage will magically have disappeared is marginally better, because with luck something will have changed in the meantime that will help you to carry on. However, in our experience the best way to proceed is simply to write your way out of the block. Doing so will take willpower, and it might involve organizing your life so that you can spend some concentrated time at a desk, but basically all you have to do is to decide that you are not going to give up and keep at it, writing and writing until, in the end, you write yourself into something worthwhile.

5   The importance of style

The switch to professional writing • Success as an
academic author • Good academic writing
• Developing your own style

[Scientific discourse consists of] a personal story told so
that the narrator appears in the guise of a modest but
competent subscriber to the moral order of which he or
she wishes to be seen to be a member.

(Harré 1994: 99)

The switch to professional writing

A major problem that many people have in starting to write for publication is
adapting to the change in expectations that comes with the move into professional writing. What is expected from them now is fundamentally different
from what was expected of them as students. In a way, it is a little like the
move from amateur to professional level in a sport, or in other pursuits such as
music or drama.

Typically, students write for a specific audience in the form of their teachers
or examiners, against the backdrop of a declared syllabus. Whatever they write,
whether it is an exam answer or a thesis, one of the central expectations on
students is that they should demonstrate their knowledge and understanding.
For those undertaking research at doctoral level, things are hardly different,
even when they are pursuing highly original work, because even at this stage
they usually write in a way that leaves as few opportunities open for critics as

possible. This often leads to bland, rather dry and defensive text, which manages in most cases to dull or disguise the excitement of the chase, almost as if what is being reported was a straightforward and methodical process with no hiccups or disasters en route, and no loopholes or fuzzy edges to show that the candidate has spent at least some time wading through risky intellectual waters.

Most students live in fear of being 'found out' as knowing less than they really do. That is why, although some of them write well and with authority and passion, they often end up writing in a style that is so densely packed with information that it is difficult to distinguish the wood from the trees, and so over-defended, that it is almost impossible to read. And that is why most postgraduate work ends up unloved and even unread on dusty shelves in university library stores.

Writing for academic and professional publication is more than a mere expression of knowledge: it is about sharing new thinking and the results of research. It is an art in the sense that it requires the mastery of skills combined with the wit and the imagination necessary to use those skills effectively. Ideally, writing skills should be learned in a co-writing situation, in which a more experienced author models both literary and secretarial aspects of the writing process, including:

- Different approaches to the development of text.
- Drafting, reading and revising text.
- Playing or experimenting with text to find the most effective way of communicating particular ideas.
- Copy editing and proofreading.

We discussed some of these skills in Chapter 4, 'Beyond the blank page'.

Success as an academic author

Our job in trying to facilitate your development as an academic author would be easier if we were able to inform you authoritatively, that success depends solely upon developing a good writing style. It would be easy because then all we would have to do would be to tell you (after a sensible amount of research) what the elements of good academic style are and to offer you advice about how you could go about developing it in your own writing. Unfortunately, success as an author also depends on other factors, including the need not only to fall into line with the general expectations of your discipline, but also to adhere to the house style of whatever publishing house or individual journals you hope will publish your work. We will say a little about house style, and about requirements in relation to the citation of sources, before turning to the question of what good academic writing consists of.

House style

Academic publishers will always expect authors to adhere to their house style, about which they will provide guidance, either in printed form or via a website. Such guidance varies from publisher to publisher, but may refer, for example, to aspects of punctuation and grammar. Often it will contain requirements about spelling, and especially about whether authors should adopt American or English spelling – that is, whether, for example, you should write about 'colors' or 'colours', and about 'Americanized' spellings or Americanised ones. Most often house style will give directions about the citation of sources, which we discuss in the next section. Finally, it may lay down expectations about how authors should deal with the possibility that certain ways of speaking will be offensive to some people.

Later in this chapter we discuss the particular problems of gendered language, which is probably the most common area in which you might come across such expectations. However, you might come across others in relation to a number of areas where using the wrong language might be considered offensive, including disability and race. Nowadays, for example, the expressions 'learning difficulties' and 'learning disabilities' have largely replaced the terms 'mental handicap' and 'mental retardation'.

Even without consulting guidance from outlets to which you intend to submit your work, however, you should be able to form a clear impression of their expectations, because crucial aspects of accepted style will be clearly visible in the things they publish. This is particularly true in the case of journals. Taking a close look at several articles from different volumes spanning several years, and scanning many more will usually allow you to form a fairly reliable picture of what they expect. Though there is considerable overlap across the range of academic journals in relation to the kind of written style that is acceptable, individual journals often have their own very particular ideas about style.

The stylistic advice, or requirements illustrated by the extracts in the box on page 54 cover a range of topics, including spelling; accessibility to readers outside the journal's specialist area; the use of jargon; the avoidance of discriminatory language and respect for human dignity. Many journals are more concerned with the style in which manuscripts are presented, some in a distressingly detailed way. Consider, for example, the following request from the editors of *Education Today*:

Please use British rather than American spellings. Use 's' not 'z' where there is a choice (eg organise, realise). Avoid the use of unnecessary capital letters. Acronyms and abbreviations should only be used where they are instantly recognisable; for preference, use the words in full on first

Stylistic advice, or requirements, from various publishers

The use of non-discriminatory language is encouraged and spellings should conform with that used in the Concise Oxford Dictionary of Current English.

Health and Social Care in the Community

Technical correctness is only one criterion for acceptance. Clarity and the general interest of the manuscript are very important. Authors should ask a colleague to read and critique their manuscripts before submission. Authors whose native language is not English should make sure that someone with an excellent command of written English read their manuscript to improve the grammar and usage.

American Journal of Physics

References. These should be kept to the minimum. Books are italicized (underlined in typescript), e.g. F. L. Carsten, *Princes and Parliaments in Germany* (Oxford, 1959). In second and subsequent references to a work, an abbreviated title should be adopted, e.g. Carsten, *Princes*, p. 72. A reference to an article in a periodical should include (after the author's name and the title of the article and the title of the journal) the volume number (arabic), date in brackets, and relevant page numbers, e.g. 'The False Joseph II', *Historical Journal*, 18 (1975), 467–95.

German History

All submissions are expected to demonstrate respect for human dignity and accountability to society.

Scandinavian Journal of Caring Sciences

Use active voice, rather than passive voice. For example, "A study was conducted" is passive voice. In contrast, "We conducted a study" is active voice. Active voice is generally easier to read and clearly distinguishes the work that the author completed from the work of other researchers cited in the paper.

Current Research in Social Psychology

The style of writing we are looking for might be called "informal" academic – that is, scholarly but as much as possible, jargon free – addressing the reader as a co-learner and working towards a community of scholars within the confines of a journal.

Analytic Teaching

Contributors should ensure that their articles can be understood by readers from any academic discipline, or from no discipline at all.

Bioethics

occurrence. Numbers under 10 should be spelt out in full except where attached to a unit of quantity or a percentage (except in tables and figures). Per cent should appear in full (except in tables and figures). Dates should appear in the form eg 23 July 1996. Contributors should avoid sexist formations.

Citation and referencing

Citing sources gives readers the opportunity to explore matters more deeply, to check the accuracy of what you have said, and whether it is about quoted figures and data, or about arguments used by those you have cited. It also gives them an opportunity to gain a richer understanding of the context within which you are writing. Virtually all book publishers and journals will be meticulous in checking your list of cited work. In the case of journals, papers may be turned down if citations do not accord with their strict style. The reason is easy to work out. As the leading American psychologist Bruner has put it, an inaccurate or incomplete reference 'will stand in print as an annoyance to future investigators and a monument to the writer's carelessness' (Bruner 1942: 68).

Whatever academic area you are working in, and whatever your topic, you will have to take account of the formalities and standard practices in relation to citation and referencing of sources that are normally expected in academic writing, and also in much professional writing. There are two basic systems you may be required to adopt:

- In the 'numerical' system a number appears in the text referring to the full citation in footnotes or end notes, sometimes in combination with additional text that is tangential to the main thrust of what is being said, or comments on it.
- In the 'author–date' approach to citation and referencing, the name of the author and date of publication appear in the text, and a full reference to the source appears in an alphabetical list at the end.

To some extent the system you are required to adopt will depend on the discipline within which you are working. However, there is a good chance that you will be required to adopt one of the variations of the author–date system, among which the Harvard system is probably the most common, though you may be required to use another variation, such as the 'Vancouver' system.

Most publishers and most journals will specify not only the style of citation that you should adopt, but also the way in which you should punctuate and organize the information in your reference list. It is curious to note that even among those who promote Harvard-style referencing there are many variations in the layout required. For example, the journal *Learning in*

Health and Social Care requires references to journal articles to be laid out like this:

> Smith S. & Hay E. (1990) Clarity, communication and culture: conceptual considerations and practical applications. *Current Opinion in Psychiatry* **3**, 359–367.

By contrast, the *Journal of Further and Higher Education* would require the same reference to be set out like this:

> SMITH, S. & HAY, E. (1990) Clarity, communication and culture: conceptual considerations and practical applications, *Current Opinion in Psychiatry*, 3, pp. 359–367.

Whatever system for referencing you are using, try to ensure that, as far as possible, you adopt the precise layout dictated by the publishing outlet to which you are submitting your work, even if this contradicts your own preference. Rather than giving directions themselves, some journals will refer to other documents where such guidance can be found. For example, psychology journals and many others will usually refer you to the APA (American Psychological Association) style guide, which is now built into the tools of some word-processing software.

The APA format has been developed in microscopic detail. It is a variation of the Harvard style, and defines, down to the last comma and semi-colon, how references should be listed in the alphabetical list at the end of the publication. It covers the required format for everything, including single-authored books; journal articles and chapters in books of readings, right the way through to how to reference personal communications and web pages. The examples below give a flavour of the sort of detail that is required. They are drawn from the *Publication Manual of the American Psychological Association* (American Psychological Association 2001).

For references to books, the APA requires the following:

> Author, I. N. (Date). *Title italicised or underlined with the first word capitalised.* Place of publication: Publisher.

For example:

> Henningham, J. (1988). *Looking at television news.* Melbourne: Longman Cheshire.

> Bate, D., & Sharpe, P. (1990). *Student writer's handbook: How to write better essays.* Sydney: Harcourt Brace Jovanovich.

Note here the comma before the ampersand (&) and that the first letter after the colon in the title is capitalised. The ampersand is required, by the way, in the reference list but other rules apply to how joint authorship is indicated in the main body of the text.

For journal articles, other subtleties intrude. The name of the journal is italicized, but not the title of the article. Like the journal name, the volume number is italicized or underlined and the issue number (where used) is in brackets and is followed by the page numbers, with a comma between each element. For example:

Johnson, A. (1975). Perceptual comparisons through the mind's eye. *Memory and Cognition, 3*, 635–647.

Becker, L. L., & Seligman, C. (1981). Welcome to the energy crisis. *Journal of Social Issues, 37(2)*, 1–7.

There are also now detailed guidelines on how to cite material from the internet. For instance:

Smith, C. (1996, April). How can parents model good listening skills? [On line] Available: http://parentsplace.om/readroom/feature2.html Accessed June 2004

There are good reasons for all this pernicketyness, as any librarian will tell you when helping you to locate a publication. For example, broadly, the document that will be listed in a library catalogue will be italicized. (In the days before word-processors the way of indicating to a typesetter that text was to be in italics was to underline that text, and that tradition still exists.) So the book title is in italics, but for a journal it is the title of the journal, not the article. This means that you know where to look in the library catalogue. With the advent of material available over the internet this is all becoming more complicated and the need for accurate citations therefore even more important.

Good academic writing

The requirements of academic style cannot be simply spelled out in a way that all or even most academics would accept. Partly this is because style is a matter of individual taste. But partly it is because academics and professionals have different beliefs about what constitutes good academic writing, depending on both their subject and their area of specialism. Even within subjects there is a divergence of views. So, for example, although in some areas of psychology the use of the first person is now common, in others, including experimental psychology, it would be unusual.

The best academic writing is characterized by the ease with which it communicates, which depends to a large extent on its being structured in helpful ways (structure is the main focus of Chapter 6). It need not be elegant and engrossing. It just needs to be clear. It is not that elegance is not appreciated, simply that it is unnecessary. One of the positive consequences of these lowly ambitions for academics in at least some areas is that it can be perfectly acceptable for an aspiring author to model her early writings on what others have written, especially when she is reporting empirical research.

Offering detailed advice about how authors in particular disciplines should write, in order to meet the expectations of the academic and publishing community in their discipline, would take encyclopaedic knowledge. It would also take a book of encyclopaedic proportions, given that there are probably as many nuances of accepted style within the different groups that make up each academic discipline, as there are differences between the disciplines. However, we want to outline at least some of the general characteristics of good academic writing. In doing so, much of what we say will be generic in nature. However, you should bear in mind that the members of the academic and professional culture within which you are working, or of which you wish to become a part, are likely to share a set of particular expectations and unwritten rules about what is acceptable in your specialist area.

Some of the claims listed on page 59 are, it is hoped, self-evident; others may need a little explanation. For example, while it is obvious that good academic writing should have something new to say that will be of interest to its target audience, it is perhaps less clear that good academic writing should be 'layered with meaning'. In using this expression we mean to draw attention to the way in which careful writing can convey meaning by implication, as well as by laboriously spelling it out. The best writing is certainly like this. It says more than the words on the page say. There is something about the ways the words are used that allows the author to imply more than the words themselves. As readers, when we come across such writing, we say that we 'read between the lines'. Of course, in some cases, not all that we seem to be able to read between the lines will have been intended by the author. That is why, when you are writing, it is important to check not only that what you have written says what you intended to say, but also that it does not say (or imply) anything that you did not intend to say or imply.

Good academic writing

Good academic writing:

- Communicates what its author intended to communicate.

It is.

- Coherent, clear and concise.
- Engaging and easy to understand.
- Well structured, with adequate 'signposting' in place to facilitate the flow of meaning.
- Interesting and accessible to its target audience.
- Layered with meaning.
- Committed, because the author makes her views plain and does not 'sit on the fence'.

It has:

- Something new to say, whether as the result of original research and thought, or as the result of critique of or interaction with earlier work.

It uses:

- The third person, where it is helpful to do so; it does not shy away from the first or second person when they are appropriate.
- The active voice where possible, and the passive voice where it is helpful.
- Short sentences where possible.
- Simple words where possible.
- Citation, in a way that helps to build the text, rather than merely decorating it, or attempting to give the impression of authority.
- Examples and illustrations effectively, in a way that facilitates understanding of points being made.

It avoids:

- Ambiguity.
- The use of jargon and technical language, except where it helps to convey meaning.
- The overuse of the passive voice.
- The overuse of colloquial expressions.
- The use of stylistic mannerisms.

Good academic writing should be committed. There is nothing more tedious than an account or argument that is so overburdened with caveats and implicit apologies that the reader wonders why the author thought it was worth writing. Authors need not only to state their point of view but also to explain why they hold it and to make clear how it adds something new to the vast pool of scholarly knowledge and thinking. Clarity and coherence combined with confidence are of the greatest importance if academic writing is to be successful in conveying its message.

Some of the other claims in the box above demand more attention. One of these, the claim that good academic writing is well structured, is so important that the next chapter is devoted to it. For the remainder of this chapter we want to address some of the other issues that are raised:

- The use of the first, second or third person.
- The use of the active or passive voice.
- The problems of gendered language.
- Legitimate and illegitimate uses of jargon.
- Using citation to build the text.
- Stylistic mannerisms.

First, second or third person?

Many academics, especially in the sciences, think it is important to present themselves as having no personal involvement with the phenomena and topics about which they are writing. As a result they enter into ritualized forms of storytelling, intended to create the illusion that they are disinterested observers of phenomena, or thoughtful (but somewhat aloof) commentators on the topics with which they are concerned. They seek to achieve this in two closely entwined ways: by adopting the passive rather than the active voice, and by writing in the third person. In the next section we will discuss the relative merits of adopting the active or the passive voice. For the moment we want to focus on the question of whether the third person is necessarily the best choice for academic writing.

You may well find, at least when you are writing for refereed journals, that you are expected to write in the third person. This may be the case not only in the sciences but also in other disciplines in which it may be favoured by academics who think that serious writing must have an air of 'objectivity' about it, and who want to emphasize their impartiality and hence trustworthiness. Whether the apparent objectivity implied by the use of the third person is a guarantee of either objectivity or of trustworthiness is an important question, though we do not intend to address it in any detail in this book. In spite of this, it is worth pointing out both that it is possible to demonstrate objectivity in what one says without slavishly using the third person, and that the use of the first person does not necessarily imply that one is inward-looking and biased in one's views. Indeed, the first person is often used very effectively in the rigorous development of arguments of all kinds. Nonetheless, even in disciplines such as psychology, education and nursing, where its use is quite common, the first person is often frowned upon.

Moving between the first, second and third person
Many academic authors will move between the first and third person easily. Consider, for example, the following extracts:

> These propositions seem to express our intuitive conviction of the primacy of justice. No doubt they are expressed too strongly. In any event I wish to enquire whether these contentions or others similar to them are sound, and if so how they can be accounted for.
>
> (Rawls 1971: 4)

> Quality of life frequently figures in discussions about life and death; about, for example, whether a life is likely to be of such poor quality that it can be justifiable (even merciful) to deny its bearer treatment that will prolong it. I propose to contrast the importance that quality of life is given in such situations, which occur mostly at the beginning of life, with the importance it may be given at the end of life.
>
> (Fairbairn 1991: 144)

In the first example, which is drawn from his celebrated book *A Theory of Justice*, the American philosopher John Rawls switches effortlessly between the third and the first person in both its singular and plural forms. By referring to 'our intuitive conviction of the primacy of justice', he makes clear that his readers are included in the group whose 'intuitions' he wishes to address, while his use of phrases like 'I wish to enquire . . .' and 'I shall begin by . . .' makes clear what he, John Rawls, intends to do. In the second passage, Gavin introduces his topic using the third person, but moves into the first person when he announces the particular issue he intends to address.

Sometimes authors will move between first, second and third person in a very short space, for example:

> Tremble (2003) argues that at times a doctor's responsibility for the welfare of her patients is more important than her duty of confidentiality to them. He illustrates his view with reference to a story about a patient, Mr Jones, who is HIV positive, and does not want his wife to know, because he is convinced that if she hears about his HIV status, she will realise that he has been unfaithful to her, and leave him. Tremble believes that in this case, if Mr Jones cannot be persuaded that he must tell his wife about his condition, the GP should inform her. In my view Tremble is right, because Mrs Jones's physical welfare is more important than her husband's fear of the consequences of her finding out about his infidelity. In coming to your own conclusion about this situation, you might want to consider . . .

This paragraph begins in the third person with a statement of Tremble's view about the balance of a doctor's responsibilities, moves to the first person in the

fourth sentence when the author shares his opinion of what Tremble has written, and ends in the second person, as he turns to address his audience
directly.

In this book we move freely between the use of the first, second and third
person. Much of the time we adopt the first person, writing, for example,

> We believe that . . .

> Unfortunately, as we have said, success as an author also depends on
> other factors . . .

By writing like this we identify ourselves directly as those who are speaking.
However, we sometimes write (more distantly some would say) in the third
person, for example:

> Some people who want to publish, fail to do so.

> Academic writers can be characterized according to the approaches they
> favour . . .

Lastly, we sometimes address you directly using the second person, for example:

> You might want, also, to reflect on the extent to which, in your own
> academic writing, you actively attend to stylistic considerations of these
> kinds . . .

> Lastly, we sometimes address you directly using the second person . . .

Closely related to our decision to move between the first, second and third
person, was our decision about how we should refer to ourselves in this book,
which was necessary because we make frequent references to our experience of
academic writing and publishing. After toying with various alternatives, we
agreed that we would refer to ourselves by our first names when it helped to
explain who had done what.

You have to decide whether, given the choice, you should write in the third
person, or whether, where appropriate and possible, you should at times adopt
the first person, thus owning at least some of the experience, ideas, beliefs,
arguments, actions and theoretical constructions you are discussing. Remember that use of the first person can walk hand in hand with a rigorous and
scholarly approach to thinking about most things. After all, you can own up to
having a point of view by using the personal pronoun 'I', while contextualizing your position by relating it to those held by others, and testing your
views against theirs. However, while commending it to you wholeheartedly,
we do so with a couple of academic health warnings.

The first concerns the danger of lapsing into an overpersonal style, in which
you fail to relate your views to what others have done, believed or concluded.

The second concerns the danger that you might end up using a variety of curious constructions, all of which are really disguised forms of the first person:

> In the opinion of the author . . .
>
> The researchers decided to employ qualitative methods . . .
>
> The authors thought that . . .

If you find yourself using these and similar constructions, it will be almost as if you are playing a game of hide and seek, in which the aim is to avoid being identified in an authorial role, even though it would not take Sherlock Holmes to work out your identity.

Active or passive voice?

Many academic authors, especially in the sciences, prefer the passive voice. Like the use of the third person, using the passive voice to describe what one has done can help to convey a feeling of objectivity and distance. Whether the work being presented was actually objective, the use of the passive voice thus provides authors with a way of drawing a veil over any subjective thoughts or biases they might have brought to their work (and they will usually bring many, however hard they try to deny it), thus giving the impression that what they have written is unbiased and not influenced by their individual perspectives or concerns.

Active and passive voice	
Active voice	**Passive voice**
The steering group approved the ethics form.	The ethics form was approved by the steering group.
Surgeons performed the first human brain transplant yesterday.	The first human brain transplant was performed yesterday.
We used non-parametric statistics to analyse the data.	The data was analysed using non-parametric statistics.
Beckford (1969) argued in favour of a new approach to road safety.	A new approach to road safety was argued in favour of (Beckford 1969).

In general it is harder to write well in the passive voice, which is less direct and to the point, and often increases the possibility of awkward constructions that can make even relatively simple ideas more difficult to understand than they need be.

The authors of technical and scientific articles typically use the passive voice, especially in situations where it is irrelevant who performed an action. For example, a medical scientist using the passive voice might write: 'A series of randomized controlled trials was conducted.' Doing so would allow her to focus attention on the methods employed, the data gathered and the analysis of results, rather than drawing attention to herself and the other researchers, as would happen if, for example, she wrote: 'We undertook a series of randomized controlled trials.'

Even in disciplines in which the active voice is often used, such as psychology and education, some academics clearly prefer the passive voice, and many use it some of the time. For example, a psychologist might write: 'Attitudes towards asylum seekers were investigated via a survey of registered voters.' Of course, it could easily be part of a mixed economy in which it sat alongside others in the first person, active voice. For example:

> Attitudes towards asylum seekers were investigated via a survey of registered voters. In this article I describe the procedures by which I gathered my data, and say a little about the ways in which it was analysed and interpreted. However, my main purpose is to shed light on the ethical problems that arise for anyone who is gathering information from this population.

Empirical scientists are not alone in utilizing the passive voice. For example, by writing, 'Arguments are offered in support of the view that abortion can never be justified', an ethicist could distance herself from the view being argued for, almost as if she did not hold it. By contrast, one who favoured the active voice, as well as choice in the matter of abortion might write: 'I want to argue in support of women's right to choose abortion.'

In our view, the active voice is preferable to the passive voice in most non-scientific writing. Fewer words are required to express action in the active than in the passive voice, and sentences in the active voice thus tend to be clearer, more concise and more direct than their passively constructed counterparts. Even in scientific writing, overusing the passive voice, especially in long and complicated sentences, can cause readers to become confused, or even to lose interest altogether.

Minding your language

One particularly thorny area for most academic authors relates to the use of gendered language. Problems arise because of the offence that some people feel, both at the generic use of the male pronouns – he, him and his – and at the generic use of words such as 'chairman', to refer to the individual who chairs a meeting even when she is a woman, and 'mankind' to refer to the human race, even though it includes women. Whatever your view of the significance that is to be attached to the way in which our language has developed, you will have to adopt some strategy to address the problem of gendered language if you want to get published by most academic publishers, or in most academic journals.

Most academics have allowed themselves to be stylistically influenced by the critique of male-dominated language – including the generic use of male pronouns – often to the extent of being bullied into adopting inelegance for the sake of political correctness. However, this is not universally true. The English philosopher Michael Dummett's discussion of this topic, though muddled at times, makes interesting reading (Dummett 1993: 106–110).

Unfortunately, in academic and professional life the campaign to avoid the generic use of male pronouns often results in clumsy writing. Partly this arises as a result of the so-called solutions to the problem that are adopted. We are talking here about the use of plural pronouns such as 'they' and 'them', when a singular is intended; the use of 'his or her'; 'he or she'; 'him or her'; or 'his or hers', and the use of the forms 'he/she'; 'she/he' and, worst of all, 's/he'. In the wrong hands the results can be disastrous, both in terms of readability and in terms of clarity. For example, consider the following example from a draft module handbook, which was smuggled out to us by a lover of the English language working in an English university:

> When the student hands in his or her essay he or she must ensure that he or she receives a signed receipt from his or her tutor, because that is the only way that he or she will be able to prove to his or her tutor that he or she gave his or her essay to him or her.

This sentence was obviously written by someone who has been thoroughly indoctrinated into the idea that he or she should write everything, including his or her module handbooks, without using the pronouns 'he', 'him' and 'his' or even the pronouns 'she', 'her' and 'hers' in a generic way. We are glad to be able to report that it was modified before the handbook was printed.

Addressing the problem of gendered language
Even though most academic journals and most book publishers will nowadays expect their authors to use a particular strategy for dealing with the problems of gendered language, they may allow you to adopt your own approach, provided that you apply it consistently. For example, in an earlier Open University book, Gavin and his co-author used their own strategy, which suited the book in question:

> When we are referring to specific individuals we use pronouns that are appropriate to their gender. However, when we are referring to non-identified students we usually refer to them using male pronouns, and in general, when we are referring to non-identified academics or writers, we use female pronouns. Although this strategy may have some odd results – including the possibility that it might induce a casual reader into thinking

that we believe that most students are men while most academics and writers are women, this seems less important to us than the attempt to avoid offence while maintaining some kind of stylistic integrity.

(Fairbairn and Fairbairn 2001)

One problem with adopting an individualistic approach to addressing the gender issue is that you may come up against people who do not appreciate what you have done, or even fail to notice it. What is worse, they might notice it, but 'read' it wrongly. On one occasion Gavin received a letter from a journal editor which, despite strongly favourable reviews of an article, pointed out that he would have to address one reviewer's concern that his 'generic use of male pronouns' was likely to be viewed as sexist by many readers. Interestingly, when he returned to his text to sniff out the offending material he found that whereas there was only a single use of the pronoun 'he' and no uses of any other masculine pronouns, there were recurrent uses of all the feminine pronouns.

David has encountered another problem in relation to his research in criminal psychology where at times all of the prisoners being described are male. This makes writing a little easier, though he usually explains his apparently generic use of masculine pronouns by a simple footnote saying: 'Throughout this paper the male pronouns refer only to men, because they are.'

In this book we have tried so far as we can to embrace a mix and match solution, making the attempt to alternate between masculine and feminine, so that you will find us switching between generic use of 'he' and generic use of 'she'. We also, occasionally, use 'he or she' and the plural 'they' to refer to one person, because it is helpful to do so, though generally we dislike these forms almost as much as we dislike the use of 'he/she' and the unpronounceable 's/he'.

Appropriate and inappropriate uses of jargon

Some uses of jargon in academic writing are helpful because they make the communication of technical details between specialists much easier; sometimes its use can even be helpful for non-specialist readers, provided that it is introduced in a way that allows them to grasp its meaning. Unfortunately, jargon is often used inappropriately. At worst some people import into their work jargon from other academic areas in an effort to make their work seem sophisticated and important. Sometimes it is simply overused by academics and professionals who want to make their writing appear more scholarly and difficult. Here, it is just one of a range of devices that such individuals use in attempting to claim authority for their work. Others include the use of long words and complex syntax that obscures meaning rather than enhances it.

Whenever you think of using technical terms you should consider whether the audience for whom you are writing will understand what you are saying.

If there is a chance that they will not, and the technical terms really are essential to what you want to say, explain such terms before introducing them into your discussion. Even then, we suggest that you should ask yourself whether the jargon terms you are using actually facilitate the communication of your ideas, rather than simply make your text look or sound fancier. If there is any possibility that using ordinary words could convey your meaning just as well, and just as concisely, use them. That way you will reach the largest possible audience. No scholar worth his salt will object to ordinary terms if you do this.[1]

Using citation to build the text

Our suggestion that good academic writing uses citation in a way that helps to build the text, arises from our strong belief that there is no point in citing sources unless doing so either is necessary to contextualize your work by relating it to what others have done, or helps you to build the arguments you want to present. Much of the citation that appears in academic writing, particularly in journal articles, serves little purpose other than allowing the author to demonstrate how (apparently) well read he is. We know of journals that will refuse articles that are 'not academic enough', because they do not include sufficient references. We also know that at least some of these journals will be satisfied by resubmissions that have more references, even when those references have no importance for the views being presented, but merely make the article look 'more academic'.

In poor academic writing the literature is reviewed as if by a twelve-year-old who has recently learnt to read. There is no critical analysis. The reader is not told when, where, how or what. The strengths, weaknesses, peculiarities or insights of cited material are not specified. No indication is given about whether the cited work contributed to the author's decision to do what he has done or might do in the future.

One way of ensuring that every citation pays its way in terms of helping with text building is to write in such a way that you include the names of those to whom you wish to refer in your text. Doing so is helpful because it nearly always means that you have to say something about the author in question. This is a good way of developing your text, as well as making it easier to follow, and helps to ensure that there really is a reason for making the reference in the first place. For example, if you were referring to an article by Barker, which was published in 1998, you might write,

Barker (1998) argues that . . .

---

[1] If you want to explore the ideological and political battles that are often hidden behind jargon and other aspects of academic style you could do worse than reading the delightful book by Andreski, first published in 1972, with the splendid title *Social Sciences as Sorcery*.

By citing Barker in this way, you force yourself to say something about what he argued. Something similar would happen were you to write that Barker 'believes that'; 'asserts that'; 'draws attention to', or 'has carried out research that suggests', and any number of other things you might say about Barker, thus allowing you to build up your text simply by telling your reader a little about what this author has written and done.

It is worth reflecting on the huge difference that adopting this style of author–date referencing can make to the ways you write. It is easiest to see if you compare a reference in this style with one in what is probably the most common way of making author–date references within a text, in which the author's name and the date of the publication are kept strictly locked up inside brackets, and no information is given about what he actually did, said, thought, argued, suggested or proposed. For example,

> Tompkins (2000) has argued that the use of paper-based literary technology will soon be a thing of the past.

> The use of paper-based literary technology will soon be a thing of the past (Tompkins 2000).

Whereas simply by reading the first of these citations we know something about Tompkins and what he does in the cited source, reading the second fails to illuminate because we cannot tell from it whether he argued his point, or carried out research that demonstrated it, or whether perhaps he even disagrees with it. The latter form is, we believe, akin to those 'kite marks' that you see on clothing and other products to tell you they are, for example, real wool, or approved to a British Standard. It tells you nothing more than that someone else has dealt with a related issue.

You may find yourself wanting to reject our advice, because you know that lots of articles use the form of referencing in which nothing is usually said about what the cited author has done, or believes or has found out or argues. If you do, reflect on the fact that doing so commits you to being the kind of academic writer who leaves her readers to guess at the reason that you are citing the people that you cite.

Stylistic mannerisms and bad habits

Most of us, however careful, manage when we are drafting our work to pepper it with unhelpful stylistic mannerisms. We all have such mannerisms, which somehow seem to multiply unless we are uncommonly vigilant in removing them from our work as we draft and redraft. Sometimes they amount to little more than the overuse of particular words, or of particular forms of punctuation that we particularly favour, but when overused make our writing particularly difficult to read.

Perhaps the most irksome species of stylistic mannerism that can be found in academic writing is the habitual use of words and phrases that are neither necessary nor helpful in making your points and thus do not really add any value. For example, do we really need the word 'really' in the previous sentence – or in this one, for that matter? Such words are usually little more than padding. Sometimes, however, they act as a kind of 'winding up' for the main event. We have both had students who write really well, but do not recognize how they 'write their way into' what they want to say. They will, for instance, start at the beginning of sections or even paragraphs with the phrase, 'When considering X, it is important to . . .'. To take one of many examples, one of Gavin's students recently wrote: 'When considering Person-centred approaches to planning it is important to recognise that they began as . . .'. In this case, it would have been much stronger to have written: 'Person-centred approaches to planning began as . . .'. This is more immediate and it saves nine words.

In our experience it is nearly always easier to identify habitual uses of words and phrases, which are neither necessary nor helpful, in other people's writing than in your own. However, with practice you should be able to spot them in your own writing, provided, as we suggest in Chapter 4, that you manage to develop the skill of reading your own work as if it had been written by someone else.

Most authors have their own 'favourite' stylistic mannerisms – empty words that recur frequently whenever they write – though they are usually unaware of using them. They appear like uninvited guests at a party. Here are a few examples:

So	On the other hand
Clearly	It is clear that
Indeed	There is no escaping the fact that
Obviously	Therefore
For all intents and purposes	Literally
In my/our opinion	Ultimately
It has long been believed that	Of course
However	In light of
For the most part	It has to be said
It would seem that	At this moment in time

Many of these words and phrases can be used meaningfully,[2] though some of them are fairly limited, especially the phrase 'at this moment in time'. One we have not listed has become so common that it was recently listed as a new word – 'attheendoftheday' – in a tongue-in-cheek article about new words, written in response to a newly published *Future Dictionary of America*, in the *The Independent Review* (Dickson et al. 2004). Sometimes such words are

---

[2] More than one of the items in this list appears several times in this book, though we have successfully evicted it from a number of locations where it had forced its way into the text against our will, and clearly added nothing to our meaning.

used wrongly. For example, 'therefore', 'so' and 'however' are often used to imply an argument where none exists. However, their use often serves no purpose.

Some of these inappropriate usages derive from a lack of careful consideration of the meaning of words and how they are employed effectively. Consider, for example, an author who wrote: 'The problems created by the new legislation were literally tearing many social services agencies apart.' How literal do you think he was being here? Especially when you start to write seriously for publication it is good to have by your elbow a book on English usage, such as Partridge's famous volume, or a dictionary that includes comments on usage, such as the Collins Concise Dictionary, and not to be afraid to make use of it. Of course, ultimately, at the end of the day, it would seem that at this moment in time there is no escaping the fact that the use of such useless stylistic mannerisms is second nature to many people.

Developing your own style

The fact that we have devoted so many pages to a discussion of academic style is an indication of how important we think it is for academic authors to take care over the ways they write. If you are near the beginning of your career as an academic author, you might find it helpful to reflect a little about what we have said, and in particular to look again at the list of features of good academic writing that we offered on page 59. If you agree with us that features of this kind do mark out good academic writing, try to work out why you think these features are important, whatever the discipline. You might also want to reflect on the extent to which, in your own academic writing, you actively attend to stylistic considerations of these kinds, and about whether you think you are successful in doing so.

Even if you agree with all the indicators of good academic writing that we have proposed, you might not attempt, in your academic work, to live up to them. For example, you might agree that academic work is best when it uses simple words where possible. Nonetheless, you might not take the trouble to write as simply as you can. Indeed, even if you believe wholeheartedly in a simple style, you may write prose that is as difficult as you can make it, because that is what is expected by the journals that you read and want to write for. We experienced some problems here, because we want to offer advice about writing well, but at the same time we want to offer advice about getting published, and these two aspirations undoubtedly conflict at times. One reason for this is that, as we have already said, some academic journals, seem to encourage a difficult and unhelpful prose style because their editors mistakenly believe that unless it is difficult, an article cannot be saying anything of importance.

If you are to maintain integrity as an author while achieving success, you will have to strike a balance between writing as well as will satisfy you, and writing in a style that suits the journals that you hope will publish your articles, or the publishers for whom you wish to write or edit books. We all have to strike such a balance.

How are you to develop your style as an academic author? One way you might attempt to do so would involve modelling your work on that of authors who write well in your discipline and in the places in which you aspire to publish, emulating those aspects of their writing that seem to enable them to communicate clearly and easily. This sounds simple, but it is harder than it seems. For one thing, it would involve developing an eye for what successful authors are doing, in terms of both the language they use and the ways in which they structure their ideas, including the order in which they present them and the devices they adopt to ensure that their readers can follow their train of thought. For another, it would involve deciding what constitutes good academic style in the first place.

Standard forms and turns of phrase

Whatever your field of interest, there will be turns of phrase that appear regularly, and form a kind of standard lexicon for the area. We will refer to them using the term 'cliché'. This term usually has a derogatory meaning, as a label for tired old phrases, that have lost their punch through overuse, and often mean very little. Or as Partridge (1991: ix) put it so well in the preface to his *Dictionary of Clichés:*

> Only those of us who are concerned to keep the language fresh and vigorous regard, with dismay, the persistence of these well-worn substitutes for thinking and the mindless adoption of new ones.

However, in academic circles we think there is a case for rehabilitating the use of clichés in a sense more like the original French meaning, when used by printers to refer to words and phrases that they used so often that they kept ready-made printing blocks for them close at hand. By getting to know the clichés that are common in your discipline, and the ways in which they can be used as an aid in structuring your writing, you can draw on them as tools of your trade. Once you have befriended them, do not be afraid to use such phrases and forms, which can help to create the scaffolding on which you can build an article, chapter, or even a longer text.

Looking closely at, and trying to emulate, the way in which other authors write about topics that overlap with those you want to discuss, and in particular at how they report on empirical research that has some similarity to yours, will not help you to win any prizes for style. Nonetheless, it can be beneficial in helping you to get that all-important initial version drafted.

It is important to emphasize that our suggestion that it can be helpful to model what you write quite closely on material produced by others, is intended merely as an interim measure, to help you to get beyond the blank page that we discussed in Chapter 4, which can be so daunting that it results in many would-be authors giving up the idea of writing for publication. Once they have seen how others do it and have tried to emulate their style, beginners who try this strategy will gradually be able to modify and adapt their writing until they develop a style that feels and reads right for them. If you decide to act on this advice, you should remember that it is important to select wisely which authors – and which sections of their work – you use as a model. Remember, a lot of what is published is bad or just scrapes through the review process. Only model yourself on the best.

6 The importance of structure

Marco Polo describes a bridge, stone by stone.

'But which is the stone that supports the bridge?' Kublai Khan asks.

'The bridge is not supported by one stone on another,' Marco answers, 'but by the line of the arch that they form.'

Kublai Khan remains silent, reflecting. Then he adds: 'Why do you speak to me of the stones? It is only the arch that matters to me.'

Polo answers: 'Without the stones there is no arch.'

(Calvino 1997: 82)

The importance of structure

Jean-Luc Godard, the innovative French film director, whose films were often characterized by strange jumps in time and complex, non-sequential story-lines, was once challenged about the lack of a conventional structure to his films. 'Surely', he was asked, 'you should have a beginning, middle and end to your narratives'. 'Yes, of course,' he said, 'but not necessarily in that order.' His point was profound. There is always a structure to every story, but how that structure is handled is part of the storytelling process itself; it can either help or hinder the process by which you grasp the elements of the whole.

The order in which information is presented in the stories through which we learn about the people with whom we live and work, is important in a similar way. If a colleague tells you about something dreadful that happened at work today, she may follow it up with an account of another incident last week that she thinks was its cause, then move on to say a little about her predictions about what will happen next unless some drastic action is taken. She is telling you a story out of sequence, because that is both the best way of grabbing your attention and the best way of helping you to understand her concerns.

The ways in which we structure what we write are particularly important, because the reader has nothing other than the words on the page to help him to grasp whatever we want to say. If we are reporting our experiences, or our research, or trying to persuade others of our point of view at a conference, the members of the audience have the opportunity to ask for clarification. This opportunity is absent when we do the same things in writing. That is why it is important to take care, not only about what we say, but also about the way in which we say it, trying so far as we can to ensure that we do so in ways that people will understand.

Although the content of our academic stories is important, it could plausibly be argued that the way in which we structure them is even more important because it will determine the extent to which they are understood. In a real sense it is better to create a text that says only a little, but says it clearly in a well-organized way, than to write something that says a lot but is so badly written, and so badly structured, that no one who reads it can understand what it is about.

Poorly structured pieces of writing can take many forms. Often, it is not that they have no structure but that they have one that is unhelpful to their cause. Sometimes it is the desire to cover all bases, leaving nothing to chance by including all the information that they can throw into their writing, that leads authors to produce these inappropriate frameworks. Or it may just be ignorance of the sorts of stories academics write. Slightly tongue-in-cheek, we have summarized in the box below some of the inappropriate narrative structures that we have come across.

Narrative structures to avoid

The Whodunnit

The Whodunnit keeps the reader guessing, never really allowing him to know what the writer is trying to do. Typically, there are hints of the general area in which the writer is operating. Large numbers of questions may be raised and perhaps answered, but the text doesn't seem to go anywhere, and the reader is given few clues as to its point. The only clue to the questions that the writer is trying to answer may be a sentence many pages into the introduction.

The Logbook

In this form, the writing is organized broadly in terms of what the writer read and did, in the order in which they read and did it. At its most extreme, the Logbook is nothing more than a step by step account of what was done, with no attempt to indicate that there was ever any thought behind it, or following from it. For example, it might contain sentences like: 'The data was put into a computer and Freelance was used to produce a bar chart', rather than more helpful (and engaging) ones like: 'As can be seen from Figure 2, all the female victims were younger than the male victims.'

Leaps into the Unknown

It is remarkable how often in accounts of empirical research, an extensive review of a literature comes to a sudden halt and the reader is told about the data collection without any clear connection between the two. In the Leap into the Unknown the reader might be expected, without any argument, to accept that because a litany of literature has been listed, it must be relevant to the data that has been gathered. In a similar way, the analysis might rush at the reader unbidden, and without any hint about its purpose.

Opaque Illusions

In this form, we get to the end of story, the dénouement, without any build-up and before we know anything about any of the characters or their setting. Many researchers are so steeped in their particular methodologies that they end up living under the illusion that the whole world has a detailed knowledge of what they do and how they do it. In the Opaque Illusion, the conclusions or discussion sections also often exist in their own private purgatory. They do not refer back to the opening of the paper, they may introduce entirely new material, either literature or findings. They neither discuss the findings nor round up the paper.

Structure is important in all good writing, whatever the academic genre, from abstracts for conference papers to full-scale books. It is important at all levels, from the sentence to the whole text, whether it is a single page or 200 pages long. It is multifaceted, and includes the order in which ideas are presented; the length and complexity of sentences; the ways in which the text is broken into paragraphs and sections; the way in which direct quotations are presented – whether, for example, they are signified using speech marks within the main body of the text, or are separated out from it in a block indent. A particularly important feature of structure, and one to which too little attention is often paid, is the use of the signposts, trailers and reminders, that tell readers where they are and where they are going, as they journey through a text.

So how should you structure your writing? There is no definitive answer. For any piece of writing there will be several possible structures that would work, as well as many that would not. Your job as an author is to find the right way of structuring your text for your particular purposes, and to develop a structure that is as helpful as it can be in assisting your readers to understand what you want to communicate to them.

Learning to structure your academic writing

Although it is impossible to provide a catch-all guide to structuring academic work, in many areas of academic study, fledgling authors can learn a lot by looking closely at what works for others. You may even be able to model whole articles on work produced by others, because the kinds of stories that you want to tell about your work will have similarities in form, if not in content, to others that are already in print. To do this you will have to learn to analyse published material that you consider to be clear and authoritative, working out how it is constructed, and what it is about its structure that is helpful in conveying its meanings. When you have done that, you will be able to draw a sketch of its structure, which you can then use as a template.

For any academic purpose there will be a number of related structures that could achieve the same ends in different ways, each of which might have many nuances, depending on the topic in question. So, although it is unlikely that you will ever find an article that will provide a model that exactly fits your requirements, you should be able to develop the skill to sniff out basic underlying frameworks that seem to work. There are only a few basic forms of academic story, even though the detail that surrounds them will disguise their underlying shape and structure. In order to illustrate the kind of thing we are talking about, we will give a couple of examples of typical structures that you will be able to detect in academic articles in many disciplines.

A basic framework for an empirical research article

Most authors who want to report on empirical research projects will be able to utilize a basic model around which to construct their articles.[1] The outline we discuss below provides a structure for any such article, whether it relates to research in one of the natural sciences, in psychology, economics or education, and no matter the species of research – whether, for example, it was experimental, survey, or case study research.

1 **What I was thinking before the research**
   In this introductory section, the author will often tell the story of what is of particular interest and focus to her topic, arguing for its importance by citing issues that have emerged from what others have done and written in related areas. In this way, she begins to let readers know not only what she is thinking, but also why she is thinking it, thus contextualizing her own work against the backdrop of related work by others.

2 **What I wanted to find out, investigate, test or check**
   Having set the scene, the author will usually offer some information about the purpose of the study undertaken. Depending on the research being undertaken, she might present some hypotheses to be tested, or key questions she wanted to address. These should derive from the confusions or disagreements in existing findings or understanding that were outlined in the first section.

3 **How I decided to conduct my investigation**
   Here the author will typically describe the methods that she used to find answers to her research questions, or to test her hypotheses. Some justification for the use of these approaches may be offered, either outlining arguments for their appropriateness, or referring to their use in similar situations.

4 **What I found (the information or data I collected)**
   The findings or results are reported in this section. Depending on the research methods adopted and the data gathered, this might take the form of tables of figures, graphic representations, or clustered lists of central concepts derived from interview transcripts, along with illustrative examples from those transcripts.

5 **What these results suggest, demonstrate or lead me to wonder**
   This section offers a perspective or opinion on the results obtained, offering arguments about why the author's research was worthwhile, presenting the conclusions she has reached as the result of her study, and making whatever claims she can about the contribution that her work makes to the sum of human knowledge and understanding.

6 **What I am thinking now**
   Here the author will typically sum up the ways in which her view has

---

[1] Possibly as the 'first page' of their writing as we discussed on page 43.

changed as a result of the research. At this point she may well revisit her discussion of earlier work, showing how her research adds to, or illuminates it. Finally, she may draw attention to any weaknesses in her approach.

In general, it is good to keep in mind that most studies have implications of three different sorts. The first is for knowledge and understanding of the issues under exploration. The second is for the development of methodologies for studying those issues. The third is for practical or policy matters. This threefold framework is often quite useful in a concluding section.

Of course, this framework provides only a simplistic template because it makes the assumption that the article will report the project as a whole, whereas many articles about such research will focus on only one aspect, for example, on the methods adopted, or on a discussion of the results; and some will set out to compare a number of studies and to argue in favour of one over the others. Nonetheless, many inexperienced academic authors with empirical studies to report will be able to utilize this storyboard as a way of structuring an article. An alternative, at least in the early stages of writing, would be to locate a published report of research that is similar in relevant ways, and to use it as a model for their own work. Often it will be possible to utilize sentences that are very close to the introductory and concluding sentences in sections of such a model.

Scaffolding an introductory paragraph

At a slightly more detailed level, it is also possible to draw up an outline, or scaffold, for crucial sections in a longer piece of work. For example, it is often possible to begin articles reporting empirical research in the social sciences using an opening paragraph that has the general form:

> Previous research [references] suggests that X. However, not all studies support this. For example, A [reference] found that [what A found] and B [reference] suggests that [what B suggests is the case]. In this study we investigated [what was looked at] by [how investigation was carried out].

For example, a social psychologist who, as an aficionado of good coffee, is surprised at the extent to which customers tolerate the offerings of coffee houses throughout the UK, might begin an account of his investigation of this phenomenon like this:

> Previous empirical studies carried out by Donaldson (2001) suggests that customers' toleration of poor coffee in designer coffee outlets depends on whether they are provided with a comfortable seat on which to sit while they drink it. However, not all studies support this view. For example, Landgren (2000) carried out a survey of twenty coffee shops, ten with comfortable seats, and ten with uncomfortable seats, and found that

when customers were served horrid coffee, the rate of complaints was comparable in each case. On the other hand, Stanko (1999) argued that customers' responses to horrid coffee actually depends on whether the coffee shop in which they drink it is aesthetically pleasing or ugly. In this article we report on a field experiment comparing customers' responses to horrid coffee in four coffee shops, judged to be 'comfortable and aesthetically pleasing'; 'comfortable but ugly'; 'uncomfortable but aesthetically pleasing', or 'uncomfortable and ugly'.

It is important to notice that the model we have offered, on which this paragraph is based, is very flexible. As a result, the basic pattern could be translated, very easily, into a model for an opening paragraph for an article in many other areas, which need not describe empirical work. Consider, for example, this paragraph about a contentious topic in the ethics of health:

A number of philosophers (see, for example, McMinn 1993 and Leigh 2001) have argued that everyone should have the right to refuse medical treatment with the intention of bringing about their death, even when their death is not otherwise imminent as the result, for example, of a terminal illness, and their present ill health is the result of an easily controllable condition. However, this is not universally accepted. For example, while Thomas (2000) agrees that refusing medical treatment with the intention of achieving one's death should be allowed, he argues that it should only be allowed in the case of those who are suffering grievously from an incurable and terminal illness. And Stokes (2001) argues that while everyone should have the right to refuse medical treatment, this right should be withheld in the case of individuals who are suffering from any impediment to the ability to reason clearly. In this article I argue against the right to choose death by refusing treatment on the grounds that the right to death implies a duty on the part of others to act in ways that bring that death about.

The narrative aspects of these introductory paragraphs may also help you to understand how they make their case. In both cases there are protagonists that are set against each other in what could be seen as mortal combat. They are conflicting arguments or competing hypotheses. Their battle is worked out through the developed paper, with the victor paraded in the conclusions.

Getting the structure of your writing right

If you are going to get the structure of your writing right, you will need to attend to several things, which we now discuss.

The needs of your audience

First you will need to attend to your audience. Even in circumstances where you have every right to expect that those who read your work will share much knowledge and many common understandings with you, it is important to think about their needs as you write. For example, it is important to give them sufficient information about sources that you cite, to allow them to under-stand the use you are making of them. However, it is probably even more important to be aware of your audience when you are structuring your work, for example, by remaining aware that they do not know what you want to tell them; that, after all, is why you are writing, and, with luck, it is why they are reading what you have written. This is so obvious that you might think it does not need to be said. However, many academic authors – both the inexperi-enced and the long-in-the-tooth – are so close to their subject matter that they write as if they expect that their readers are already familiar with their ideas.

The whole picture – learn to stand back and view it

Secondly, you will have to learn to stand back and view the whole picture. This is necessary in order to allow you to notice how the parts of your text stand in relation to one another and how successfully they build up a coherent message. In Chapter 4 we talked about the importance of learning to read your own work as if you were a stranger to it; that is what we are talking about here: the ability to read (then read again) what you have written as if you do not know what it is supposed to say. Only by doing so will you be able to work out whether it says what you intended it to say. In particular, it is only by being able to read it as if for the first time, that you will be able to tell whether it says things in the most helpful order.

Signposts – get them right

'Signposts' are elements of texts that help to make their structure clear and to guide readers as they make their way through the ideas that they contain. They come in different shapes and sizes and, whereas some are 'official' – including headings and subheadings – some are 'unofficial', for example, endings of sections that hark back to what went before, or opening sentences that hint at what is to come, before announcing what is going to happen now.

Headings and subheadings can act as helpful signposts to make the structure of a text clear. However, there is no point in using them if they do not accur-ately reflect what is going on in the text, and therefore great care has to be taken in deciding both what headings and subheadings to use, and where to place them. It is also important to be clear about the relationship between subheadings of various kinds, because knowing this will help you to assess whether your text is really saying what you think it is saying, or intended it to say. Sometimes you will find on writing a new draft of an article, say, that you extend a short section in a way that makes it seem like a stranger under the heading where it began its literary existence, and feel the need to reorganize your text, perhaps adding a new subheading, or taking one out, or merely moving existing material around into places where it sits more comfortably.

Distinguish the wood from the trees

Whenever you are writing about a complex topic, it is important to ensure that your readers will be able to 'see the wood from the trees'. In empirical research, for example, problems can arise when you are reporting on the interaction between a number of possible causes and effects. Paradoxically, in such a situation, the subsection headings, rather than the section headings, usually point to the central story. Imagine, for instance, that you are reporting on research that had investigated the relationship between children's performance on various tasks, and both their sex and their age. One way of reporting this would be to have a section about boys' performance at different ages, and another that did the same for girls; you would thus have main headings that related to sex, but subheadings that related to performance at different ages. Another way of reporting your results would be to organize what you had found, according to age; this would have main headings that related to different age ranges and subheadings comparing the performance of boys and girls at each of these ages. So the paradox is that, in the first version, although the main headings relate to sex, the dominant message that would be taken away by readers would be about performance at different ages, whereas in the second, the main headings would be about age, but the dominant message would be about sex differences in performance.

Beating about the bush

Whatever you are writing, whether it is an article or a chapter for a book, you should avoid writing yourself into what you want to say, taking paragraphs or even pages to get to the point. This is a common mistake among novice academic writers, who often use their introductory section to warm up, and then give a repeat performance at the end, using the concluding section to wind down. Even experienced authors at times devote pages to tedious scene setting, in, for example, the form of extended reviews of previous literature, which do not really help readers to understand the point of their text. Sometimes you might find it useful to include such material in first drafts as a way of convincing yourself that your topic is worth writing about, because others have been interested in it. Remember, however, that extensive literature reviews can swamp your own ideas so much that the main thrust of your argument will often emerge only after many pages, by which time readers might have lost interest.

Most successful academic authors do not beat about the bush, but aim to engage their readers immediately. The Gestalt therapist Fritz Perls is often quoted as saying that everything before the 'but' is bullshit. He was referring to the way in which people sometimes try to avoid owning the unpalatable things they want to say to others by prefacing them with lots of irrelevancies, thus delaying the moment when they say what they really want to say. For example, 'I really like the way that you are so honest about everything, but actually I can't stand you.' In a similar way, a timid academic author may beat about the bush, making lots of references to others before tentatively sketching out his own view. Such an author is in effect saying 'Look at all the clever things these other people have said, but by the way, here is a thought I had.'

Beginnings, endings and the space between

It is important to attend to the way you open and close any piece of writing, whether it is an article, a chapter or a book. These crucial parts of texts can be thought of as being like the bread that holds the contents of a sandwich together. But they do more than that. Used well, they add to a text. The intro- duction greets the reader and seduces her in. It opens up strands of rele- vance at the outset, giving the reader a flavour of what is to come. The ending or conclusion, on the other hand, wishes the reader well as she leaves, bringing together the key points you have dealt with in a convenient form for her to take away with her. Often, discussions of other people's work that appeared in the introduction of an early draft will prove more useful towards the end where they can be set against, or contrasted with, the author's own views. A good concluding section will often provide a puzzle to end on, something to remember the text by.

Whenever you write, try to hold your text together by making some obvious cross-reference from the conclusions to the introduction. One way you can help to ensure you do this will be to write a draft of the conclusions you expect to reach before you begin work on the introduction; that way you will have the conclusions in your mind as you set out.

Sentence length

Many authors use long sentences successfully. However, some use so many and construct them so badly, that they almost fail to communicate anything at all. Consider, for example, the following astonishing sentence:

> May we not argue that the way in which such conflicts should be met in our society involves (a) a cautious and conservative approach to funda- mental change; (b) a recognition that certain courses of action are ruled out, since they are profoundly offensive to many people (majority? sub- stantial minority? – so much depends on how the question is framed); (c) an awareness that there are arguments unconnected with Christian religious and ethical convictions which tend to support them, or (put it

another way) to show that they are reasonable (in this case we are working with a concept of human rights and human dignity as co-extensive with Homo sapiens)?

(de Cameron 1989)

We think we know what the author of this sentence was trying to say – almost. However, he does not give us much help. Perhaps it is simply that the sentence is a long one – it is, after all, over a hundred words long; but perhaps not. Perhaps what makes it problematical is that as well as containing a three-part list and three questions, it also has three asides, one of which has its own sub-aside. What do you think? No matter what you think of this sentence, it is worth trying to vary your sentence length. Short sentences give readers the chance to breathe.

Not all writers have difficulty with long sentences. Some, indeed manage to use them rather well, both within academia and outside it. Consider, for example, the following sentence from Elizabeth David's classic book, *French Country Cooking*:

Rationing, the disappearance of servants, and the bad and expensive meals served in restaurants, have led Englishwomen to take a far greater interest in food than was formerly considered polite; and large numbers of people with small farms in the country produce their own home-cured bacon, ham and sausages; personal supervision of the kitchen garden induces a less indifferent attitude to the fate of spring vegetables; those who have churned their own butter, fed their chickens and geese, cherished their fruit trees, skinned and cleaned their own hares, are in no mood to see their efforts wasted.

(David 1951: 8)

Unlike the remarkable sentence that we cited above, many readers will think that this sentence works well, because Elizabeth David knows how to engage her audience and carry them along. That is why, in the same book, she has managed, at times, to write sentences that are well over two hundred words long, but which read easily and well. Most of us cannot do this.

Grammar and word order

English is a curious language in that word order is remarkably flexible and meaning can be gleaned even when the order is totally confused. For example, you can work out what is meant by 'I cup of tea would like a', even though it breaks the most fundamental sequence of subject followed by verb followed by object. This flexibility provides the opportunity for changes in emphasis to be produced by changing where the words are in a sentence; it also allows the unwanted possibility of adding confusion. Consider the different implications of the following variants:

Having carefully drawn a sample the age and sex of the participants were examined.

The age and sex of the participants were examined having carefully drawn a sample.

Examining the sample of participants, which was carefully drawn, their age and sex were determined.

Which sentence emphasizes that the sample was carefully drawn? Which draws attention to the consideration of age and sex? Which is the most confusing to follow?

Of course this is a huge and complex issue that would take us into consideration of subordinate clauses, how text is held together and many other aspects of linguistics. For the present we just want to alert you to the subtle significance of word order and to point out that, often, if you are having trouble writing things clearly you can overcome it not by radically changing the words but by changing the order in which they are used.

Punctuation and paragraphing

The ways in which we punctuate our texts can make all the difference to whether they are easy to read and convey the meanings we intend. Indeed, some punctuation marks, especially the comma, can make all the difference to the meaning of a sentence. In her learned guidebook on copy editing, Judith Butcher (2002) lists dashes, space, hyphens, brackets, apostrophes and commas as punctuation marks that can cause problems. In addition in her section on common faults of punctuation she deals with full stops, parenthetical dashes, colons – with and without dashes – and semi-colons. But even she mentions that for serious consideration the reader should turn to a whole book on the topic: Trask (1997).

It is worth remembering that, even for those who find punctuation relatively easy, writing in short sentences is easier. Of course, short sentences can result in a boring style. However, this is probably better than being wrong. It is certainly no worse. It is for you to decide. In any case, practice makes perfect. Start with short sentences. Then gradually, as you become more confident, allow yourself the luxury of a more flowing style that makes use of the whole range of punctuation marks; doing so will no doubt enhance the character of your written work – making it easier (as well as less boring) to read!

Many people have difficulty with paragraphing. A sure sign that this is the case is when you look at a draft and all of the paragraphs seem to be about the same length, usually with four or five to a page. As a rule of thumb, it is worth bearing in mind that most paragraphs will have at least three sentences and that it is unusual to have paragraphs that are longer than a page. However, there is no hard and fast rule about where paragraph breaks should come, and in many cases there will be more than one possibility.

Generally speaking, a new paragraph should indicate a change of direction in your thinking, or a new idea. This means that you can use a paragraph break to indicate to the reader that you are launching into a new idea. This can add emphasis and help to clarify your argument.

Academic writing as storytelling

Although we incline towards the view that writing as clearly and concisely as possible is a worthwhile basic aim for academic authors, it is by no means the case that you must write either clearly or concisely in order to get into print. Indeed, quite a lot of academic writing seems to be deliberately contrived to be as difficult as possible. This is particularly evident in peer-reviewed journals, many of which are dominated by articles that are more complex than necessary, make poor use and too much use of citation, and use big words and jargon where ordinary language and simpler words would do. Rather than making the attempt to communicate as clearly and directly as they can, the authors of such work seem to be attempting to make what they write as dense and impenetrable as possible, almost as if they do not want people to understand what they have to say. The same is often true of academic books, though to a lesser degree, perhaps because there is less pressure for the authors of books to adopt *academese* as the language of choice. Of course, some academic writing is a model of clarity and simplicity, no matter how complex the topic being addressed; unfortunately it is rather outweighed by academic literature at the other end of the spectrum.

Writing in the overcomplex and often obfuscatory style favoured and sometimes, apparently, expected by many journals, has certain advantages. For example, using lots of big words and technical terms can help to give the impression that you are really clever; it can also have the effect of warding off possible critics, who may be wary of admitting that they do not know what you are talking about, because they are afraid of looking stupid. Nonetheless, in our view, it is always best to try to make your work as easy to understand as you can.

As we have been indicating throughout this book, one way in which you can achieve simplicity while communicating complex ideas in a clear and engaging way, is to view your academic writing as a form of storytelling. Thinking of academic writing as narrative helps in facilitating inexperienced and experienced writers alike to develop a style through which, while adopting the conventions of their discipline, they can begin effectively to communicate their ideas.

Conceiving of what you want to say as a story makes it easier to develop a sound structure for your text. Another benefit is that viewing it as a story can help to focus your attention on the people you are telling it to and their needs.

Structure is partly about setting up connections between the elements of a text. It is about ensuring that there is a narrative flow from one section to the next. This means that at every stage, whenever you are writing, you should ask whether it is obvious what the relationship is between adjacent paragraphs and between adjacent sentences – do they follow on from one another? If not, is it clear that a jump is intended?

Think of this as like editing cuts in a film. If one section of a text flows naturally into another then there is no need to help the reader understand where you are going in your argument. But if you need to jump from one issue to another in order to lay out some matters that will be relevant for a later stage in your argument, then you need to signpost that clearly, as well as give your reasons for doing it. For example, if after having specified what hypotheses you are testing you now need to deal with the data you will be examining, then you must make clear from the start of your data section why it is *that* data you are dealing with. If yours is a review essay and you have been considering one approach to a topic but must now deviate to give some background on another area before showing how it relates to your first approach, then you must help the reader to understand why the detour is necessary. As in a film, the audience will accept for a few minutes that there is some reason for the deviation, but if they are kept guessing too long they will lose the plot.

All academics have stories to tell. Whatever form their scholarship takes – whether, for example, it is empirical, documentary or conceptual research – the stories they tell will usually involve sharing information about how they came to their conclusions; about their methods and hypotheses; about the genealogy into which their work slots – its parentage and forebears, its relationship to earlier work, and the ways in which it agrees or disagrees with views put forward by others. Of course, academics of different kinds not only have different areas of interest, but also different ways of telling their stories. For example, whereas scientists and social scientists will often employ visual means such as graphs and statistical tables to show what they have found, others, including philosophers, theologians and historians, will be more likely to use detailed examples and carefully constructed arguments. In telling their stories, some academics will make extensive use of specialized vocabulary, and some will make much use of citation. The stories academics tell may thus be told in different languages, or at any rate in different dialects of the same language. However, all will be stories of a kind.

If an academic book is the equivalent of a novel, then the academic article is the equivalent of a short story. Thinking like this will help you to avoid one of the pitfalls into which authors sometimes fall: that of being unclear about the species of writing in which they are engaging. Writing a book, for example, is quite different from writing an article for a journal. For one thing, books allow much more expansive discussion of examples and illustrations; for another, their length demands that the author should say more, whether this means covering a bigger area, or covering a small area in greater detail. The short story is not a novel that has had its wings clipped. It has a life of its own; it is its own genre. An academic article is not a cut-down version of a scholarly book; articles call for a different style entirely: more immediate and to the point.

A good article knows what it is about, and even if it uses illustrations and detailed arguments, it does not say more than is necessary to support the conclusion or viewpoint that is being put forward. Although the academic article is its own genre it also has a number of sub-genres, including the research report, the review of previous literature, the critical response to previously published material, and the original argument. The shorter the article, the less room there is for detail in the descriptions of ideas, methods and results that are offered, or for detail in the arguments that are advanced, and the more need there is for concise and straightforward.

What makes a story interesting? And what makes it plausible? One simple answer is that we know who the main characters are and what they are doing. We know the setting in which they are located and how they interact with each other and those settings. Each episode in the story has a clear presence and its consequence for the characters is apparent. The parallels in academic narratives are not difficult to see as shown in the box below.

Storytelling analogies for academic narratives

Components of fictional story	Academic parallels
Protagonist	Main hypothesis or argument
Antagonist	Challenging hypothesis or argument
Episodes	Stages in the study or contexts for argument
Consequence for characters	Implications for hypothesis/argument
Dénouement	Conclusions and future directions

Certain features of successful storytelling are found in the best academic writing, but are notably missing from the worst. For example, a good narrative writer constructs her plot and the way she introduces it in a way that seduces us into reading further. She ensures that the characters who inhabit the world she is creating are sufficiently believable to motivate us to pursue the narrative to find out what happens to them. Good academic writers do similar things, though in general the characters with whom they populate their texts are not people, but theories, hypotheses, methods, results, conclusions and so on.

So one of our central suggestions for writing well as an academic, is that, whatever your discipline, you should avoid overfanciful ways of expressing yourself, laying aside difficult words and constructions and even jargon wherever possible, and concentrate on developing coherent, well-structured and engaging stories about your work. In doing so you should, of course, adopt the narrative forms that are appropriate to your discipline and to the material you are writing about. Thus, for example, if tables of results, and graphs or charts are a standard practice in your discipline, you should utilize them to allow you to show what it is difficult to express in words. If technical terms are necessary to communicate with those with whom you want to communicate, you should of course use them. However, it is never a good idea to use such devices in constructing the stories you tell about your research if those devices do not help you to tell your stories as interestingly and as clearly as possible.

Recognizing poor structure

It is always possible to recognize poor structure because, although you may be enjoying and agreeing with some of what is said, being interested in it and involved with it, you may not be able to give a lucid account of the main thrust of what is written. This may happen by the author confusing you by creating what we call 'pseudo-structure' in their text. This is often done through the inappropriate use of words that are suggestive of structure. For example, beginning sentences with words such as 'thus', 'however', 'furthermore' or 'therefore' all suggest a link to the previous sentence. 'Thus' and 'therefore' suggest that the reader is about to be made aware of the conclusion of an argument; 'however' leads us to expect that we are about to be given an alternative of some kind; and 'furthermore' suggests that we are about to be given an additional point.

The best academic authors are able to determine both the right amount of detail and when to offer it; to make wise decisions about what should be in the foreground at any time; to decide what to include and what to excise. One common problem with structure arises when an author writes in such a way that it is impossible to identify the main focus. The reader does not know which characters in the plot to pay attention to. There may be lots of information, often at different levels, but it is difficult to tell what is important and what unimportant. In such situations the problems have often arisen because the author was trying to say too much, and failed, as she worked on successive drafts, to make rational decisions about what she should develop further and what she should lay aside, or even abandon altogether.

There are never enough words to say everything that you would like to say on a topic. This is most true in relatively short pieces of writing such as journal articles and single chapters of books – and even more so, in articles for periodicals or newspapers where there is the added problem of the inadmissibility of support for one's views in the form of citation. However, it is also true at the level of whole books. The trouble is that writing tends to stimulate the mind, and so as you write and try to work out the best way to say things, it is almost inevitable that you will come up with new ideas that seem too important to lay aside. When this happens, you will have to develop sufficient self-control to leave those ideas half worked (or half baked) for use at another time.

You may, like many authors, find that constraints in the shape of word limits can exert a beneficial influence over your writing style, by inducing you to take care with language, for example by avoiding repetition and long-windedness. All of us can persuade ourselves that what we have written is really nicely put, even if it is a bit long. The discipline of staying within strict word limits can cut through the self-deceit that often plays a part in such situations, by forcing you – if you really want to get into print – to look more carefully at whether every idea and every word really is earning its place. It is always important to take the time to decide what is essential to any piece of writing, and to have the courage to omit what is inessential, even if you feel affection for it because you wrote it.

Helpful hints for structuring your work

- Vary your sentence length and use short sentences where possible.
- Check your punctuation, especially if you use long sentences at times. The facilitation of readers' understanding is more important than adhering blindly to rules.
- Don't beat about the bush.
- Whenever possible, rewrite in order to avoid complicated constructions.
- Make sure that your headings and subheadings accurately label the sections to which they refer.
- Learn to distinguish the wood from the trees.
- Make sure that your paragraphing makes sense. Does each paragraph really mark a new idea?
- Check that the signposts you use to direct readers around your work, letting them know how different sections relate to one another, are accurate and helpful. Avoid misleading use of structural words and phrases such as 'therefore' and 'this leads us into a discussion of'.
- Think of your academic writing as storytelling and make sure the different parts of your story support one another.
- Make sure that ideas flow in such a way that your readers will be able to follow your line of reasoning or catch the drift of your story without having to engage in intellectual gymnastics.

7   Using illustration

Annoying technicalities • Illustrated information
• Getting illustrations right • Shaving with Occam's
razor • Boxology • Submitting illustrations

> Attractive displays of visual information . . . often have a
> narrative quality, a story to tell about the data.
> (Tufte 1983: 177)

Annoying technicalities

For many academic authors the most tedious part of the writing process is
sorting out the technicalities of format and layout, references and illustrations,
before their text can be printed. It is almost as if they think that such details are
simply an unnecessary and rather irritating barrier to finally communicating
their ideas, theories and results to their intended audience. They are mistaken,
and it will help you in understanding what is involved in preparing work for
publication if you reflect a little on the part that such details can play in
enabling you to communicate with your readers. In some ways they are like
the orchestration for a piece of music. The melody may be pleasant enough
but until it is set for a particular set of instruments it has no life. They are also
akin to the various elements of setting and scenery that dramatists use to
create the *mise en scène* within which their story can come alive.

The settings in which academics place their stories need to have props
that are appropriate to each particular narrative and thus facilitate its telling.

The very nature of those props tells the reader something about the author, and the qualities of the story they are telling. Is the author well organized or haphazard; thorough or casual? Does the way in which the story is told suggest a scholar or a novice; a person in control of her material or someone struggling with it?

In this book there is not the space to go into all the possibilities and technicalities surrounding the use of illustrations in academic authorship. We can only alert you to the matters you should consider and point you in the direction of where you can get more detailed guidance. If you follow through on these ideas, though, you will lift your material from the mundane to the professional.

Having said that you need to think carefully about illustrations, it is nonetheless important to be clear that you can never have total control over how illustrations and related matters are handled unless you are your own publisher. Much will be determined by the publisher and be out of your control. However, word-processors enable you to alter the appearance of your text, so you can still get quite close to the published form your text will take, whether it is a book or a journal article. This can influence the way you write, because it will help you to imagine how it might appear to a reader. However, it is important to realize that, as an author, it is not your responsibility to set your text out in the way it will look when printed.

All publishers have a house style which, by and large, will be imposed upon your text and illustrations when they are prepared for publication. The fonts that will be used and other details of layout, such as the width of margins, whether the text is justified, and whether graphical illustrations appear in boxes, will all be decided by the publisher, and so any work of this kind that you do will probably be abandoned when they come to typeset your work for publication. Indeed, many publishers insist that you provide them with text that is devoid of most features of layout.

However, you cannot assume that any visual material will be redrawn or even tidied up. They may just be copied directly into the published version. Even if they are redrawn the graphic artist will have to work from your original and is unlikely to ask you for clarification of any ambiguities, just making a best guess. This can mean that if your original material is at all confusing you can have a battle at the proof stage convincing the publisher to change the illustration to accord with what you had in mind.

If you are writing for a journal you will have no chance of influencing the way your text looks on the page. However, in the case of a book, and depending on the publisher, you may be able to persuade an editor to allow some deviation from the house style. For example, you may have a preference for the way in which distinctions between subheadings of different levels of importance are distinguished, or whether different fonts or text styles are used to delineate the verbatim quotes.

Unless you are preparing what is known as a 'camera-ready' book, that is, one in which the printed pages are reproduced directly from the manuscript you submit, the detailed format of visual illustrations such as graphs, diagrams and tables will not necessarily be under your control. The degree of control will vary depending on the publishing outlet and the particular technologies the publisher employs.

Illustrated information

We are using the idea of an illustration to mean many different forms of material that capture a crucial aspect of your work in a concise form. This can be an illustration in the metaphorical sense of representing some important aspect of what you are talking about, such as an insightful quotation from a well-known author or a key respondent. Or it can be an illustration in the more direct sense of being a visual depiction of something you are describing, such as a graph of your results. So illustrations, as we are using the term here, could be stories, case histories or case studies, descriptions of experiments or observations. They can take the form of verbatim transcripts, pictures, photographs, diagrams and other graphical representations such as tables, graphs, flow diagrams, and so on.

We are using such a wide definition of 'illustrations' to emphasize their crucial role in your text. They are the nub of what you write. They both elaborate and shed light upon your central message, and in many cases provide the crucial evidence to support your argument. Illustrations will often be what people remember about what you have written, and will be the aspects they wish to cite. It is therefore often a good idea to start the planning of what you will write by determining what the main illustrations will be, and then getting them in good shape before starting to put text around them.

Of course, visual illustrations are the most powerful form to use, if used appropriately. If you have two or three percentages there is not a lot of value in putting in a bar chart to illustrate them; but if you want to show changes in rates of change (such as increases in inflation) then a graph or other visual representation will save a great deal of text and make your point more clearly than a table of numbers can. Edward Tufte does a quite remarkable job of showing the various possibilities for handling visual illustrations in the three wonderful books he published himself dealing with what he calls Information Design (Tufte 1983, 1990, 1997). The way in which the books divide up the area is an education in itself.

The first book (Tufte 1983) reviews the 'visual display of quantitative information'. This is perhaps the most usual form of graphical representation that scientists, especially, think of, but Tufte shows all the pitfalls and delights, in an of course beautifully illustrated book, that might be encountered with even the most conventional of charts and graphs, as well as some innovative approaches to illustrating quantities. One such approach is the Marey train schedule that incorporates a train timetable as a series of crossing lines linking places and times. He shows that even the apparently most minor detail, such as the thickness of a line on a graph, can help or hinder getting the message across.

The second book (Tufte 1990) celebrates 'envisioning information'. In the opening pages Tufte quotes Philip Morrison's reference to 'charts, diagrams, graphs, tables, guides, instructions, directories and maps' as 'cognitive art', claiming that the book is a partial catalogue for such a collection of art at 'the intersection of image, word, number, art'. In doing so, Tufte draws attention (in all senses) to the fact that any diagram is not just a standard chart, but a work of art, an artefact, in which every line and letter, number and symbol is doing a job and needs to be carefully considered. He shows that complex sets of material can be given impact and their meaning drawn out if the details of how they are presented are carefully thought through. In particular, if people are to make use of the illustrations and act on decisions derived from them then the ability to read them clearly is crucial.

The third book (Tufte 1997) is the most ambitious and in some ways the most innovative. It deals with 'visual explanations'. He shows how the way in which relationships are represented visually can have a huge influence on what people understand from those relationships. Perhaps his most telling example is his analysis of the crucial engineering information concerning the damage to O-rings on space shuttle craft prior to the disastrous launch in 1986 of the space shuttle Challenger. Tufte reproduced the list of numbers that were faxed as evidence of the impact of low temperatures on the O-rings: information that was ignored. He then provided a number of different illustrations that make much clearer the likely impact of low temperature, which he claims people would have understood much better and been more likely to take notice of. Indeed, think how much easier it would be for you to understand the point that Tufte is making if we had included the illustrations from his book.

Getting illustrations right

Diagrams, tables, bar charts, figures or any other illustrative material have two purposes. One is to provide more detailed evidence to support an argument. The other is to illustrate the argument in ways that are better than words. Illustrations that make things more confusing should be omitted. This is true from the humble bar chart to a complex multivariate statistical analysis.

If the point is being made that there are some interesting differences between groups, then bar charts for which those differences are visually very clear are appropriate. For example, the fact that the variables went into the analysis in the order A, B, C, D, does not mean this has to be the order of the chart. If, for instance, C is the most extreme (richest, oldest, most violent) followed by B, then A and then D, that is the order they should be on the chart unless there is something illogical or confusing about doing it that way (for example, perhaps there is some other dimension, such as age, that is the obvious one to use).

Given the ease with which different chart forms can now be generated it is essential that the appropriate form is used. Appropriate means the one that reveals the relevant patterns most clearly. Just because it looks clever or pretty does not mean it is appropriate. Pie charts, for instance, are rarely helpful, pretty though they may be when multicoloured.

If a complex statistical analysis is summarizing the relationships between a large number of variables, then the reader needs to be able to identify the actual variables (say by numbers on the diagram that refer to an appendix listing the variables in detail). Such diagrams inevitably do need to be studied, but the more the writer can help with that the better.

Which charts are put where in the report, especially which are put next to each other, needs to be carefully considered. Charts should be next to each other if comparisons are to be made between them, and far apart if comparisons would be confusing. So putting two complex diagrams adjacent to each other is usually a recipe for total confusion.

Tufte is a leader in giving detailed guidance on how to get visual illustrations into the form that makes them most effective. He draws attention to the details of exactly how the illustration is constructed. There is a tendency for inexperienced writers to ignore such matters. This is becoming an increasing problem with the ready availability of graphics software. One key to thinking about this is whether the material welcomes the reader or whether it just tells you how clever the author is in creating such a complex illustration. Tufte calls this 'friendly' versus 'unfriendly' material. We have drawn on Tufte's ideas in the box on page 95.

You will see that one of the central ideas in this box is that you can get the message and understand its main implications directly from the illustration. If this is done well, the reader can almost treat the article or chapter like a children's picture book and scan through and make sense of the main story simply by looking at the pictures. This is no mean skill of the author. It requires thinking carefully about the medium – words, numbers, pictures – that is best for which aspect of the argument and how those points can be integrated into a convincing and, ideally, pleasing whole.

Do remember, as we have mentioned, that your visual material may be used directly by the publishers and therefore is likely to be reduced in size when it is printed in a book or journal. Make sure that crucial details will not be lost, or require a magnifying glass to be seen in the published form.

Also keep in mind the suggestion we have made throughout about written material. Get a sensible associate to have a look at your illustrations and, without any prompting or help from you, get them to describe what story the illustration tells. Listen carefully to the questions of clarification that they ask.

Some guidance on making your visual illustrations readily accessible

User friendly	User unfriendly
All text spelled out	Abbreviations and cross-references to appendices
All text horizontal – left to right	Words run in different directions
Notes to explain meaning of data	Cryptic graphics requiring cross-reference to text
Labels to explain meaning of graphics	Obscure coding requiring study of legend etc.
Graphic attracts viewer	Illustration repellently full of 'chartjunk'
Components have strong brightness contrast	Many subtle colours that will get lost if greys
Type is clear, precise and 'modest'	Type is dense, demanding and overbearing
Type uses upper and lower case and serifs	Everything is in capitals without serifs
Words show how to make sense of picture	Words tell different story from picture
Main lines light in weight with effective contrast	All lines are equally chunky
Tend to be horizontal (width greater than height)	Height much greater than width
Nature of data suggests shape of graphic	Graphic's shape determined by 'artistic' whim
Words, numbers and graphics are integrated	Reader needs to jump between material

Source: After Tufte (1983: 183)

It may be possible to deal with some of these by changes in the illustration. If not, make sure that your text clearly spells out the information needed.

Shaving with Occam's razor

Clarity of illustrations is so crucial that it is worth considering a little further. As in all areas of scholarship, parsimony is the main principle. This was expressed most famously in the fourteenth century in relation to explanations by William of Occam. He proposed that the basis of science and philosophy should be that, in explaining something, assumptions must not be needlessly multiplied. An illustration is a form of explanation. Therefore a good principle is that you should not add to an illustration features that the reader will needlessly have to make sense of. Tufte uses the term 'chartjunk' to describe that content-free decoration which is now so easy to put into any diagram but adds nothing to its overall sense.

Only put into an illustration what is needed, but do make sure all the information that is needed is there. This includes a clear indication of what it is an illustration of, its source and the meaning of any symbols or axes. The units of any measurement and the sample drawn upon are also crucial in scientific charts.

Any illustration, whether it is a case study, a diagram or a picture, tells a story. You need to be very clear in your mind what the storyline is. Usually it will assume some background knowledge or information on the part of the reader, but other aspects the reader will expect to glean directly from the information that you give. It is therefore important that you determine how appropriate any particular illustration is for your purposes and for the specific audience who will be reading the work.

Implicit messages

Because an illustration is telling a story you must be alert to whether there is a sub-plot that you had not intended, which may mislead or confuse your reader. The amusing but very sound book by Darrel Huff (1954) subversively called *How to Lie with Statistics*, recently republished (Huff and Geiss 1993), is replete with illustrations of how to produce graphs so that they imply something that is not actually supported by the data. More recently, Jones (1995) has focused on how to lie with charts to good effect as well. The ironic titles of these books show that there is a great deal of *legerdemain* possible with visual illustrations. You can use this to your advantage to make your work seem all the more impressive and your results probably stronger than they really are. You can be caught out, though. Readers may turn first to the chart and, seeing that it has been presented in a way that distorts the information, dismiss the whole claim.

Singles and multiples

Often you will not be able to get all the information you want into one illustration. This raises important matters about how the different illustrations relate to each other and whether any cross-reference is necessary. At its most elementary this may mean that the orientation on the page of the illustrations is as similar as possible so that direct comparison is as easy as possible. It is particularly difficult for the reader to cross-refer from one illustration to another unless they are carefully co-ordinated.

In general, it is better to have one diagram that captures all the information you need rather than lots of related diagrams; but if you do need more than one diagram, think carefully about whether the reader needs to move between them to understand your points. The page layout may mean that it is difficult to place the two illustrations next to each other in a way that assists comparison. If you do want the comparison to be possible, make sure you indicate that in the details you give of the illustrations to the publishers.

This apparently simple idea is often missed even in the much used bar chart or histogram. For example, there may be three matters, a person's age, the day of the week and the time of day, say in relation to the use of a particular facility. Different ways of organizing this information would make quite different points, for instance emphasizing age differences as opposed to days of the week. Putting seven diagrams, one for each day of the week, may carry all the information, but could be very difficult to make sense of, whereas putting all the information into one illustration could be confusing. You need to determine the central issue and organize the visual material to accord with that. With spreadsheet software such as Excel you can explore different representations at the touch of a button, so there is no excuse for just going with the first one that the software happens to produce.

Boxology

Charts and graphs, maps and photographs are the most obvious form of visual illustration that academic authors draw upon. Many other ways of using visual aspects of text on the page are available and worthy of careful consideration. We will give space to just one of them here. This is the tendency in some disciplines to summarize an argument with a diagram that has a series of boxes, in each of which is an aspect of the argument with lines showing how they relate. These diagrams share much with the flow diagrams that would be actual designs for systems in, for example, computer science or electronics. Or they may draw upon the idea of the organization chart that lays out who is responsible to whom, most typically in a hierarchical organization like the military or the health service. When such a diagram is used to summarize a set of conceptual relationships or to lay out an argument, it becomes something rather different that may be productive or destructive depending on how it is employed.

Some academics have dismissed these diagrams as 'boxology'. This derisive term is meant to imply that, rather than developing the argument effectively, the author simply joins up the components in boxes thereby implying much more precision and logic to the argument than it warrants. Support for such criticism may be gleaned from the fact that there is not one such diagram in any of Tufte's books. He thus implicitly indicates that such sequence of boxes is typically a lazy way of illustrating an argument that may best be presented in some other form. Its prevalence therefore is probably also a consequence of confusing a number of different forms of diagram.

Perhaps the most obvious and appropriate use of boxes joined by lines is when a process is being described that has a number of different stages that can be achieved by different possible routes. This is the engineer's flow diagram translated into the more abstract world of philosophy, literature or the social sciences. In engineering there is a distinct vocabulary that can be drawn on, where different shapes mean different sorts of processes, such as an oval for a choice point and a square for the combined results of a number of choices. The organization chart is analogous to this, in that it is the flow of authority that is being mapped. In other words, the most direct, conventional use of linked boxes is where some process is being depicted that implies material, energy or power is being transmitted from one component of the process to another, being modified at each stage.

The use becomes more problematical when the links between the boxes are taken to indicate the direction of causes, the entities in one box influencing those in another. An example would be two boxes, one with the word 'gender' in it and the other the word 'ability', with an arrow from the former to the latter. This would, presumably, be taken to imply that differences in gender create differences in ability. The diagram might look tidy and a neutral summary of some established correlations, but you only have to pick up any feminist analysis of such correlations to realize the pattern of causes is certainly more complex than this.

The problem of boxology comes when the links between the boxes are implicit assumptions that are not explained or defended. A diagram with boxes and links between them is only of value if the links do actually mean something rather than just being a loose form of hand-waving to imply relationships without being at all clear about what they are.

The three main aspects assumed in any box diagram are that: (1) each component in the diagram is independent of every other, so can be treated as a separate box, and (2) the lines between the boxes indicate a direct relationship, with the direction of causality often implied by an arrow, and (3) most crucially, that the lines (and arrows) indicate the dominant (causal) relationships between the components. Often, all these assumptions are invalid, but also if you follow the lines around you realize that every box could cause every other, so the implication of causal direction is actually not even supported by the diagram that purports to demonstrate, or at least illustrate, it.

However, such diagrams can be productive in summarizing subtle and complex ideas in a way that brings the central points home and also acts an *aide-memoire*. One example of this is a particularly apposite one for this book because it summarizes the components of an argument and how they relate to each other. Figure 7.1 is taken from Toulmin's (1958) book on the analysis of argument. Here, quite a complex idea and set of relationships are clearly summarized by the indications of boxes and their relationships.

You can take Figure 7.1 and use it to form most arguments, as follows. Because it has been shown (Grounds) that people who smoke many cigarettes contract emphysema (Warrant) as published studies have shown (Backing), it is probably the case (Modality) that any given heavy smoker will be at greater

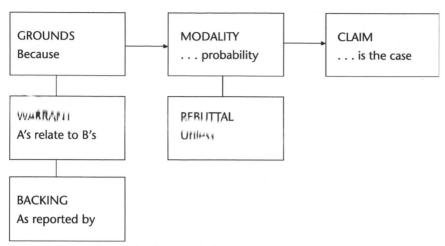

Figure 7.1 A good example of the use of a box diagram to summarize a complex idea (from Toulmin 1958).

risk of emphysema (Claim), unless that person has some particular protective factors such as never inhaling (Rebuttal).

The point about the diagram is that it summarizes a detailed book elegantly not just in terms of listing the components, but also in helping us to understand their meaning and how they relate to each other. For example, although the Rebuttal may seem to modify the Claim because it helps to indicate the conditions under which the claim would not hold, the diagram actually makes clear that the rebuttal is logically a modification of the probabilities that have to be sought back through the fundamental Grounds and the Warrant for those grounds. Furthermore, the diagram makes clear that there will need to be some Backing for the crucial Warrant on which the argument is based.

Of course this is not the place to enter into a discussion about the nature of argument, but we hope you see that a carefully considered box diagram can capture an argument (in the case of Figure 7.1 about the nature of arguments), in an elegant and powerful way that encapsulates a number of subtle ideas and their interrelationships.

Submitting illustrations

Every publisher has its own technical requirements concerning the submission of illustrations. For example, Elsevier, which publishes many journals, has a website that provides many technical details and assistance on how to submit artwork correctly (www.elsevier.com/locate/authorartwork). You do need to take account of such guidelines if you do not want all the work you have put in to preparing your illustrations to go to waste.

The developments in information technology mean that there are many formats in which illustrations can be stored: bitmaps, jpeg, tiff and gif, eps and umpteen more. Each of these converts the picture or diagram on your screen into the computer code that allows it to be transmitted and recognized by particular software. The conversion process is different, though, for each format. Jpeg, for instance, loses a lot of the information in the picture in order to make the electronic file as small as possible. It will thus give rise to a picture of lower quality than, say, a tiff image, but that latter image will require much more space in your computer. If this sort of thing interests you then the computer sections of bookshops will offer you a vast array of beautifully produced books to guide you through this arcane world in relation to the particular software you have access to. If you do not want to become a 'techy', just determine the most appropriate format from your publisher, find out how to produce it and stick with it.

8   Moral authorship

Responsibilities and rights

A range of constraints • Using material in more than one publication • Plagiarism • Joint authorship • Relationships between authors and editors • Contracts and agents • Copyright • Being a morally responsible author

A range of constraints

Writing is usually carried out in isolation. However, it is part of a social process and it becomes a public event as soon as there is an attempt to get others to read it or to publish it. When this happens, the author is expected to conform to a range of traditions, professional guidelines, regulations and legal constraints. At the heart of all of them are matters of etiquette about, for example, the ways in which well-mannered co-authors will work together. However, some are more properly thought of as ethical matters – from the wrong that one person does to others by plagiarizing their ideas, to the wrong that a publisher can do to an author (and to readers) by publishing a weak text just because it is likely to make money. Finally, the public activity that is academic publication is subject to legal constraints. Since these are significant mainly when publishing in newspapers and magazines, we will leave their discussion until Chapter 11.

In this chapter we will start with some matters for which there is no legislation but which may cause concern for the budding writer because they serve as unwritten rules about what people expect of each other; many of these are issues that we wish we had known about when we first started on the road to publication. As we move through the chapter, we will introduce more technical issues. It is important at the outset to be clear that all we can do in one chapter is to comment on a few issues, rather than explore them fully.

Authors have responsibilities to their publishers and to their readers. They also have responsibilities to anyone who has shared information that they use in their published writing. And though it may sound pompous to say so, academic authors also have a responsibility to posterity. The whole point of publishing as a scholar is to contribute to society, by setting down one's experiences, findings, ideas and arguments in a more or less permanent form. That is what distinguishes scholarly writing from many other forms of published output, including journalism, which often has an ephemeral quality. And it is why it is unethical to use the medium of academic publication in the knowledge that what you are writing is trivial, frivolous or downright wrong.

Using material in more than one publication

When you submit work for publication you are implicitly claiming that the text you submit is original and has not been published in the form in which you are submitting it before – unless, for example, all you are doing is submitting an article for republication in an edited book. There is nothing wrong with publishing work that overlaps with other material you have published, either because you are using the same material in a different way or for a different purpose, or because you are developing ideas further in the later publication. However, it is clearly a breach of the trust that exists between authors and those who publish their work, to offer for publication material that is substantially the same as existing publications, as if it were wholly original. A related, but rather different matter, concerns the submission of the same material in different forms to publications that have different audiences. This is often appropriate in multidisciplinary areas in which the different audiences may be expected to take rather different things from a study. Some audiences may be more concerned with the work's theoretical implications, others with its practical consequences. The point is that the best academic writing in any field will often have a rich central narrative that opens up a number of very different sub-narratives, aimed at achieving different purposes in relation to different audiences.

Of particular concern to most academic authors is the ways in which multiple submission to peer-reviewed journals is viewed. In general, the submission of the same article to more than one journal at the same time is frowned upon. More than that, many people consider it to be unethical to do so, and some journals will not accept articles for review unless authors make a statement to the effect that it has never been published before and is not currently being considered for publication elsewhere. Further, once the article is accepted, the publisher will require you to sign a copyright form that assigns the copyright to the publisher. So you would be breaking this agreement if the paper ended up somewhere else as well. In our experience, newspapers and magazines never ask you to sign copyright forms or other documents that make clear the ownership of the written material. They just assume it is your copyright and that in sending it to them it becomes their copyright once they print it. So if you want to hold on to the copyright you had better negotiate that with them beforehand.

By contrast, it is not uncommon for authors to submit the same book proposal to more than one publisher at a time, rather than waiting to be rejected by the first, before going to another. Although some publishers will try to discourage this practice, some think it is acceptable. The reason for this difference in attitudes towards multiple submission in relation to books as opposed to journal articles perhaps lies both in the nature of the relationship between authors and those they hope will publish their work, and in the transactions that go on between them.

Although it is inappropriate to submit articles to more than one journal at a time, it is acceptable to withdraw a submitted paper, for example if you consider it has taken too long to go through the review process, especially if decisions are not made in something like the timescale advertised by the journal. It is quite common for journals to take many months more than their own estimated times to complete the review process, which means that those who have submitted material to them are left in limbo; this is a matter of ethical importance. However, you should discuss withdrawing the paper with the editor first in order not to develop a reputation as an awkward cuss.

The relationship between author and journal editors is very unequal, with editors holding the power, and the transactions that pass between them are largely intellectual or academic ones. This holds more strongly for prestigious journals than ones which may not have so many submissions. But the editor's decision will be fundamentally academic, which is why the originality of the material is so crucial. In the case of book publishing, on the other hand, the transaction is largely a commercial one, and for that reason the relationship between authors or editors of books, and publishers can be more equally balanced. A book proposal is a potential product to sell, from which profit might be made. Publishers, as civilized as they may be, still realize that they are in a marketplace where goods are on offer to various possible buyers. If they are lukewarm about your proposal they may even suggest that you try a few pub-lishers. But be wary of sending book proposals to many publishers. If you have more than one offer to publish, you are almost bound to irritate whoever you turn down. The process of deciding whether they should accept a proposed book is time consuming and may have other costs associated with it, such as paying people to review your proposal.

As an author you want the best deal you can get, while commissioning editors have to decide whether your book will fit into their catalogue, what it is worth to them, and whether you are likely to deliver a saleable manuscript. In order to benefit as much as you can from your work, you will have to consider the royalty rate and other benefits that you might be offered. However, you will also have to think about the prestige of the publisher in question and the likelihood that they will market your book sufficiently well to allow you to benefit from whatever royalty rate they offer you. Few authors of academic books will ever make significant amounts of money from their publishing, unless they happen to write a book that will be adopted as a textbook by a large number of courses across the country, each of which has many students. (Some authors, it has to be said, seem to have a knack of identifying such textbooks; theirs is a gift worth having). However, if you are intent on making at least a little money from your efforts, it would probably be better to sign up with a market leader, even if they offer a lower royalty, than with a small company that offers a higher royalty but which has a less developed marketing machine and so may sell fewer copies.

A slightly different form of multiple publication is sometimes given the label 'salami publishing' to describe the production of many slim publications from one project, in a way that can be likened to slicing salami. It is most often used in relation to empirical research. In some instances, this may be appropriate – for example, where the tradition is of short publications dealing with one specific aspect of a study. Indeed, in some intellectual cultures, notably Japan, people are sometimes only given very small amounts of space in which to give an account of their work, possibly only two pages. They therefore have to produce one paper, say, on their methodology and a number of other short papers on aspects of their results. If your work lends itself to this form of writing, it can be an effective way of getting your material published. But you do need to make sure that each paper is distinct and that you do not attract criticism for making limited material spread too thinly.

The other side of the coin from slicing your material into lots of distinct journal articles, is pulling various publications together and writing a book using material already published in articles. This is clearly a reasonable route to the creation of the text of a book, though some sceptics will always have doubts about whether it is proper to reuse material originally published in another form elsewhere. However, it is a natural step on from writing about the same material with a different slant for different audiences, or revisiting ideas or data analysis as you develop through successive publications. A book that draws disparate material together in one place will usually be welcomed.

However, do be careful to make clear what has already been published and what is new material, so that your readers can have a clear idea of the origins of what they are studying. If you cite your earlier publications at length you may also need to be careful to ensure that you do indeed still hold the copyright, as we will explore in a little more detail later.

Plagiarism

Drawing on your own published work to produce a new document sometimes causes confusion about what the original source of the material is. But when the material you draw upon was originally produced by someone else, that is plagiarism. In essence, plagiarism involves representing another person's ideas or words as if they are your own. It is related to other matters, including copyright and patent, but differs from them in that the latter are both enshrined in law. For example, as an author, if you copy material beyond a set amount, you will breach copyright and become liable to legal sanctions, while selling certain material, or making it available freely even, can break a patent or reduce the possibility of obtaining a patent.

Patent is rather a technical, legal matter that varies considerably between the USA and Europe, and we suggest that if you are concerned that your publication will reduce your own possibility of establishing a patent for your invention, or could infringe another person's patent, you should consult a lawyer who specializes in patent law. By the way, all this is rather different from having a trademark, which can be a piece of typography, services, physical goods or brand name registered with a national Register of Companies.

Plagiarism is a great deal messier affair than breaches of copyright, patent or trademark. Because it does not carry such legal force it may not be so clear when it has occurred. You therefore need to be on your guard to avoid any hint of it. To be found guilty of plagiarism would attract severe criticism from your academic peers. In most institutions, students may fail courses if plagiarism is proven. It can arise for a number of reasons, from poor habits of scholarship developed during undergraduate and postgraduate study, through to the wilful and deliberately deceitful use of another person's writing in order to gain credit and appreciation that is not rightfully yours. One reason that plagiarism has become such a common problem on a global scale is the increasing ease with which electronic sources can be accessed then 'cut and pasted' at will.

Plagiarism does attract considerable ordure on anyone doing it, but sadly there are remarkable variations in how it is dealt with. We know of cases of students who clearly copied chunks of their supervisor's thesis into their coursework without citation and who suffered no penalties for doing so. In another blatant case, an ex-student submitted for publication a piece of work that was almost entirely a word-for-word copy of another student's work with whom he had shared a room. When this was raised with the publisher and with the university authorities, providing concrete chapter and verse illustration of the plagiarism, absolutely no action was taken. All this serves to emphasize that the limitations on plagiarism are moral constraints rather than legal ones. So if you plagiarize you may not be struck down by a bolt of lightening, nor is it certain that you will be overtly castigated by your colleagues. What will happen, though, is that the rumour mill will sweep into action and you may quickly find that no one is willing to work with you and that your submissions are rejected from journals without clear indications why.

Joint authorship

The moral and ethical demands on you increase when you start collaborating with other people. Part of the reason for this is that, as you may have noticed, there are few desks large enough to get more than one pair of knees under them. Arranging matters so that two people actually physically write together is extremely difficult. Joint authorship is thus rarely a truly collaborative venture in which two or more people create a piece of text in the same moments, say like a songwriter and instrumentalist in the typical Hollywood biopic with one sitting at the piano and the other leaning over his shoulder making suggestions. It is almost invariably a sequential process in which each co-author works on one aspect of the material alone then shares this and discusses changes which the second author may act on, producing a further revision.

It is this sequential process that produces the delights and dangers of co-authorship. Not only does it seem to halve the work (although it does not really as most authors want to be involved at some level in all aspects of the work), ensure you have a second reader, spark ideas and broaden your knowledge, but it is also likely to make the writing longer when both authors want to contribute at all points.

Collaborating with others in the production of a piece of writing can be a great joy but it can also cause headaches and stress. Most people who write collaboratively will almost certainly ask themself at some point, 'Is this worth it?'

The advantages and disadvantages depend entirely on the relationship between those who are working together. For example, where there is a big difference in experience between the parties, the expertise and 'insider knowledge' that come with longevity as an author may be complemented by the innovation and energy of youth, so that both parties can learn from each other. If one member is very junior, then working with someone who is more experienced can be a great help in getting the writing to a level that will make it publishable. For the senior party, on the other hand, there is the pleasure in helping others up the publication ladder, and perhaps the added advantage that they will be so grateful that they are happy to undertake some of the more tedious and time-consuming tasks that accompany writing – checking references and so on. Where collaborators are more equal, the added power of their combined effort and experience may open up possibilities for publication that neither person could achieve so readily on their own. This can be particularly useful in multidisciplinary areas where no one person can have mastery of the field as a whole.

Many academics begin their publishing careers by writing and publishing collaboratively with their supervisor, gradually moving on to publish on their own, and to develop new collaborations with others as opportunities arise. The success or failure of such collaborations depends to a large extent on the development of trust, and a shared understanding of the strengths that each party brings, and a willingness to negotiate different roles. Collaborators who know each other well and have worked together previously may be able to set to work without much prior discussion. However, the partners in a new collaboration would always be well advised to reach clear agreement, not only about the roles each will play but also about the approach that will be taken to the writing process, well before finger is put to keyboard. Indeed, it is not at all unknown for there to be some form of written 'prenuptial' contract between the proposed authors before even the scholarly activity from which the publication is expected to arise, is initiated. One of the main points of such prior agreements is to plan in advance what will happen if the partnership breaks down. Consideration certainly needs to be given to how a fundamental failure in the working relationship would be dealt with when agreeing to publish with one or more other people. We have both suffered from the devastating effects of not heeding this advice.

Crucial considerations for effective collaborative authorship

One issue of central concern in collaborative authorship is the ownership of the work that has gone into creating the publication. This is most clearly an issue in areas such as science, where publication will often rely heavily on data that has been collected as part of empirical research. For example, many researchers fail to realize that, while recognizing the intellectual investment of the individuals involved, most universities will regard such data as belonging to the institution. Another crucial aspect of ownership relates to the relationship between students or other junior researchers, and their supervisors. A common bone of contention in such situations is that although the less experienced partner may have done much of the leg work, and put in considerable sweat and perhaps quite a few tears in collecting data, access to that data will often only have been possible because of the supervisor's personal contacts and reputation, while understanding its likely significance will often only have been possible because of the supervisor's skill. Thus, for example, while a student may regard his supervisor's input as brief and therefore insignificant, the supervisor will recognize it as crucial. If such matters are not openly discussed before anything of note has been discovered, resentment and mistrust can cause so much conflict that nothing ever gets published from the work.

A second, and closely related aspect of collaborative authorship, relates to questions about the ownership of ideas and intellectual property. For example, an experienced researcher may be clear that his pearls of wisdom are the distilled essence of years of hard thought, while a less experienced collaborator might hold the view that while her work drew on ideas that came from her supervisor, those ideas were pretty obvious, and that in fact the crucial factor in turning them into something useable was her creative input and intellectual effort. It is always a real pity if the lack of agreement over who has the right to publish the insights that arise from research denies the academic community the benefit of the emerging wisdom. The earlier in the process that everyone who is involved can establish agreement about who has a right to ownership of ideas and products of their joint research, the better.

Finally, there is sometimes a problem in situations where some members of a collaborative team decide that they do not wish to be associated with certain ideas or with publications that present them. They may disagree with the interpretation of data, or the uses to which it is put, or the conclusions drawn from an argument. It should never be assumed that everyone would want their name on whatever is going.

The situation is rather different if the people involved have signed a contract with some third party, usually a publisher, to write a book or to contribute a chapter. Then they are jointly bound. In such circumstances, the withdrawal of one party could require the whole contract to be renegotiated. Such a renegotiation can be especially important if the publication will result in royalties or other income.

Possibly the most contentious issue in academic circles over joint publication relates to the way in which authorship is to be attributed. It is a matter of some puzzlement to non-academics to discover that the order in which names are listed on any publication can have deep significance. The first name on the list is usually seen as the most senior in terms of the importance of his or her contribution, though sometimes the order of names implies no more than that the first named author, or editor, was the one who originated the idea. Some institutions have a clear set of guidelines on such matters, that reflect the notion of apprenticeship in authorship, so that while a student's first paper will often be published with the supervisor as first author, things will gradually change as his contribution grows, so that the student eventually becomes first author, and eventually flies solo with only an acknowledgement to the supervisor.

These matters are relevant to all scholarly collaborations. The parties need to be clear before too much water has passed under the bridge as to who has ownership and rights of access to data and other source material, what the agreement is on intellectual property, and how authorship will be handled. We should, perhaps, finally, point out that, in our experience, these are not often contentious issues, but when serious disagreements do emerge they can be devastating to all concerned.

The issues of ownership and intellectual property should not be the only thing to discuss with any co-author. Compatibility of style and approach to the work should be sorted out before too much ink has been spilt. At the very least you should read your co-author's work before collaborating to ensure that she tackles matters in a way with which you are comfortable. If your co-authors have stylistic habits you do not like, it is best to discuss this with them as soon as you can.

The actual mechanics of how the work will be co-written also need to be considered carefully. People have remarkably different ways of working. Some cannot write a second sentence until the first has been perfected. Others like to produce pages of notes dealing with many aspects of the topic at hand and then refine them. If writers assume that the person they plan to work with has the same habits as they do then they may get an unwanted surprise. These differences, though, do mean there can be no general prescription of how to collaborate.

However, we have found in our various collaborations, especially with the advent of e-mail, that the development of a detailed skeleton for any work that is agreed and then used as the basis for the actual writing does ease matters and speed them up. The skeleton can be initiated in a very sketchy form by one person then passed back and forth, evolving along the way, until it reaches a level of detail where everyone now knows what they will write (more or less). By carefully numbering the sections and subsections of the skeleton there is a clear point of reference. It can even be a great help to indicate broadly how long each part of the document should be. Consequently, the writing is not forced to proceed from the start of the document to the end, but can unfold as the authors find most comfortable. For example, for this book we identified fifteen chapters across a total of four sections. We agreed that each section would be about 5,000 words (or around ten pages). We also listed about ten topics for each section. This meant that when we started writing we knew to some degree what each page of the manuscript would cover. Of course it did not end up like this. At one stage the book had nineteen chapters, and the sectional structure is no longer openly declared. Our detailed skeleton did mean, though, that we could get on with the writing and pass sections back and forth as we wrote them, without confusing ourselves or needing lots of meetings to work out where everything fitted.

It is also worth noting that the management of joint authorship possibly increases in complexity geometrically as the number of co-authors increases. Three co-authors are much, much more difficult to pull together than just two. Once the number goes beyond three then an overt organizational structure is necessary. People actually need to be assigned roles that they agree to, and someone needs to take a leadership or management role to ensure the job is being done as agreed and that all the contributions fit together. This 'manager' in our experience usually ends up finalizing the draft of the document.

Checklist for agreeing co-authorship

- Agree a skeleton of the work in as much detail as possible
- Clarify how the authorship (especially seniority) will be identified
- Agree on any subsequent use of material after initial publication
- Discuss styles of writing
- Determine mechanics of development of text
- Understand complementarity of contributions
- Establish what will happen if one author withdraws

Relationships between authors and editors

Once the text leaves your desk and becomes part of your contract with a publisher or editor, you are entering into a morally, and often legally, binding agreement about the nature of the work that goes beyond the assumption that it is an original contribution of which you are the intellectual property owner.

Sometimes publishers exert influence over the form the writing takes – over style and the issues addressed – frequently as a condition of agreement to publish. This is really a matter of power and authority. The more significant you are in your field the more likely are publishers to bow to your wishes. But you should never forget that, except in very few cases these days, publishing is a commercial venture. The publisher will be assessing how to ensure that the publication will sell. This can relate to views on what an appropriate cover should be, even the title of the work, but certainly to price and what is called the print run, that is, the number of copies that will be printed, which is an indication of how many the publisher considers can be sold in a reasonable period of time.

As we discuss in a number of other places, most publishers – both of books and of journals – have an established house style. In the case of books, the description of these specifications usually runs to many tens of pages, and sometimes to hundreds. At times it can seem like more effort is used to ensure that your text obeys the niceties of house style, than to write the text in the first place. If you are writing a book, or are the author of a single chapter in an edited book, it will be part of your contract that you follow the guidelines laid down by your publisher. At times it will be possible to persuade them on some nuances, but you will rarely be successful if you try to do so from mere preference or taste, but only if you can convince them that what you want to do will enhance the quality, relevance or attractiveness of your work to influence sales enough to overcome all the added problems associated with doing something different from what they usually do. These problems include their staff being unsure about what is correct and the possibility of setting a precedent for future publications.

Hassling the publisher/editor

What counts as appropriate nudging and what as unprofessional hassling? The answer to this question lies in custom and practice with a dose of 'taking the role of the other'. When we were young and eager it was considered counterproductive to nudge or remind anyone whom you wanted to make a decision in your favour. But that was when ten students in a university class was a lot and academic staff thought they were ill done by if they were asked to teach more than one class a week. Nowadays the pressures are much greater on everyone, not least because of the instantaneity of e-mail. This means that it is much easier to send a gentle reminder but also that such a reminder is likely to join dozens received that day.

As we explain in the next chapter, most academic journals are edited, and have submissions to them reviewed, by people who do not get paid to edit or review and whose full-time job does not give high priority to these tasks. This does mean that submissions can sit on desks for months, awaiting the moment when the reviewer or editor can find spare time to process them. In these circumstances a polite nudge can assign priority to something that was not seen as significant up until that point. It should also be borne in mind that administrative mistakes are made and documents get lost in the post, so checking that something has arrived is perfectly reasonable.

The crucial point is to determine what the publication expects to be its processing time. This is often declared in notes for contributors, but editors will nearly always be willing to indicate what they expect. If this time is substantially exceeded then it is reasonable to check what has happened to your work. Similarly, if you are asked to review material within a given time frame, expect to be reminded with increasing ferocity if you miss that deadline. Reviewers are regularly kicked off editorial boards if their reviews come in very late.

Redressing grievances

Remember: human beings with faults and foibles, biases and prejudices do the whole processing of manuscripts. So if you believe you have a genuine grievance you should approach the appropriate person and explain the situation. It is surprising how fruitful this can be. Recently David submitted a manuscript to a highly regarded journal only to get a very dismissive letter from the editor together with two critical reviews. Close reading of these reviews showed that one of the reviewers admitted that he did not know the area very well and that the other review was not at all logical and appeared to be more an attack on the presumed audacity of the author to tackle the topic at all. The reviews were not in the objective spirit that is the basis of academic discourse.

Knowing the reputation of the journal, it seemed that the editor could not have studied the reviews or the paper carefully. David assumed that in his busy life the editor had noted the recommendations of the reviewers and just sent a standard rejection letter.

He therefore took it upon himself to write to the editor, indicating that perhaps he had not had the opportunity to look at the paper closely or to consider the rather unprofessional approach of the reviewers. The editor accepted this possibility and undertook to review the paper carefully himself and the reviewers' comments. Eventually he agreed that the paper was a good one, and the reviewers' responses had been inappropriate, and after relevant revisions it was published.

In most areas of publication the greatest redress available comes from being able to submit your work elsewhere. It is remarkable how often something considered worthless by one publishing outlet is accepted by another. We may sound like cynical old men, but our experience is that rejection has relatively little to do with the inherent quality of the work, and more to do with fashion or style that the particular outlet considers appropriate. As in all storytelling, the key to success is to know your audience.

Contracts and agents

When it comes to getting a major publisher to publish work for a wide audience, then it is very helpful indeed to have a literary agent. Agents act as go-betweens. They know the world of publishing and many publishers. They know how to present the author and the work and who are the appropriate people to approach for any particular type of book. Most importantly of all, they know about contracts.

It is unusual to use an agent for academic publishing because, frankly, the financial gains are so small that it is not worth an agent's time to promote such work. Also academics are notoriously slow in producing their books (they have real jobs after all), so the throughput of work is just too limited to make it worth their while. But for popular, trade books, getting an agent can be the crucial first step towards finding a publisher.

Agents typically take 10 per cent, or sometimes 15 per cent, of all the money the author obtains from the publisher (and usually put VAT on top of that too).

But in our experience of publishing books for a mass market, having an agent on board is a very useful foil to protect the author against the publisher and also to act as a sounding board that is much more supportive and less risky than going straight to a publisher.

Copyright

The one legal matter that is always relevant in academic publications is copyright. This is part of a general right under the UK Copyright Act 1998 not to have your work treated in a 'derogatory manner'. This includes not having your work distorted or modified in any way that challenges your reputation. In addition, under the same Act you have a right not to have work attributed to you that you have not produced, and a right to be identified as the author for what you have created, which is what most people understand as copyright. Within the law there is also some right to privacy, that is, not having certain material published – usually photographs or films produced purely for domestic purposes – but 'public interest' defence and legal precedent, as well as big variations in how different jurisdictions handle the nature of privacy, mean that this is a goldmine for lawyers.

Interestingly, the copyright law also gives authors the right to approve all changes to their text. But there are plenty of exceptions written into the law, and publishers usually make sure their contracts allow them to do what they want with a text, although, with the exception of newspapers, they will usually keep the author informed of modifications, if not actively seeking the author's agreement.

Authors need to be aware that publishers hold the author responsible for any infringement of copyright, and most publishers require contributors to sign a contract making that clear. Most publishers also expect the author to pay for any permission that may be needed to use copyright material. However, copyright only lasts for seventy years after the death of the author under UK law. It is rather more complicated in the USA, and other countries have yet other rules. But in general it is a minimum of fifty years after the death of the author.

Copyright may be more onerous than is often assumed. Much material that is used as part of a research process may be copyright and therefore not available for publication without authorization from copyright holders. Such material can include photographs, maps, previously published questionnaires and many of the other bits and pieces that researchers draw from each other. The law is not simple and has grown up through precedent. It includes some interestingly unexpected rules like that which is at the heart of A.S. Byatt's wonderful novel *Possession*. The twist in the plot of that book is the little known fact that letters are the copyright of the person who wrote them, and their heirs, not, as might be expected, of the person they were addressed to.

Getting permission to use published material is not necessarily straight-forward or cheap. When David wanted to quote in his book *Mapping Murder* from a *Times* obituary of Stuart Kind, it took a few weeks for the newspaper to get back to say that they wanted a few hundred pounds for the privilege, although that obituary was drawn almost entirely from Kind's own autobiography and was reproduced in a very similar form in a number of newspapers. As this would have come out of David's rather limited royalties, he simply paraphrased what Kind himself had written, making clear what the source was, without needing to pay anyone.

David could quote the odd sentence in Kind's own words because under UK law it is acceptable to publish small amounts from other sources provided citations are 'not substantial'. Material may also be quoted without permission 'for the purposes of criticism or review'. Under certain conditions, UK law also allows work to be reproduced without permission for use in schools. The US law on exceptions to needing permission to publish is couched in an even more vague reference to 'fair use'. So the basic rule is that, if you are not sure if what you seek to quote or use is covered by copyright, ask for permission. Similarly, if you hold the copyright on some work and someone else uses it without the appropriate permission, you can assume that they were probably doing that illegally.

As mentioned, who actually owns the copyright depends on the contract between the creator of the material and the publisher. It is not unusual for the publisher to require the author to assign the copyright to the publisher as part of the agreement for publication. The publisher may, however, in the tradition of fair play, check with the author when a request for use of the work arises. So if you are seeking permission you may need to get both the publisher and the author to agree.

The familiar '©' copyright notice has emerged from international agree-ments under the Universal Copyright Convention (UCC) to protect copy-right ownership. So although under some countries' legal frameworks it is not essential to print the copyright notice because the author automatically holds the copyright – as in letters mentioned above – it is a sensible safeguard to do so. The format is to have the notice 'placed in such a manner and location as to give reasonable notice of a claim of copyright'. This is usually taken to mean on the title page or immediately following it. It should take the form of the '©' copyright symbol immediately followed by the name of the copyright holder and the year the work was first published, all on one line; for example:

© *David Canter, 2003*

Having obtained permission to use copyright material, you will need to check whether there are any requirements concerning how the source is acknowledged. These requirements form a legal contract in granting permission to republish the material.

Crown Copyright and the US Freedom of Information Act: some curiosities

Funded research also raises issues of copyright. The funding agency may hold the copyright. If it is a UK government department, then it will not only hold on to the copyright but also insist that civil service personnel approve any text before it can be published. This contrasts with the USA where the laws of the land forbid anyone who is government funded from obtaining commercial benefit from publications that arise directly from that funding. In other words, the reports of the work are not copyright. Broadly speaking, the civil service cultures of the two nations can be characterized by the fact that the possibility of publishing government-funded work in Britain falls under the Official Secrets Act 1989, whereas in the USA it falls under the Freedom of Information Act. However, the recent introduction of the Freedom of Information Act 2000 in the UK may change all that. We'll see.

Privately funded studies often include a provision of confidentiality as well as control of copyright. The subtle implications of this were nicely illustrated by events that happened while writing this chapter. David was telephoned about a report he had completed some months earlier, which had been commissioned privately by a large organization. At an internal union meeting of the organization, the report had been cited and the local newspaper had decided to produce a front-page article quoting from this meeting, claiming the organization was at crisis point. Once the newspaper had published this account, without any cross-reference to David to check the facts, local radio got in touch asking David for some comment. The newspaper had taken the union view, a perspective not really supported by the original report. This presented an ethical/professional dilemma: should David try to set the record straight by doing the radio interview?

The first thing he did was to get in touch with the organization and ask them how they wished to tackle the published account. He offered them his understanding of the circumstances, but made it clear that because this was a private report to that organization it was up to them what information they released about it. If they wanted him to explain matters to the media he would, but as the organization had already acted on some of the recommendations in the report it was not now especially appropriate for him to comment.

The crucial issue here is that the report in question was not a published document. If it had been then David would have had a right, and possibly an obligation, to explain its content to journalists. Such a public document would have been published in relation to any agreement between the organization and David, which may well have included careful anonymity. In other words, the process of publication would have taken into account the possibilities of further media interest. As the document was not in the public domain, but a third-hand account from a private meeting, any account that found its way into the mass media was an issue for the original organization, who technically hold the copyright anyway. As it turned out, the organization eventually thought it would be appropriate for David to give a balanced account of the study to counteract the very biased viewpoints that had found their way into the press. He was under no pressure to give such an interview but was informed by the organization's press office that they would welcome it if he did. He decided to give the interview.

Being a morally responsible author

The main message to take away from these explorations of the morals and ethics of authorship is that you and the people you interact with when writing and submitting text have rights and obligations to each other. Some of these are implicit, such as the work being your own, and some are explicit, as in ownership of copyright. In the broad run of writing, these moral, ethical and legal constraints are not usually onerous. It is only when matters become fraught and contracts have to be challenged that you need to have mastery of the details of yours and others' obligations. But this is one context in which the old adage says it all: To be forewarned is to be forearmed.

Table of moral issues

Moral issue	Ways of addressing it
Is it your own work?	Be as scrupulous as possible with citations
Is it original work?	Determine what you want to write and submit it to the most appropriate outlet
Are you working well with any co-authors?	Agree working arrangements before you start detailed collaboration
Are you following the contract?	Read any contracts carefully and negotiate *before* signing
Do you own the work?	Be aware of copyright

9 Writing for journals

The nature of journals • Peer review • Blind review: ensuring academic standards? • Deciding on a journal • Having an impact • Maximizing your chances of acceptance • Horses for courses

Becoming a published author in an academic journal is these days the *sine qua non* of being a scholar, a real academic, rather than being a teacher or lecturer. It is the publication of an article that shares with your colleagues the results of your speculations or studies that is the main means by which you join the academic club. Professionals such as doctors, engineers, lawyers, therapists, and many others, also contribute to the growth of their professional discipline by writing articles for journals. In this chapter we explore how to select a journal to submit your work to and the general strategy for improving your chances of having it accepted.

The nature of journals

It is useful to distinguish between a document that is written as a one-off, stand-alone publication – which, for simplicity, we will grace with the old-fashioned term 'book' – and those publications that form a part of a rolling sequence, that are issued periodically – prosaically attracting the generic term of 'periodical'. These latter include weekly or monthly magazines, which can be found on high street bookshops, as well as what are known as academic or professional journals. Academic periodicals may be published very frequently, such as *Nature* and *The Lancet*, and be available in bookshops, or be issued just two or three times a year and be available only to the few members of a learned society.

The term 'journal' is thus a rather ambiguous one, referring to a regularly published, 'serial' publication in contrast to a 'book' or monograph that becomes available only once. Of course, even this distinction can be fudged. For instance, a 'part-work' is published as a series that goes to make up a large book – say on the History of War, or (perhaps more appropriately) Serial Killers – or perhaps a series of books that covers a range of topics in a given area. But in academic circles the term 'journal' tends to refer to professional or scholarly publications that contain contributions from experts in a specialist discipline. These contributions are referred to as 'papers' or 'articles'.

It is helpful to keep in mind that academic journals started life as proceedings of meetings of learned societies, and many such proceedings are still published to this day. They recorded the details of lectures given by eminent members of the society when they reported their discoveries or insights into topics of special interest to that society. It is still the case that in some of the natural sciences it is the proceedings of a conference, the written account of lectures that have been given, which are regarded as of special significance. Thus journals are the means by which the scholars and professionals keep in touch with each other about their research findings. This includes reports of empirical research, in which data is collected and analysed, documentary analysis of archive material, and conceptual research of the kind that is common in arts subjects.

Although they emerged as the proceedings of learned societies, most English language journals are nowadays published by commercial organizations. In other language cultures there is still a strong tradition of journals being published by research centres or universities, more as in-house documents than as widely available publications. Publishers typically seek out a distinguished figure in an area that they want a journal to cover and invite the person to edit a journal. Or, equally often a distinguished figure or learned society will approach a publisher and ask them to support a journal they have in mind. Editors, who are usually full-time academics who will be paid very little by the publisher for carrying out the task, will have a contract with the publisher to provide articles for publication. Their job is to oversee the quality of the material. In the great majority of cases the editor will not handle the production or copy editing process. All of the technicalities will be dealt with by the commercial publisher. If the journal 'peer reviews' submissions, as we discuss below, editors are supported by an editorial board of colleagues who help to review papers, as well as by other occasional reviewers that the editor calls upon.

Journals vary in many ways, for instance, whether they are aimed mainly at a professional or an academic audience, or whether they are specific to a distinct sub-discipline within an area of knowledge, or are more general in their coverage of topics of broad interest to people across one or more disciplines. This variation in the nature of journals is one of the subtleties you will have to master if you are to choose appropriate outlets for your studies.

It is often considered that there is a hierarchy of prestige among journals depending on how selective they are in the papers they publish, how widely cited the material is that is published in those journals, how broad is their readership and how international is their make-up. However, these aspects can confound each other, and in any discipline there will be notable exceptions. One curiosity of how the academic community operates is that 'international' often means American and that some journals with wide readership are not nearly as selective as those with a very narrow readership. No two academics will agree on what the most prestigious journals are in their discipline, but of course that does not stop them trying. Indeed, from time to time distinguished scholars will go on record as saying that it is the content of the material that should be evaluated and not the quality of the outlet in which it is published.

Peer review

Peer-reviewed journals are the principal focus of academic debate in most disciplines and tend to appear two, three or four times a year, though some appear bi-monthly or even monthly. Academics and other professionals use such publications both as a way of testing their ideas or findings through the peer review process and as a way of relating their own work to that of others who have published on related topics. Above all, articles in peer-reviewed journals are usually regarded in most disciplines as the fundamental building blocks for the theories, methods, results and applications that define a subject area.

Less academic prestige generally attaches to publication in non-reviewed journals and periodicals. These publications tend to have a less scholarly focus than peer-reviewed journals, are often lighter in tone, and usually appear more frequently – perhaps once a month or even once a week. The material in them will often be written by people who are professional journalists giving an account of the work of others, rather than by specialist experts reporting on their own thoughts or deeds. The writing for these non-reviewed journals is selected in terms of how well written and well informed it is, not whether it is an original contribution to knowledge. It runs into the area of publication we have called newspapers and magazines that we deal with in Chapter 11.

But, as in all aspects of human endeavour, the reactions that people have are often more complex than the 'peer review = good' formula would imply. There was one memorable occasion when David as a young academic had an article written about him in a weekly national newspaper and this was commented on most favorably by his head of department at a staff meeting. Yet that same week a colleague in the same department had an article published in the prestigious scientific journal *Nature* that heralded a breakthrough in understanding human speech perception, but the head of department did not even mention it.

Nonetheless, peer review has become one of the 'sacred cows' of academic publication, giving the journals that use it much more credibility than periodicals that do not. The process of peer review is generally regarded as a way of determining if an article really is an original and worthy contribution. It is also, interestingly, one bulwark against plagiarism, although not wholly successful in this. In the strangely communal process that is science and scholarship it is believed that, by subjecting journal submissions to the scrutiny of other scholars who have the focused expertise needed to evaluate the submission, the quality of work that is accepted for publication will be guaranteed. Whether this is true is open to some debate.

A number of studies have questioned the essentially conservative nature of the peer review process. For example, in one recent paper in *Advances in Health Sciences Education* (Hojat, Gonnella and Caelleigh 2003) three researchers from American medical colleges identified half a dozen processes that lead to distortions that take the peer review process far from the objective determination of merit that it is assumed to be. They report, for example, a number of studies that show that articles resubmitted to journals that had already published them, but resubmitted under the names of less prestigious authors or from less prestigious institutions, were usually rejected under their new authorship, the journal editors having not spotted that they had already actually published this material.

Many journals attempt to avoid such biases by keeping the details of the authorship secret from the reviewers in what is called a blind review process. In this process they typically also keep the identity of the reviewer secret from the author. This is intended to avoid personal prejudices and reduce the emergence of academic vendettas. But it can be only partially successful. As researchers at New York University have demonstrated convincingly, the authorship of papers can be established relatively easily merely by considering which papers they have cited. Other distortions, beyond that brought about by believing that an established authority's work will be of a higher standard than that of an unknown novice, have also been identified by many researchers. These include such normal human predilections as supporting work that agrees with what is already the received wisdom, or that shares an ideological stance with the reviewer. Material that is clearly and confidently presented will also get a better reception than much more significant work that is difficult to follow or confused in its details. Indeed, as a journal editor for many years,

David knows from his awareness of the different biases of each reviewer that he could determine the acceptability of many papers simply by the choice of reviewers he sent them to.

Papers that take advantage of the jargon and concepts that are prevalent within any sub-discipline may well be more acceptable to many journals than the same material presented in a stripped down day-to-day language that makes it seem all too obvious. Some areas of scholarship are more prone to this than others, but in the spirit of objective assessment we leave you to form your own opinion of who are the worst culprits (However, Andreski's delightful 1972 book *Social Sciences as Sorcery* illustrates these issues with an emphasis that are certainly relevant a quarter of a century later.)

Recognizing that the judgements made about material submitted to peer-reviewed journals are not the totally clinical, unbiased analyses that the scholarly community would like to think, can be used to your advantage. You can learn how to present your material in a way that will play to the biases of those who make the decisions rather than, often needlessly, raising their hackles. You have to be aware of the nature of the enterprise in which you are engaged and not enter it with the naive faith that if what you are doing or saying is good it will inevitably be accepted. To return to our narrative model for publication, you have to learn how to tell the sorts of stories that other academics want to hear.

Blind review: ensuring academic standards?

Blind review means that the people reviewing the paper are not given any direct indication about who the author is. Likewise the author is not given any indication about who the reviewers are. Besides the obvious clues in the citations that we commented on above, in some disciplines this 'blindness' is also more notional than real because there are so few experts in a given area and their opinions are widely known.

Some journals, especially in the area of medicine or engineering, where published work can have life and death implications, or in legal contexts where the work may be drawn upon for court decisions, require that authors are either members of a professional body or that they supply a brief biography with the paper. The reasons for this throw light on the interesting fact that a lot of what is presented to a journal in a paper has to be taken on trust. The editor and reviewers cannot check that all the references every author cites really exist. Although they will check submitted articles for obvious mistakes in argument and in scientific methodology, they will not be in a position to vouch for any data and its analysis. Therefore they must assume that authors are professionals who have done an honest and competent job. A few scientific journals even request that the data on which the results are based be made available to subsequent researchers. However, data can always be massaged or be fraudulent, so this is only a partial check.

In his fascinating book *The Undergrowth of Science*, Walter Gratzer (2000) shows that chicanery and incompetence are much more prevalent in academia, and related scientific laboratories, than many of us realize. The main defence against these human frailties is replication. As further studies mount up, particularly when they are attempts to reproduce results or challenge accepted arguments, weaknesses in science and scholarship are eventually exposed and rectified. But there are areas, especially of professional application as we have noted, where the editors of journals rightly believe that they cannot wait for the slow tests and retests of academic debate to take their course while unprofessional conclusions are allowed sway. These journals are therefore not satisfied merely with reviewing the material submitted to them. They wish to establish the credentials of the author as well.

Deciding on a journal

There are many books and lists available of the journals that are published. Your own reading and discussions with your colleagues will also alert you to what journals are available that may be relevant to you. Browsing through any libraries you have access to also will open your eyes to possible outlets for your publications.

Aims and scope of a journal

In order to form a clear view of what the editor of the journal thinks the journal covers you should study carefully any information given in the journal about the sort of material it seeks to publish. Sometimes this is in a section that gives an overview of aims and purposes, often inside front or back cover, but certainly on websites. Sometimes these are called 'Mission' or 'Aims and scope', but other times they are not labelled at all. For example, within its 'Instructions for authors', the *Journal of Psychiatric and Mental Health Nursing* makes clear in a section entitled 'Scope of journal content':

> The editor welcomes authoritative contributions from people working, or otherwise involved, in psychiatric, mental health and learning disability nursing. Articles must be original and focused upon nursing. They will be well-referenced, or the material will be a practice-based first claim to knowledge that is outside the current literature. Papers commenting on published articles may be solicited. Points of view are welcome.

Analytic Teaching has a mission statement that includes the comments:

> *Analytic Teaching* from its first issue, set out a broad agenda within the context of Philosophy for Children. This tradition continues. Areas of interest to readers and contributors included Philosophy for Children, teachers and teacher trainers, but also included those interested in the role of narrative in teaching and learning, liberation pedagogy, Vygotskian psychology, and cognitive science, among other areas.

It goes on to indicate how the journal contents are 'shaped by the interests and talents of its readers and contributors', with more details on the sorts of articles it publishes.

To give just a couple of other examples, the *Journal of Further and Higher Education* gives an overview of what it publishes but does not label it in any way. The *Journal of Environmental Psychology* swallows the details of what the journal covers in a few sentences within its 'Instructions to authors'. By contrast, the *Journal of Investigative Psychology and Offender Profiling* has a lengthy section on its back cover entitled 'Aims and scope'. But wherever they are located, these details are your first consideration when choosing a journal.

To maximize the chances of getting published, it is important that you choose carefully among the journals available. You should ensure that the subject matter, style and form of the article you wish to submit really are suitable for the journal you choose. Has the journal published on similar topics before? Have you found that you are citing work written by the editorial board? In addition, it is important to bear in mind the audience at which you are aiming. For example, it is no use sending a paper about professional practice to a journal that prides itself on the contribution it makes to the building of theory, or a highly theoretical paper to a journal that focuses on the development of practice.

By looking at back issues of the journal you can learn a great deal about it. This includes not only what the journal publishes but also who the editor is and the make-up of the editorial board that supports the editor. You can gain further information from various reference texts that list from time to time the rejection rates of journals. Many journals also note when papers are submitted so that by looking at when they were eventually published you can see how long it takes the article to find its way through the review process and into print. Some things to consider in assessing whether you should submit your work to a particular journal are summarized in the box on page 124.

Notes for contributors/instructions to authors

Besides the types of content the journal wishes to cover there will also be details of the forms of paper it accepts. For example, *Analytic Teaching* publishes 'articles, classroom dialogues, research reports, stories, reviews, and essays'; and the *Journal of Information Technology for Teacher Education* states

---

Matters to consider when choosing a journal to which to submit your work

The editor	What is his/her approach and expertise?
The editorial board	Discipline and publication history?
Notes for contributors/instructions for authors	Study carefully in order for details of acceptable content and the requirements of format.
What kinds of articles have recently been published?	Are there any articles you can use as models?
Other journals it may distinguish itself from	What are the special qualities of this journal?
Its prestige/rejection rate	How selective is it? What are the chances of acceptance?
Estimated time to process submissions, including reviews and an editorial decision	Will you wait years to get a response?
Estimated time to publication after a positive editorial decision	Does this fit with your plans? Or would it be better to aim for a less highly regarded journal with a quicker turnaround?

---

that, 'contributions are published in the form of original theoretical works, research reports, literature reviews, software and book reviews, conference reports, and announcements about the development of information technology theory and practice in teacher education.' However, many other journals are narrower in the style of contributions that they will consider publishing.

Notes for authors also give advice about the length of articles that is preferred and, sometimes, the length that is expected for articles of different kinds – original articles, reports of research, brief discussions and so on, and for other contributions such as letters to the editor. Although many editors will exercise some discretion about the length of articles they will send out for review, it is wise to take stated word limits seriously, ensuring that if you edge over the limit a little, you do so only because it is not possible to say what is necessary within the words allowed. Editors and reviewers may frown on long-windedness. Whatever happens, there is no point in sending an 8,000 word article to a journal that has a word limit of 3,000 words. To do so is to invite rejection.

The requirements that journals have can be very detailed. Some may specify a maximum number of citations that authors should use, whereas others actually specify a minimum number of references that authors must use. However, it is as well to be aware that there are cultural differences in expectations. For example, in journals in the USA, there is an implicit expectation that authors will reference everything that may relate to their work, whereas in the UK the expectation is often that you should include only citations that are directly relevant to the case or argument being considered.

There may well be word limits or format expectations for the abstract or synopsis at the start of the paper; we have even come across journals that require the synopsis to start with a particular part of speech such as a verb. You will save yourself a lot of time and effort, and avoid annoying the editor, if you ensure that you submit articles exactly the way the journal specifies. This particularly applies to forms of citation that we have discussed in Chapter 5.

Some journals are rather vague about what they expect of authors; and sometimes, despite the fact that notes for contributors are given in detail, it is necessary to guess at what is expected, or at any rate acceptable, by looking at the kinds of articles that appear in recent issues. You may have to work out whether it would be best to adopt a formal, third-person style of writing, or whether a more informal style, utilizing the first person at times, is likely to be acceptable, if this would be your preference. There is no point whatever in trying to get an article accepted by a journal if you are unwilling to adopt the accepted style; you will only be inviting rejection.

Having an impact

It is ultimately the journal's editor who acts as judge or referee when assessing any recommendations from reviewers. The quality and nature of a journal thus owe a great deal to the editor. He or she decides whether to accept reviewers' opinions and whether reviews are objective or biased. This is such a personal mission for each editor that you would need to read carefully what is published in any journal to be sure the contributions were of a standard and a form you considered appropriate.

To get beyond this individual analysis of all possible journals, attempts are made from time to time to create lists of the 'impact' or prestige of journals. These assessments are based on overt, mathematical calculations instead of actually reading the articles published. But precisely because these are based solely on numerical analyses they are open to great debate.

The usual way in which these 'impact factors' are determined is by relying on citation indexes. These indexes are created for the admirable, even honourable, reason of enabling researchers to follow up who has cited any given paper so that they can explore the subsequent research that built upon that earlier work. However, what this produces is a detailed, systematic record of which works are cited in subsequent papers and how frequently. It is therefore a straightforward computation to calculate which papers are most often cited. A further short step will indicate which journals carry the most cited papers. The number of citations is taken as an indication of their 'impact'.

Of course, you would not expect academics to leave the calculation as a simple frequency. These serious minds immediately realized that there would be many features of journals and journal papers that would make these figures misleading. The size of the discipline is one such obvious distortion. If you are publishing in an area that has many thousands of researchers, such as renewable energy or the work of Kant, then you are far more likely to be cited than in a very small area of scholarship such as left-handedness in tennis players. An interesting illustration of this is the American journal *Psychology, Public Policy and Law*. For many people this would be regarded as a rather narrow, somewhat specialist journal of limited significance. So it may be surprising to discover that its 'impact factor' is listed in the top ten of psychology journals. The reason, we suggest, is simply that psychology and law are such huge professions in the USA that it needs only a small proportion from *each* of these to cite papers from that journal for that journal's 'impact' to go up.

The mere longevity of a journal will also have a big influence. The longer a journal has been around the more people will have got to know it and the more time there will have been for articles to be cited from it. Another distortion is brought about by self-citation. People tend to cite themselves. So journals that publish the work of people who publish a lot will have more citations from people that they publish than journals that publish authors who are not so prolific.

The various ways of calculating the impact of a journal try to take account of these and other biases that can make the numerical calculations misleading, but as far as we can establish, no one has produced a way of calculating impact factors which the majority of people in a discipline believe give a fair assessment. However, for the fledgling academic thinking about making a publishing impact, all of the biases we have mentioned can actually be harnessed as we have listed in the box below.

Ways to increase the impact of your journal articles

Criterion	Procedure
Authoritative	Joint publication with established expert
Wide reach	Choose an area with many scholars
Significance	Connect to a widely studied topic
Acceptance	Support commonly held viewpoints
Comprehension	Use the language (jargon) of that sub-discipline

---

Maximizing your chances of acceptance

Whichever journal you decide on, you can maximize the chances of having an article accepted for publication by making sure that it is as well written as possible – though what this means will vary from journal to journal. Some will expect that you should write in a particular style, perhaps utilizing only the third person, and some will have an expectation that your work is heavily referenced. We have had work rejected on the grounds that it was not sufficiently 'academic', because there were 'too few references'. This is curious, given that some of the most prestigious journals in the world, such as *Science*, actually restrict the number of references that are permitted.

Sometimes, inexperienced authors develop the idea that before putting in the effort necessary to write an article, it would be worthwhile submitting an early draft to an editor 'just to see whether they will take it', or to send a term paper or thesis and ask if it is appropriate for the journal. If you have entertained this idea, it is as well to abandon it. Submitting unpolished work to 'test the waters' will not further your cause in the slightest; to do this is to ask editors to do work that you should have done before submitting anything to them. Most will be not only unimpressed but also irritated. Most editors, you must remember, have other full-time jobs and will not have time to respond to your explorations, or will simply process it as a formal submission and the reviewers will wonder what has been sent to them and reject it out of hand.

When you are thinking of submitting to a journal that you read regularly, or find you are citing often in your own work, it should be fairly easy to assess the journal's nature and what it requires of its contributors. When you are considering submitting work to a journal with which you are less familiar, it is essential to take the trouble to familiarize yourself with the range of subject matter that tends to be addressed by articles that it publishes. Submitting material to a journal you have never even seen is a recipe for failure. There is nothing that irks editors and reviewers more than receiving contributions that demonstrate ignorance of their journal, especially when those contributions fail to acknowledge material on related topics that have recently appeared in it.

Never forget that everyone who is involved in the editing and reviewing process is an ordinary human being. These people may strive to bury their prejudices and give objective, professional opinions, but some may actually abuse the process by attempting to impose their own biased views. That is why anything you can do in your writing to help the former and undermine the latter will increase the chance of your work being accepted. If there have been articles in the journal of your choice that are relevant to the topic you are writing about and you do not relate what you say to that earlier work, you open yourself to the claim of ignorance. Possibly more invidiously there is a real chance that the author of that earlier article will be sent yours for review. You will not get off on the right foot with this person if you are clearly ignorant of his or her work.

We do not wish to paint a totally cynical picture of prejudiced academics wheedling their way into positions of power in order to impose their biased opinions on subordinate colleagues who have no redress, so that unless you toe a particular line you will never get published. There are far more checks and balances in the academic community than this pessimistic picture portrays. Any journal that developed a reputation for such bias would soon lose all credibility, contributors and subscribers. Furthermore, except in the smallest and most arcane areas of scholarship, there is always more than one journal to choose from, so healthy competition keeps editors and reviewers alert to accusations of bias or unprofessionalism. Not only that, but in our experience the great majority of academics try to do their job honestly and objectively. They are academics because they attach value to the principle of unprejudiced, open debate. But they are human as well; and so ambition, jealousy, pride and other debilities will also be part of their make-up, even if they are usually kept under control.

Horses for courses

The central message that we want to get across is that there are many journals out there. They all need material to continue their existence. They also need to differentiate themselves from similar journals. You will therefore be able to find an outlet for any article you write that is worth publishing. The task when you start is to find the most appropriate outlet. There are plenty of clues available as to what any journal is looking for, but by far the best is the actual material published in the journal taken together with the journal's own declaration of its aims and objectives.

10 The journal process

Submitting to a journal

If you are to succeed in getting published in academic and professional journals, you need to understand the system for submission and selection, and in particular, the peer review process. Doing so will give you the greatest chance of success.

Journals are usually edited by academics whose main employment is in full-time teaching and/or research. Editors are supported by an editorial board made up of academics and professionals who have a claim to expertise in the topic or field that the journal addresses, and by a wider circle of reviewers or referees, whose contribution is to read, comment on, and make recommendations about articles – both about whether they make a worthwhile contribution to the field and about whether they are well enough written to be acceptable for publication in their present, or an amended, form.

Most important journals are produced and marketed by commercial publishing companies, though journals that are published without the involvement of publishing houses have become more common since typesetting with computers became relatively easy and inexpensive. Such journals are usually published as part of the business of a university department or research institute. As mentioned in the previous chapter, journals grew out of the meetings of scholarly societies, but this was soon augmented by research institutes publishing their own regular accounts of their work. Both societies and research institutes do still publish their own journals, especially in professional areas and in many countries outside of the Anglo-Saxon sphere of dominance.

The editorial boards of these 'in-house' journals will be drawn from the members of the society. The editor may even be elected by society members, or they may be senior figures in the research institute that publishes the journal. For journals published outside of these remits the editor and the editorial board are more likely to be a rather ad hoc group drawn together by the publisher and the editor and those who work closely with him/her.

Nowadays, there are also increasing numbers of electronic journals, accessed via the internet, which can be printed out as required, and many journals are now produced in both electronic and printed forms. Sometimes new academic journals are launched initially in electronic format as a way of testing their likely ability to attract readers, or produced in-house as a way of establishing the degree of interest necessary to persuade a commercial publisher that they are financially viable.

Whether they are available both on the World Wide Web and in hard copy or in just one of these forms, all peer-reviewed academic journals process papers in more or less the same way, summarized in Figure 10.1.

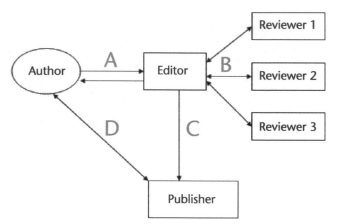

Figure 10.1 The main stages of peer review for an academic journal (see text for an explanation of the four stages A to D)

The process of getting a paper published in a peer-reviewed journal has four main stages.

First, you submit your paper to the editor, as indicated by channel A in Figure 10.1. You should submit the paper in the format the journal requires and with the number of copies the journal wants, or increasingly, in an electronic format via e-mail, or possibly through a designated website. It is a common courtesy to include a letter to the editor with your submission that supplies all your details as well as the title of the paper and a note declaring that you have not submitted the paper elsewhere and that it is indeed your own original work.

Most social science and arts journals will accept submissions from anyone and evaluate them on their merit, but journals whose publications can have life and death implications, for example in medicine and engineering, may require contributors also to submit a résumé so that the editor can be sure the author is bona fide. In some few cases this control is exerted by only accepting papers from members of specific professional bodies. You need to check notes for contributors to be sure about all this.

Also be aware that if the editor is going to send the paper for blind review, that is, where the reviewers will not have a clear indication of your identity, it is essential that your manuscript has a title page with your details on that can be simply removed, making the remainder of the manuscript anonymous. In electronic format this can be more tedious because the word-processing software may embed the authors' details deep in the file, making them difficult to remove without a lot of bother. Just remember that the more quickly your paper can be processed with minimal intervention from the editor then the more quickly you will get a response. If he or his secretary has to fiddle with your paper to make it anonymous then it may sit on one or other of their desks until they get the time to sort it out.

After submitting a paper there may be some initial correspondence to require you to modify the text in accordance with the journal's format and objectives, but if it is a highly regarded journal the editor may send it back and just ask you to submit in the appropriate form. She may even ignore the submission. On the other hand, if you have looked carefully at previous issues of the journal and absorbed and acted in accordance with whatever instructions are provided for authors, this should not happen. Sometimes editors decide, having looked at an article themselves, that it is either not suitable or not worth considering seriously, and reject it outright. On very rare occasions they may even accept it without sending it for review.

Review

If your submission is judged worthy of serious consideration, the editor will send it for review, typically to two or three reviewers in your particular area. This is shown in Figure 10.1 as channel B. These people, like you and the editor, are usually gainfully employed full time in some other job, so the editor may need to chase them for their reviews. Some reviewers may decline an invitation to review because of pressure of work; sometimes requests for reviews get lost in transit; and sometimes, no doubt, prospective reviewers just fail to respond. From time to time editors have to seek other reviewers. Reviewing times vary, depending on the journal, but it would not be atypical for six to eight weeks to be suggested as a turnaround time. Some very popular journals, though, will consider six or eight months, or even longer, as a reasonable turnaround time.

If you are lucky, this means that you may receive a decision from the editor about three months after you submit your paper. However, it can easily take more than six months for a decision to be made, and if you are very unlucky, it may even be six months before the reviews are completed, which means that the time until you hear from the editor will be even longer. It is always wise to be polite to editors. Nonetheless it is not a bad idea to e-mail or write to them if a few months have elapsed, asking whether there is any news of your paper. Although the odd editor is rather pompous, most are just ordinary people like you and like us, and most will respond positively to a little gentle chivvying, along the lines of, 'I wondered whether you had any news yet about the article I sent you on 15 January?'

Guidelines for reviewers

One good way to understand how peer review works is to look closely at the sorts of guidelines that a reviewer is likely to be sent by the journal to guide the comments that are required. Before you submit your work, you should review it against the kinds of things reviewers are asked to consider, thinking how you would review the paper if it had been sent to you, then modifying it to deal with the criticisms you think a reviewer might offer.

Journals differ in the things they ask reviewers to consider. Sometimes they ask quite detailed questions, but sometimes they simply want them to make a judgement about whether an article is acceptable as it is, should be accepted with amendments, or whether the author should be invited to resubmit after substantial rewriting.

Below we will take an actual example of a review protocol with comments as an illustration of the kind of thinking a reviewer might go through in assessing an article.

Overall review

Here the reviewer is asked to summarize the essence of the paper and its main strengths and weaknesses. It is *very* helpful for the author to see what reviewers really think the paper is about. It may not be what the author thought was either the main point of the paper or its strengths and weaknesses. If this is the case then the author does need to consider carefully how the central arguments of the paper are laid out and how these are reflected in the title and its overall structure.

A typical response might be:

> This is an acceptable paper describing a well-conducted study clearly. It gives an account of the relationships between the physical contexts in which crimes occur and the particular patterns of behaviour that occur in those contexts. Generally, though, I found it rather uninteresting and unsurprising. The results are reasonable enough but perhaps because I've seen so many other similar papers with similar results I would like to see something that moves us all forward in a more significant way.

Here the reviewer is saying that the article is presenting a story he has read about many times before, and that although it is plausible it does not excite him. We can glean right away from this that whether the editor will accept the paper will depend on (1) whether the replication of these findings is important, and (2) how desperate the journal is for material to publish.

Particular questions

Next the reviewer will be asked to respond to a number of particular questions, as set out in the box on page 134, with some typical responses.

Example of a reviewer's report

- *Are the title and abstract clear and appropriate?*

Yes

- *Is the argument theoretically and logically consistent?*

Yes – though there is little theory here. Like I say, I'm totally unsurprised by the lack of evidence of a relationship.

- *Is the style of writing clear and comprehensible?*

Yes.

- *Is the organization of the paper clear and comprehensible?*

Yes. Though I'm guessing the editors will want a paper that clearly explicates the methodology described here as it is still not a widely used or understood procedure.

Commentary

Here the reviewer is really pointing out to the editor that there are some strategic, policy issues that she cannot resolve. The editor would therefore be obliged when writing to the author to comment on this point. If the editor does not, then it is a reasonable assumption he has not read all the reviews through carefully.

- *Are the references appropriate and complete?*

To be honest they are not especially up to date. For the sake of completeness the authors may wish to conduct a more recent review – for example, I think Relodge and Piers have done a recent paper on profiling characteristics from crime scene actions.

- *Is this an original contribution?*

Not especially – it says what other papers have said before but it's useful to drive the point home that contextual features are likely to have a strong impact on behaviour – it would certainly be useful to have other papers that have found other evidence to suggest that this technique of direct mapping is likely to prove fairly unproductive.

- *Does it have applied/professional relevance?*

Only in so far as telling us what not to do (though that is very valuable).

Commentary

This question is, of course, special to this journal that seeks to build bridges to practice. Another journal may emphasize contributions to theory or methodology.

- *Are the illustrations, figures and tables appropriate and correctly labelled?*

Yes.

- *Is the literature review minimal and comprehensive?*

See above

- *Does it advance relevant knowledge?*

Yes, but mainly confirms previous studies.

- *Are the methodologies employed sound?*

Yes.

- *How important is the paper to this Journal?*

It points to the recommendation that more has to be done beyond current practice. I think the author(s) might be a little braver in their conclusions and a little more vigorous in pointing out the low utility of the methods they review. It would be even better if they were able to suggest a plausible alternative.

Commentary

On the basis of the answers they have given to some specific questions of this kind, the reviewer will then be asked to make a recommendation about whether the article should be accepted or rejected, by choosing from a number of options.

Reviewer's recommendation

Please choose ONE of the following options:

> *Accept subject to minor revisions*
> *Encourage revision and resubmit for review*
> *Reject as unworthy of publication*
> *Reject as inappropriate for this journal (Please suggest an alternative journal if you have one in mind)*

Commentary

Finally, the reviewer might be invited to add any additional comments she would like to make, along with any comments she might wish to make to the editor that she would not like to be shared with the author.

Additional comments
Please type any additional comments or recommendations you may have regarding this paper.

I would encourage the author(s) to pursue this line of work. Although the results they report are not a great surprise, it is important that we continue to explore these issues.

Editorial comments
Put here any comments you have for the Editor that you do not wish to have passed on to the author.

I suspect I've seen this paper in other versions submitted to other journals. The author seems terribly keen to publish what is really a rather slim piece of work.

Commentary
You will never get to see these final 'closed' comments. It is here the reviewer may be very rude about the work or raise suspicions he cannot substantiate, for example of possible plagiarism. More likely it may be a comment that the author has already published something very similar to this and does the editor still want it, or that the reviewer has reviewed the paper when it was submitted to another journal so it might be fair to pass it on to a different reviewer. In some cases it may be a discussion with the editor as to whether this type of paper really is suitable for the journal in question. Presumably the statutes that are emerging around the world providing 'freedom of information' may make such comments eventually available to authors?

Editorial decisions

Once editors have amassed all the comments that they feel necessary from one or more reviewers then they will make a decision. This means they will contact you again (channel A in Figure 10.1) usually enclosing all the comments from reviewers together with a letter to you that indicates what their decision is on your paper and their own emphases on why that decision has been taken. Typically they will indicate one of the following decisions:

Accept without revision

For many journals this is a rare occurrence. In 20 years of editing *Journal of Environmental Psychology*, David can only remember two occasions when this happened.

Accept with some minor modifications

This in effect indicates that the paper is suitable for publication once these corrections have been made. Normally the revision will only be reviewed by the editor. The details of the modifications will often be provided as precisely as possible, although they may include comments such as 'tighten up the text'. The editor may also say that the paper will only be published without further review provided the revision is returned within a specific time, for example a month. In rapidly developing fields this ensures that the paper is not made obsolete by more recent publications.

Require the paper to be revised and sent out for review again

This is a decision that the paper is appropriate for the journal but that too many questions are raised by the reviewers to allow a decision to be made without the revised version being reread by the same or different reviewers to ensure that the author has adequately addressed reviewers' comments. In this case the details of what will be required are likely to be specific and may include a suggestion that new forms of analysis should be undertaken, that additional arguments should be addressed or presented, or that new perspectives or models should be included in the discussion.

Reject as of too low a quality for the journal

The details of the weaknesses of the paper will be listed and this can be enormously valuable. We have found that the more reviewers attempt to undermine a paper in detail the more valuable are the comments in helping us to develop our ideas and subsequent publications.

Reject as irrelevant to the journal

Possibly this could include indications of what a suitable publication might be. If this happens you have probably not done your homework in determining the appropriate journal to submit to. Or you may have been unlucky and a change of editor or editorial board has occurred since you last studied the journal with a consequent change in policy and mission.

Revising your article

Once you have heard back from the editor, if your paper has been accepted in some form, most probably with major revisions and a request for resubmission, then your task is to study the corrections you have been asked for. There is no point setting off on writing a completely new article that may have to start the review process all over again, unless you have got an out and out rejection – which we'll consider in a minute. In preparing your revision, remember that editorial decisions come from editors and not from reviewers. Some busy editors in popular journals hardly read reviewers' detailed comments and just act on their overall recommendations, but others are independently minded and may put their own interpretation on the reviewers' comments. If you are invited to resubmit, remember that it is the editor's comments that you must respond to. Read the editor's letter carefully and see how much of what the reviewer says the editor is supporting.

In general, editorial decisions are pretty cut and dried. This means that once an editor has decided that he does not want your article, he will probably stick to his decision. However, it is sometimes possible to enter into a certain amount of discussion with editors if you are uneasy about a decision that has been made, though if you want to become a successful academic it is as well to be somewhat circumspect about challenging editorial decisions; in general it is probably less painful just to accept that your article has been rejected. If you do decide to write to an editor raising a query about a negative decision, be polite, be clear about what you want to say and remember they hold the power and it really is not worthwhile falling out with them.

In one case we queried a decision because it was clear that an editor had not studied very carefully the reviews that he had endorsed. The reviews were *ad hominem* and admitted ignorance of the topics we were covering. When this was politely pointed out, the editor agreed to reconsider the paper and, although he had originally rejected it totally on the basis of the reviewers' comments, in the end he accepted a revised version for publication.

On another occasion an editor wrote saying that although he and all three reviewers had enjoyed and substantially agreed with the arguments presented in an article, it was being rejected on the grounds that it was somewhat too long. Given that the article, though long, was actually considerably shorter than many that appeared in the journal in question, this seemed an unreasonable reason for rejection. It was resubmitted the day the decision was received, after a whole section had been removed (to be utilized in another place), thus reducing it by about one-third. A telephone conversation with the editor the following day confirmed that this was a good move because it was then accepted.

When you prepare the revision you are shaping the paper to accord with the views of your colleagues as expressed by the editors and reviewers. But your response to their comments does not need to be slavish. The paper will have your name on it so must reflect what you think is sensible. When you send the revision to the editor it is often the custom to include a letter that indicates how you have dealt with the reviewers' comments and, if you have not seen fit to act on them, why. You may get asked for further revisions until the editor is satisfied the paper is worthy of publication. Tolerance and patience and some degree of humility are therefore essential traits to help you get through what may often seem to be (and probably is) nitpicking and pretentiousness, merely reflecting the importance that some journals ascribe to themselves.

Dealing with rejection

One of the most dispiriting experiences faced by people starting to publish is a destructive review of their work, especially when it is part of a rejection of a paper they have submitted to a journal. We know people who have been so distressed by what they see as pernickety, or just plain wrong-headed criticism, that they have vowed never to submit a paper again and in some cases have faded out of academic life as a consequence (usually to the greater benefit of the professional agencies they subsequently joined). In a sense this is an appropriate decision because if you do not have the psychological make-up to cope with the slings and arrows of outrageous criticism, you will find the cut and thrust of academic debate around your work very disturbing.

However, it may help you to know that absolutely everyone who has submitted work to journals has had work rejected, or at the very least has been required to make extensive revisions. As an editor of a journal for many years, David had to pass on rejection criticisms to extremely distinguished and experienced colleagues. No one is immune from this experience. One way of looking at it is to see developing the skill of publishing in a journal as rather like learning to ride a bicycle. You can read a lot about it and study carefully how it is done, but in the end you will only master the skill by getting on a bike and, in the early days, understanding what it is that causes you to fall off.

So, if you have the resilience to deal with this challenge and to take the inevitable knocks, there is much you can learn from the rejection. Some questions to ask yourself are listed in the box on page 140.

Questions to ask yourself on dealing with rejection of a paper submitted to a journal

- Was this an appropriate journal to send the paper to?
- Which of the criticisms might have been anticipated and dealt with before submitting the paper?
- Is this an outright rejection or has the editor made clear that a resubmission would be acceptable? (Or at least left the door to resubmission open)
- Do the reviewers have a particular bias that can be dealt with in any revision?
- If the comments are acted on will this create a paper more suitable for a different journal or should it be resubmitted to this one?
- After the initial shock and rereading the comments, what are they actually saying? What has the editor emphasized? Which of the comments does the editor seem to be ignoring?
- Are there some fundamental flaws in what has been done or written that mean this paper should be started from scratch, or is this a paper that can be salvaged?
- Are there any jobs available at fast-food outlets?

Direct contact with the publisher

Once you and the editor have agreed on the final version of your article, and there may be a number of cycles through channels A and B (see Figure 10.1 on page 130) before that is achieved, he will send it on to the publisher for preparation for publication (channel C in Figure 10.1).

When the publisher is in receipt of the text that has been accepted by the editor, the fourth and final stage in the process (channel D of Figure 10.1), will be opened in order to conclude some formalities, such as getting you to assign copyright to the publisher, though usually with the proviso that you will automatically be granted permission to use the text in other ways, provided that the publisher's role in first publishing it is acknowledged. Sometimes you will also be required to declare you have no commercial interest that influences your submission. You will also usually be offered a set number of reprints of your article for free, typically twenty, and be offered a further number at fixed prices. Some journals will not accept papers unless you are willing to buy a designated number of reprints.

Once you have signed an agreement with the publisher you will then eventually get proofs of your paper, which are a representation of your article as it will appear when it is published. These proofs will sometimes come with detailed questions about confusions or omissions, problems with citations and references, and so on. At this stage you will not be allowed to change any of the substance of your paper, only to correct errors and respond to the publisher's queries. Once you have responded – both to the proofs and to the publisher's specific queries – and any necessary corrections and changes have been incorporated, you will eventually see your work in print.

Why does it all take so long?

The time from having a paper finally accepted to seeing it in print can be remarkably long, from a few months to a few years. The reasons for this are many, to do with printing and publishing processes, checks on text and bringing together papers for efficient production, but often it is simply a matter of the journal moving through a backlog of papers that are queuing up to be published. Newer journals that do not have a backlog of papers to publish will get your material into print sooner, but as we discussed earlier, that benefit needs to be balanced against notions of 'impact'. With internet access, more and more journals are putting papers online as soon as the corrected proofs are available. This gives much quicker access to accepted work. Any delay on your part in returning corrected proofs can lead to you losing your place in the queue or to other, similarly dire, consequences.

If the time it takes from acceptance to publication is added to the time the submission process takes and then on top of that the time it has taken you to write the paper, you can see why in some disciplines it can easily be five years between a piece of work being finished and its appearing in published form.

Figure 10.2 summarizes the process in a simple flow diagram, showing the life cycle of a journal article, which emphasizes the author's involvement. As you will see, there are a number of feedback loops in this, where ideas or documents move back and forwards. The internet and associated information technologies are speeding up these interactions, compared with the days when everything went by post, but material still gets lost in virtual reality and some aspects, such as the signing of the copyright form, are still usually done on hard copy through the postal system. Also the actual time to read and comment has not changed, we would guess, since people first read and commented. Patience and a long-term perspective are therefore essential if you are to cope with publishing in journals.

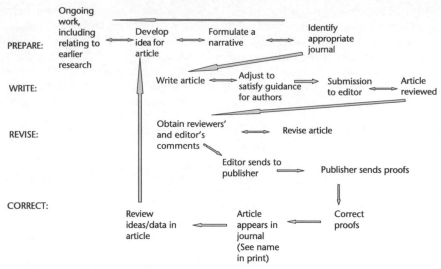

Figure 10.2 The life cycle of a journal article

Checklist for publishing in a journal

- Choose the journal with care
- Study the aims and objectives of the journal
- Read previous issues and identify articles that –
  may act as a model for yours
  should be cross-referenced with yours
- Prepare your article with close attention to the journal's notes for contributors
- Submit to journal with brief covering letter to the editor
- Wait patiently for editor to send reviews and decision. (If you do not get an acknowledgement that the paper has been received by the editor, do make sure it has not got lost in the ether)
- Politely ask editor after eight weeks when you might expect a response (optional)
- Cope with comments from editor/reviewers
- Revise article in the light of reviewers'/editor's comments
- Resubmit with a short note explaining how you have responded to the comments
- Once accepted, sign copyright agreement and send to publisher
- Correct proofs sent from publisher as quickly as possible
- Make careful note of the full published reference to go on your CV and be cited in future publications

11 Newspapers and other forms of publication

Beyond academic journals • Why write for newspapers? • The challenge of journalism • Getting a toe in the door • The essence of journalism • Legal constraints to publishing • Reports for clients • All writing is authorship

Literature is the art of writing something that will be read twice, journalism what will be grasped once.

(Cyril Connolly)

Beyond academic journals

Writing for publication in academic and professional journals is the main form of authorship for most researchers and other scholars. This should not hide from you the possibilities of other forms of publication. These include what loosely can be called the printed 'mass media', which covers daily and weekly newspapers, local and national, as well as magazines of many forms, from general lifestyle monthlies, to those that specialize in hobbies and leisure pursuits. It is also important to recognize that another sort of publication that is very different from 'academic' writing is the preparation of commissioned reports on topics that are defined, often very precisely, by clients.

These forms of publication make their own demands on authorship. Although there is still the need to be as clear as possible and to have something to say, there are other demands that come from the nature of the publication and the audience that will read what you write. These differences require that the material is written in a rather different way from the usual academic format, often to the point of structuring the material in ways that might feel alien if you have only ever written scholarly material. Yet both these forms of authorship, for the mass media and for clients, have many benefits that make it worthwhile considering them seriously. They can also be a useful bridge between the limited audiences for academic pursuits and a wider public whose lives may be touched, and even changed, by your writing.

Why write for newspapers?

Many of the reasons for becoming an author in academic outlets apply, but with different force, to writing for newspapers and magazines. Writing for the mass media is a way of reaching a wider audience, and if you have anything to say you might question why you should say it only to people within your immediate discipline. You may make a little money out of it and the small amount of kudos attached to having your name so obviously in print may impress your students even if all it does for your colleagues is to make them jealous.

Trying to write for a newspaper can be a very good way of improving your writing style. Rather than having a limit of 3,000–5,000 words, for example, you may be allowed 800 words, if the paper thinks it is an important topic, in which to say what you want. The discipline involved in trying, within such a small space, to say something meaningful, is well worth developing, as is the discipline of writing about serious academic topics without the use of standard citations and references. It can help to make a great improvement to your writing when you have more words available, because it will help you to hone your writing skills to be sure that every word counts.

It is also worth remembering that your colleagues read newspapers and magazines – and probably more thoroughly than they read academic journals. Therefore, writing in the mass media is a surprisingly good way of reaching out to other academics and professionals. It has consistently been our experience that we get more response to issues we have raised in newspaper articles than to pieces in journals.

We are not saying that all academics can be expected to master journalistic skills. In our experience when writing for daily newspapers the journalists and sub-editors at the papers have invariably reworked our writing both to fit in with the style of the paper and to emphasize at the start of the article what they consider newsworthy in what we had to write. This was certainly a salutary exercise, but we were always impressed with what survived of our original argument and made the writing look totally in place within the newspaper. Over time we have become more able to write pieces that the sub-editors did not feel the need to rewrite, giving real satisfaction to seeing our own words so rapidly in print.

The challenge of journalism

Becoming an author in a journalistic context such as newspapers or magazines is a rather different kettle of fish from contributing to academic publications. So although the skills you develop in writing for academic journals is relevant, and the processes you go through in deciding on where you would like to publish more popular material for a lay audience has many parallels with choosing a journal to write in, there are some differences to keep in mind.

The first point to realize is that newspapers and magazines need copy. A daily or weekly paper gobbles up material at a great rate. Magazines need lots of text to spread out the pages between the advertisements from which they usually make their money. There is also an increasing appetite in the mass media for commentary from people who can claim some sort of informed opinion. Editors of these outlets may be quite appropriately anxious that academics will not communicate effectively with their publication's readership, but they will always be more interested than you might have thought in well-written, informative articles from people who are not full-time professional journalists.

The majority of the material in newspapers and most magazines is written by people who make their living, or a substantial proportion of it, as journalists. Such people will often not only have a relevant university degree, say in English, but also a postgraduate qualification in journalism. After that they will have two years of supervised apprenticeship and will have had to pass professional examinations (that have a 60 per cent failure rate), before they become fully fledged journalists. They learn how to extract the essence from a topic – which is invariably thought of as a 'story' – and how to identify the central grabbing point that will be the opening sentence.

People moving into journalism are far from the haphazard scribblers, hacks, that are so often caricatured. They have training as long as lawyers and more than many other professional groups. So if you want to be taken seriously as part of this profession you do need to absorb and accept some of its rules of engagement. You are joining the ranks of those people who make some of their living writing for newspapers and magazines without having a specific allegiance or employment with one particular publication: a freelancer. Some academics manage eventually to write regularly for a particular newspaper, but this is rare. One-off stories from time to time are more the norm.

Getting a toe in the door

If a journalist asks you for an interview on a topic, offer instead to write the piece yourself. This is a good way of getting to write for newspapers or magazines, and one which David has used from time to time. It also has two distinct advantages over an interview. One is that you can formulate the comments in your own words. Even though these will be edited by the newspaper they will still be closer to your own formulation, to the story you want to tell, than that derived from the journalist's shorthand notes. The second is that while it is rare, although not unknown, to be paid for an interview, you will get a small but welcome sum for the article you write yourself (provided you invoice the newspaper for it). The disadvantages are all to do with needing to operate within the realms of journalism rather than academic publishing.

The essence of journalism

The famous comment attributed to Groucho Marx, Mark Twain and other authorities is worth repeating here: 'I am sorry this letter is so long but I do not have time to write a shorter one'. It is often, and perhaps usually, easier to write more than it is to write less. When we have a longer word limit, most of us have a tendency to be less careful with words than we would otherwise be; we might use two words where one would do, we might unnecessarily make the same point in more than one way, or use longer examples and illustrations than are strictly necessary. Where the number of words available is low, we find ourselves having to prune back to what is essential, often making the text clearer in the process. The pruning is a distinct process that adds time and intellectual demands to the art of writing.

The first and most crucial point to keep in mind is that what you write is for mass consumption. Whether it be a monthly computer magazine or a daily newspaper, the publication wishes above all to reach its audience, and as many of them as possible. For an academic paper in a specialist, scholarly journal, the crucial issue is whether it is a contribution to knowledge. A journal article may require close and careful reading to understand its main findings and it may assume a great deal about the capability and background information on which the reader can draw, but it is a bonus if it is interestingly written. The opposite is true of any form of journalism.

Perhaps this distinction should not be as great as it usually is. It would be wonderful if most journal articles were engaging and easy to read. It may also be healthier if the articles in newspapers typically assumed more of their readers' background knowledge rather than less. Indeed, in the sports and financial sections of newspapers there is often the assumption of accepted jargon and background knowledge that would be similar to that found in a scientific journal. So the distinction we are drawing here, like most distinctions, are only to help you understand the central issues rather than being hard and fast principles.

Reaching the readership of a newspaper or magazine in a lively way does require much more consideration of writing style than does writing for an academic outlet. Short words and sentences are *de rigueur*. Avoidance of unusual words is essential. Names and specific references to incidents have to be clear and unambiguous, even when something generally known is being mentioned; for example it will not be unusual in some papers even to write 'Tony Blair, the Prime Minister', just so the readership is aware without doubt which Tony Blair is being mentioned.

The second point to accept is that popular periodicals and newspapers of any kind have to operate around very strict publication deadlines if they are to be effective. David has been telephoned at 10.30 am by national newspapers and asked for six hundred words on a topic that has just hit the news, to be e-mailed by 4.00 pm that same evening. There may be negotiation around these deadlines but often of no more than half an hour or so. This can be an exciting challenge, especially when your desk is littered with half-written journal articles that you have been working on for the past three years, but it is a challenge that cannot be shirked. If you miss the deadline not only will the piece never appear in the newspaper, but it is unlikely you will ever be asked again. You cannot search the literature for days, or even hours, under these conditions, nor can you afford to write draft after draft and discuss it with colleagues. You have to get a clear idea of the point you want to make and make it as strongly and directly as you can.

Length is also crucial. Some newspapers may be willing to cut down your 1,500-word article to the 300 words they need. But what they are most likely to do is to use the first couple of paragraphs. The easiest way to reduce a piece of writing to the length needed is to chop it from the end to the required size. Look again at any newspaper article and you will see that it is written in such a way that it could end with each paragraph. The important information is at the start, and as paragraphs are added they elaborate or develop the material in the earlier paragraphs so that the piece always makes sense no matter where it is stopped. The really clever journalists do manage to keep their pieces alive all the way through so that the sub-editor has a hard time cutting off the punch line in the last paragraph, but do not expect that to be a trick you can easily pull off.

The other big difference from a scholarly journal that you must accept if you are to survive in the heady world of popular publishing, is that exactly what appears in print is determined by the editor. The final version of the piece is not under your control. Some editors, if time allows and they want to check they have not distorted the piece too much, may send you a copy of the revision for your approval. In our experience, though, this is extremely rare. David's daughter, Lily, who is a professional journalist – and has guided the writing of this chapter, for which we are extremely grateful – regularly complains that some details in what she has written have been distorted in the editing process. She is working full time within a newspaper environment, so imagine how much more problematic this may be for you at a distance from the day-to-day business of bringing out a newspaper.

For academics, the most frustrating part of the editing process is often the headline that is put on their paper. Not long ago David wrote a piece for *The Times* that was arguing how inappropriate it was for the diagnostic label of Asberger's syndrome to be applied to some offenders. The headline seemed to imply the opposite of his point, resulting in a complaint to his professional body that he had inappropriately criticized people suffering from this condition. In dealing with this complaint, the professional body's letter to David accepted that he had not done anything wrong, but advised that he should 'be careful what he writes in the future'. This indicated that the professional body was apparently ignorant of how newspapers are put together and that David had actually been very careful about what he had written but had no influence over the headline. In effect their comment implied that he should not write for newspapers because there was always the risk of his work being headlined or edited misleadingly. This stand on not writing for newspapers may be one that you take if you have similar experiences.

Of course, the reason that a newspaper or magazine would wish to publish your material, besides its being interesting to read, is that it gives access to facts, opinions or understanding of a topic that they cannot get any other way. Therefore, unless, you are an established journalist they will be concerned to ensure that you have some authority. David still laughs over the answer he got when asking a journalist writing for *The Sun* tabloid newspaper, why all the people they quoted were described as the 'top' people in their field. (He was implying that many of them were clearly not.) The answer came back without hesitation 'because "leading" has too many letters'. The main point here is that the newspaper always wished to make its readers believe that the material coming from someone who was not a journalist was being cited because that source had some privileged, quality access that set it apart from what would be available from any other source. You will need to convince a newspaper or magazine editor that you can provide such credibility.

The range of outlets that we have included under the heading of newspapers and magazines is enormous. The comments above and in the box that summarizes them opposite therefore do have to be regarded as crude generalizations. As we have discussed with academic journals and will explore with book publishers, you have to select your publication outlet in relation to your objectives for publication. Some newspapers such as *The Times* supplements for Education or Higher Education will be closer to academic journals in their desire to include scholars as contributing authors, and the consequent interaction around the final version of the article (although headlines will still be

---

Some criteria for operating as a freelance journalist

Criteria	Implications
Readable	What you write is easy to read and understand, with minimal grammatical or syntax errors
Simple	Few polysyllabic words; short sentences
Engaging	The reader wants to read the material because it draws them in
Relevant	Deals with issues that are of interest now
Accurate	Any article finishes usually in the word length guidelines that are given. This will often be to within an error of ± 5 per cent of the total required
Timely	Deadlines can be to the nearest 30 minutes and are fundamental
Informed	The article is authoritative in providing privileged or specialist information
Valid	There is a genuine basis for the claims or opinions on offer
Chop-able	The most significant information is earliest and the article can be readily cut at any point to fit length requirements
Malleable	Accept that the editor's decisions on the text are not negotiable

totally outside of the author's control). Other outlets may just use the copy you send them as a starting point and rework the piece into their own style. Some will pay quite handsomely, others will be rather mean. Do not forget though, this form of publication is a commercial venture. They expect to pay you and, as in all areas of commerce, negotiation over rates is acceptable even if often unsuccessful.

Legal constraints to publishing

In Chapter 8 we dwelt on the morals and ethics of publishing, but when you move into the mass media the legal constraints that encompass all publishing become particularly significant. These constraints vary from country to country and from time to time, but they are most pertinent to the popular publishing we are discussing in this chapter, and journalists need to be familiar with them. The box on page 150 lists the most pertinent laws in this respect. We then look briefly at some of the issues they raise.

Laws relating to publishing

- Sexual Offences (Amendment) Acts 1976 and 1992 – both to do with not identifying victims
- Children and Young Person's Act 1933 – not identifying victims, witnesses, or the accused under the age of 18 if they are/have been involved in a court case
- Defamation Act 1996 – to do with libel, slander and how to defend libellous remarks
- Rehabilitation of Offenders Acts 1974 and 1984 – not publishing spent convictions
- Copyright, Designs and Patents Act 1988 – who owns the copyright, and penalties for breaching it

Most notable are the legal constraints relating to libel and slander. Libel is anything published that discredits another, provided the person (or group) libelled is alive. In special cases it can also be illegal to libel a dead person. Slander is a similar law about what is spoken. Publishers are highly sensitive to the possibility of being sued for libel. When David wrote about well-known convicted murderers in his book *Criminal Shadows* he mentioned people with sobriquets such as the 'Son of Sam' or 'The Yorkshire Ripper', naming the people who had been convicted of those crimes. Even though the names of these killers are widely published, David was still given a forty-page report from the publisher's lawyers that included requests for assurance that the people named had indeed been convicted of the crimes as claimed.

Defamation is also part of this issue, but is rather more complicated. Defamation and libel can arise, for instance, if you were attacking the research of a colleague in a way that threatened his career or livelihood. It would only be illegal, though, if you could not support your claims with firm evidence. You therefore need to be aware of the possibility of a lawsuit if you name any individual in a derogatory way, and seek advice from an appropriate lawyer if in doubt. Much of the law on defamation has not been tested, so it often comes down to the jury's interpretation of words and their meaning.

There is the related matter of 'negligent misstatement'. This is when something that is published, or something that is omitted from a publication, could be acted on and those actions could give rise to physical injury or financial loss. Electrical wiring diagrams that are unsafe or food preparation that would create poisonous conditions would be obvious examples. There are certainly areas of medical publication in which general claims may mislead those who are not well informed, and so caution should be exercised in getting such claims published. Authors should be aware that the publisher holds the author responsible for any such negligence unless it can be clearly shown that the error was introduced as part of the publication process. The publisher will keep a careful record of all contact with the author on matters that might relate to libel or negligence, so all authors are well advised to do the same.

What might not have been so expected is the number of legal constraints in the UK over what can be published about what goes on in the courts, particularly with regard to victims and children. These matters of contempt of court will not be directly relevant to most academics, but any would-be author should consider whether the principles of protecting the innocent, or those who cannot so easily protect themselves, are relevant to their own publication. Newspapers and magazines have active legal advisers who specialize in this aspect of the law. The editor will be alert to the need to check for possible legal constraints with the publication's lawyers, but if you have any doubts you should raise them with the editor directly.

The most crucial constraints that relate to proceedings within the courts concern not identifying individuals who are involved in court cases, or commenting on their characteristics. This includes a victim of sexual crime, defendants or people whose prior convictions have been 'spent', that is, are no longer regarded as legally significant. Newspaper editors are of course aware of these legal constraints and would not allow inappropriate publication, unless they could claim it was in the public interest. But they may rely on you in some cases for determining whether the material may be unpublishable because it relates to ongoing legal proceedings and is therefore *sub judice*. If you get it wrong, you and the publications could be charged with contempt of court because you have caused to be published something (for example, comments on the accused's character or previous offences) that will prejudice a pending court case. This is one aspect of the law that varies considerably from one country to another. In the USA much more may be published about ongoing trials and especially about defendants than would be acceptable in the UK and most of the rest of Europe.

Reports for clients

Many different individuals and organizations will commission reports for a host of reasons. They may, for example, request a review of knowledge in an area relevant to their business. A solicitor may request a review of information that can form the basis for evidence in court. In some cases, public relations organizations will commission an account of scholarly views that they can use to gain editorial space that includes their client's name. An illustration of this was when David was asked to produce a report on the psychology of fear that Madame Tussaud's could use as a vehicle for announcing the refurbishment of its Chamber of Horrors. These reports are paid for like other commissioned research, but the important point is that the output is not the findings as such but the actual document that is produced. These documents may be eventually reworked for publication to a wider audience, but initially clients are paying for a piece of text that can be used for their specific purposes and may often not have more than a handful of copies produced.

Although the report to a client would normally take a very different form from other publications, it does have many parallels with writing for newspapers. It needs to speak to its audience directly and to present the crucial information at the start of the document, not have it buried in dense conclusion sections. Clients want, essentially, to know what the implications are for their actual activities. Deep academic background and relationship to previous studies and the like, which are essential for a journal article, are irrelevant to the client unless they have direct bearing on what he or she does. Best practice in such reports is therefore to start with a clear summary that emphasizes the implications of the report and likely actions that could follow from it: what is often known as a management, or executive, summary. The work that was done in brief form would follow, and after that the main results.

What you are doing here is drawing the readers in, like a newspaper article, so that they get the crucial information first and then will want to follow that up in more detail and eventually get to the backing for your conclusions. As much of the technical detail as possible will go into the appendices as it would be expected that only advisers to the executives would want to study that material. All the many people who may have helped with the report are best acknowledged because the chances are they get no other recompense for the help they have given you. The order of contents of such a report might be:

1 Executive summary
2 Remit of the report
3 Work undertaken
4 Main results
5 Results in context
6 Recommendations
7 Action plan
8 Summary and conclusions
9 Acknowledgements
10 Bibliography and references
11 Appendices

You could never publish this document in the form described here. It is in some senses 'inside out' with regard to what would be usual in an academic publication. An academic publication starts with a definition of the problem to be studied, contextualized within the way that problem has been considered, or not, in the past. The recommendations for action are typically asides as part of the conclusions, not the opening points in the summary as proposed here. Therefore, if you have aspirations to eventually publish this work you must build into it the material that you will eventually need for an academic account. At the most elementary level this means you may have a much fuller reference list and citations than are strictly needed for the executives to whom you are reporting. The context of the results against examinations by other people and an earlier literature has to speak directly to your clients, but you need to keep an eye on how that material could be readily reconstructed for scholarly publication. Similarly, the methods that you employed may not be given in much detail in section 3 of your report, but it is worthwhile putting them in detail into your appendices so that you can lift them out into the main body of the text for the journal of your choice. Of course, all this presupposes that your arrangements with the client will allow for publication.

Contracting with a client on future publication

If you hope to recycle reports written for clients it is essential to have a clear contract with them that deals with such possibilities. In our contracts we usually have the following form of words:

> The Client will enjoy full access to all of the results from the research and no Researcher or associated colleague or student will take advantage of any confidential knowledge without prior agreement of the Client.
>
> The Client will also allow the Researcher royalty-free, non-exclusive, irrevocable, perpetual licence to use the all results and any intellectual property. The researcher shall be allowed to keep the anonymized data collected for the purposes of future research and development of the data with prior agreement of the Client. The Client has the right to object to statements made about itself by the Researcher and both parties undertake to resolve such issues by negotiation.
>
> The Researcher shall protect the anonymity of any individuals involved in the research as well as the identity of any individual informants within the Client Organization.
>
> The Client recognizes that it is the intention of the Researcher to publish any aspects of the results of the work that have academic merit, but that the Client will have the right to review the work prior to its being submitted for publication and to request any modifications or omissions that in the client's view are necessary for commercial, security or other appropriate reasons. The Researcher undertakes to act on all such reasonable requests provided there is no undue delay in their being made to the Researcher after submission of the draft publication.
>
> In the event of failure to resolve any issues raised in the above agreement provision shall be made for arbitration.

In our experience most clients are happy to agree to such a contract but they may put in further limitations, such as requiring that subsequent publication will not be for at least twelve months, or that they be acknowledged (or not) in published accounts of the work.

All writing is authorship

Anything you write has the potential for publication. Some people are painfully aware of this, revising and editing even e-mails to make sure they are as succinct and elegant as possible. But you do not have to go that far to be alerted to the fact that when you create text you are on the first steps towards becoming a published author. Articles in newspapers on the issues of the day, or in magazines explaining your particular perspective to an interested but untutored audience, draw on your expertise and scholarship and so are as worthy of writing as a learned paper that only a handful of colleagues around the world will fully understand. Similarly, summarizing an area of knowledge for a particular client can have enormous effect on the individuals who commission the work.

All of these 'non-academic' forms of publication merge with each other and with the pieces you may write for journals. At their heart are similar skills of communication and understanding your audience. Challenges of how to structure the text to make it most appropriate to your audience are also present in whatever you write. You need to master the different media, though, and respond to their different demands, but in doing so you will be enriching the portfolio of writing skills on which you are drawing.

These skills and various pieces of writing provide you with more tools and resources to take with you on your journey as an author. They will accumulate until, perhaps unexpectedly, you realize you have a body of knowledge and expertise that transcends single articles. This may be the point at which you consider writing a book, to which we turn in the next chapter.

12   Doing a book

Why write a book? • Turning a thesis into a book • What about editing a book? • The challenges of editing

Why write a book?

Once the effort is over and the hours have been put in, there is something curiously satisfying about seeing your name on the front of a book, especially if it has an attractive cover and there are a decent number of them in your university bookshop. But more importantly, writing a book will sometimes be the most appropriate way of publishing your ideas – if, for example, you want to make a series of arguments in favour of a new way of thinking or a new approach in research; or if you want to explore a wide range of aspects of a topic. Or you might find that, having published a number of articles relating to an area, you now wish to gather those ideas together with others that are as yet unpublished, to create a more comprehensive picture of your area of interest and your particular take on some of its facets. Another source of ideas for some aspiring authors of books, especially for first books, will be the work they carried out for their postgraduate degree.

Writing a book is usually exciting, as you discover ideas you had never dreamt you had, and try to find not only what you want to say, but also the best way to say it. However, it is also time consuming. The actual writing of a book will typically take between a year and eighteen months, if you are able to give a reasonable amount of time to it, and double this, or even more, if you are not. More surprisingly, persuading a publishing house that the book you want to write is one that they want to publish, can easily take up to a year or even longer.

Even after you submit your manuscript, nowadays almost certainly in electronic form, there is still a long way to go as your text is subjected to various indignities (including copy editing and being nudged towards your publisher's house style) during its transformation from raw text into bound copies that please your editor, and hopefully satisfy you. Typically this will take around nine months to a year, so the entire process from first approaching a publisher to seeing your book in its final printed form will often take at least a couple of years, but may take twice as long as that.

Once your book is in print, you will probably find that some people are impressed by the fact that you have published it. However, you may well find that you gain less academic credit than you might have expected, given the considerable effort – the hours of thought and research; the drafting and redrafting; the checking and changing; the commitment, toil and sweat – that you have put into its production. One reason for this could be that although all publishers subject book proposals to quality control of a kind, by taking advice from other academics with expertise in the relevant field, this is usually focused at least as much on marketability as it is on academic rigour. In other words, the reviewing to which book proposals are subjected is often less intellectually rigorous than that carried out for journals. In addition, reviews of book proposals are just that – reviews of *proposals*, rather than of completed texts, as is the case with the peer review process to which journal articles are subjected.

In spite of all this, in arts subjects such as philosophy and history, and sometimes in the social sciences, books may be valued as a legitimate way of reporting on important ideas and findings, alongside articles in peer-reviewed journals. However, in some areas, particularly in the sciences, the publication of a book is often given little credibility as a marker of academic and intellectual achievement, which is why most academic scientists would never consider the possibility of writing a book, even if they have written hundreds of journal articles.

Academic science books most often take the form of compendia of ideas, theories and findings from a broad swathe of academics, compiled for the benefit of students, rather than extended presentations of original ideas, arguments and research. That is why publishing a book in the sciences will usually count for less in gaining promotion than a single article in a prestigious reviewed journal, even if the material in that article was a version of a single chapter in the book. As a result of the pre-eminence of the sciences in academia, books of all kinds, and in all academic areas, are often viewed as if they are of little intellectual merit and unlikely to make a serious contribution to scholarship.

It is important to note that our account of the way in which academic books are often devalued relative to refereed journal articles is very much centred on the UK, and that there are other countries in Europe – Poland, for example – where the book is still very important in judging academic merit. More than that, not everyone would agree with our view that academic books are frequently denied the credit they are due. For example, in his recent book *Getting Published*, Wellington (2003) begins a chapter on book publishing by examining Powell's view that, 'in many circles book writing has been seen as the pinnacle of academic achievement' (p. 76). However, he recognizes that some people believe that 'academic status is now conferred more by a commercially published book (especially a textbook) than by articles published in "eminent, high status journals" ' (p. 77).

Interestingly some of the most distinguished scientists nowadays have turned their hand to writing books that are intended to sell to a general market; and many of them are excellent (see, for example, Dawkins 1989; Fortey 1998; Jones 1999; Rees 1999; Greenfield 2002). Usually, however, although they write well for the general reader, thus raising the profile of their disciplines, such authors already have established reputations, and their popular works, no matter how well written they are, may well add nothing to their professional reputation. David had a degree of popular success with a book entitled *Criminal Shadows* (Canter 1995) which was published as a trade book and won the Golden Dagger award for crime non-fiction, and the US equivalent, the Anthony award. It was a serious scientific book that put forward original ideas. However, the fact that its subject matter gave it appeal that allowed it to attract a wide audience while still often being cited in PhD theses meant that he had to argue fiercely for its inclusion in his department's submission of published work in the Research Assessment Exercise.

Turning a thesis into a book

Although the most effective way to capitalize on their postgraduate work is to use it to inform articles in refereed journals, people who have completed a research degree often think about publishing their work as a book, and it is easy to see why they might. After all, they will probably have devoted several years to their research, and it will often be the most significant piece of work they have carried out to date. Not only that, but they may feel certain that their proposed book will be of interest to at least some people in their field, and perhaps even beyond, since their examiners obviously thought not only that they had something worthwhile to say, but also that they had said it well enough to merit a pass. Suddenly their shiny new postgraduate qualification does not seem sufficient to justify the privations they endured during those long, lonely years.

Attempting to publish a thesis in book form is not to be recommended if you are a totally novice author. Sometimes, turning a thesis into a book works well, especially when the author set out to write a thesis with the intention of turning it into a book. This is exactly what Gavin did with *Contemplating Suicide*, which was a reworking of his PhD in applied philosophy, with a different audience and purpose in mind, and took almost as long to prepare as if he had written it simply as a book. Sometimes, unfortunately, publishing a thesis does not work well, especially when the book is little more than a modified version of the thesis on which it is based.

Books are usually more direct than theses. They have less gratuitous citation of the kind that is typical in postgraduate work. Books tend also to have a more confident note. They avoid the apologetic tone that often invades theses as candidates try to cover their backs by giving advance warning of what they have not done.

If you decide that your thesis would best be published as a book, you will thus have to be prepared for the considerable effort that you will have to expend in restructuring and perhaps largely rewriting it. More than that, if you actually want people to read your book, you will have to be prepared to abandon at least some of the ideas and results over which you slaved, possibly for years, because, however important to you, they are unlikely to be sufficiently interesting to others to make them worth publishing. Such is the enterprise into which you wish to step, because the only reason that truly justifies publishing anything for academic and professional audiences is that it can make a contribution to knowledge, thinking or practice (though many academic and professional authors publish for less worthy reasons). For example, a book will rarely be attractive if it contains an extensive review of literature of the kind that is present in theses, much of which is often only marginally relevant to the research undertaken. If you have conducted empirical research it is likely, also, that you will want to cast aside the contents of some of the pages, including pages that you probably devoted to presenting data and results.

Make no mistake, converting a thesis into a book is a substantial task, involving lots of gardening – pruning (and sometimes wholesale clearing out) of material that has outlived its usefulness, as well as careful cultivation of ideas that you put to one side in preparing your thesis but which may be of interest to the wider audience that you hope your book will attract. To switch metaphors, converting a thesis into a book requires a lot of repackaging, to produce a product that is saleable, rather than passable.

> **Some things to bear in mind if you decide to use your thesis as the basis for a book**
>
> - Books can afford to be much more challenging, and even provocative, than theses.
> - Whereas theses are written to be judged by others with relevant expertise, books are usually read by people whose expertise is likely to be less developed than that of the author.
> - You can take stylistic risks with a book that you cannot afford to take with a thesis.
> - There is no need to include in your book every example, research approach or analytic method that appeared in your thesis. If you do, your readers may fall asleep.
> - Remember that, whereas your examiners were paid a little to read your thesis, many people who read your book, or attempt to do so, will pay for the privilege; make it as interesting, accessible and worthwhile to read as possible.
> - Books are usually less formal in style than theses. Make yours easy and attractive to read.

What about editing a book?

Many people seem to hold the view that editing a book necessarily offers an easy way of getting published. This is an illusion since, in most cases, editing a book takes a great deal of effort, and may even take more effort than authoring a book. Everything depends on two things: the kind of edited book, and the attitudes and beliefs of the editors. Admittedly, some people publish edited books without putting in much effort, usually because they have the view that once they have selected their team of authors, their job is merely to 'top and tail' the volume in question by writing a brief introduction and perhaps a short concluding section. However, others see the responsibilities of editorship differently and believe that it is their job not only to help individual authors to say what they have to say as well as they can say it, but to ensure that their individual contributions fit together in a volume that has some coherence.

Any 'edited' book that takes little effort was probably thrown together with little thought and in the absence of much by way of editorial guidance or involvement. It is because so many people believe that all edited books are of this kind that such books are often looked down upon by academics who believe that they do not take a great deal of effort or creativity. In order to understand why negative views of the intellectual value of edited books are common, it is necessary to reflect on the differences between edited books of different kinds, including books that comprise papers from a conference, books of readings (often known as 'readers'), and what might be called 'conceived edited books'. Doing so will also help you to determine which of these forms of edited text, if any, you might wish to take on as a publishing project.

Conference proceedings

Many conference organizers publish proceedings, in which they aim to include all contributions, as a standard part of the package participants buy when registering. Proceedings are often published 'in house', in a form that does not match the quality of most book publishers' offerings. Nowadays, proceedings may well be published in electronic rather than paper form. Papers usually appear in the form provided by conference presenters, who may be required to format them in a standard way to allow for easy reproduction. In many cases there is no selection or review process, and the editors do little more than gather the papers together with perhaps a short introduction saying a little about the event at which they were presented. In some of the natural sciences, however, conference proceedings are highly prized and contributions are more carefully selected than journal articles.

Sometimes the papers from a conference or series of conferences are used as the raw material from which an edited book is created. Sometimes such books are little more than conference proceedings. However, many involve more significant input from editors in selecting the papers they want to use, and perhaps in working with contributors to develop their conference papers into properly conceived chapters, fit for publication.

Books of readings

Typically, books of readings gather together material from different sources, including journal articles and extracts from earlier books. Readers are often produced for pedagogical purposes, to give students easy access to high quality professional writing in a specialist area. Many editors of such collections are motivated by their involvement in a particular course or courses, and the material they select will thus reflect their views of what is centrally important in the area on which they focus. Their book may become a central plank in their teaching and, as a result, they may hope that their own students will buy it; with luck, it will also be bought by students from other, perhaps competing, courses. Good examples of such edited texts may be found in the many 'course readers' produced by the Open University, to meet the needs of its distance learning students.

Sometimes the advent of a new university course gives birth to a reader that belongs to a different sub-species, one that consists entirely of newly commissioned work aimed not at a professional academic audience, but at students. So, for example, there has recently been a rash of new books for students undertaking the 'foundation degrees' instigated by the Blair government (see, for example, Bold 2004). Editing such a book could provide a steady source of income, because they are typically produced in response to a perceived need in a mass market; however, the academic credibility they are likely to convey to their editors may be limited. On the other hand, where edited books of this kind relate not only to new courses but also to emerging subject specialisms, they may also have significant academic merit. Such books overlap with the next, and most academically significant, type of edited book.

Conceived edited books

'Conceived edited books' offer both editors and contributors the possibility of making a significant input to academic debate. They take a number of forms, depending on whether they consist of newly commissioned or previously published material. Although edited academic books are perhaps less common than they once were, there is an increasing trend to produce very large edited overviews of broad academic areas, with titles such as the *Encyclopaedia of Applied Ethics* (Chadwick 1997) and the *Encyclopedia of Law and Economics* (Bouckaert and De Geest 2000). These are produced in much the same way as other edited volumes except that there may be an editor-in-chief who commissions all the myriad individual contributions.

In a conceived edited book, the time the editor spends in putting a proposal together, signing up contributors, guiding them and commenting on their submissions, as well as writing key chapters and an introduction, will often take the same sort of time that it would have taken her to write the book herself, and is often far more onerous. The advantage is that by engaging other authors who have the detailed expertise to write parts of a book, it is possible for editors to produce a powerful and important book addressing issues that they have spotted as important, even though they do not have the range of expertise and indeed the perceived authority to write the book on their own. Rather than being a pale imitation of a 'real' book, as some people think, conceived edited books can thus offer a much stronger and more honest approach to both the explication of ideas and the exploration of issues, than attempting to write in a watered-down kind of way about topics that are not fully within your grasp. The same is true of edited books that gather together previously published material with the intention of delimiting an area of concern. The creative intellectual input in such a book comes from spotting the fact that a number of researchers and authors are working in related areas, and putting together a selection that is somehow 'more than the sum of its parts'.

The challenges of editing

From what we have said so far, it should be clear that the amount of work involved in preparing edited books of each of the species we have outlined will depend upon the view of the editors. Some editors will avoid becoming over-involved with the mundane business of supporting contributors in developing their chapters, because they want an easy life. It is such 'editors' that give edited books a bad name. Others, on the other hand, will steer clear of decisions about the text of individual chapters, because they believe these are best made by the contributors. However, their serious attitude towards editor-ship will be evidenced both by the careful selection of authors and topics, and the coherence that this can lend to the work as a whole, and also by the introduction and perhaps the linking narrative that they write. Admittedly these are two extreme positions and there is a range of possibilities between them. However, the point remains that book editors differ in their views of the nature of editorship and of the kind and amount of work involved.

Edited books undoubtedly have a strong contribution to make in many academic areas, as we have made clear. Nonetheless, edited books are often unjustly denied the credit that they deserve, so much so that many academics would rather write a single article (or, somewhat ironically, a single chapter in an edited book) than edit a book, even one that will make a serious and important contribution. That is why we think you should think carefully before deciding on this route to publishing.

13   From idea to reality

A book's journey to print

An idea for a book • Stages in publishing a book
• Stage 1: Forming a convincing shape • Stage 2:
Deciding on a publisher • Stage 3: Proposing to a
publisher • Stage 4: The review process • Stage 5:
Signing a contract • Stage 6: Developing the text
through successive drafts • Stage 7: Submitting your
manuscript to the publisher • Stage 8: Responding to
copy editor's queries and suggestions • Stage 9:
Correcting proofs and providing an index

An idea for a book

So you have an idea for a book – a book, what's more, that you believe the
world is ready for; a book for which there is a definite niche in the market.
More than that, you have an urge to write it. You might well feel, as some
people do, that you have had this book inside you for years just waiting to
be written. Or maybe you just have something that you really want to write

about – some ideas or arguments, a point of view, or a theory that you want to share, but could not manage to share in an article. Perhaps you want to write a textbook because you think you have the ability to write about the central ideas in your area of expertise in a way that will excite students and help them to learn. On the other hand, rather than experiencing the urge to write a book, you might experience a compulsion to harvest ideas from people you know, admire and trust, in order to create an edited book to fill a gap that you perceive in the intellectual universe but which you do not feel qualified to fill on your own.

What are you going to do about your urge to write or edit this book? One thing that you should avoid is to just start writing your book or gathering contributions for an edited volume in the expectation that, once you have finished, all you will have to do is find a publisher. If you do, you will probably be wasting your time because most publishers like to help plan any books from the outset and rarely accept unsolicited manuscripts. We both know colleagues who have poured their souls into books without any prior contact with anyone who would print it and then wasted years unsuccessfully seeking a publisher.

Very few authors of academic texts will find publishers for books that they have already written. One exception to this would be a very well established author who, on the strength of track record and celebrity, could persuade a commissioning editor that she would be foolish to turn down the opportunity to publish his book, on the grounds that if her company does not do so, some other publisher will. But few authors even with an established track record would risk the gamble of writing a book without a contract from a publisher.

In order to get our books into print, most authors and editors have to approach publishers with a proposal, rather than a manuscript. Indeed, proposing to a publisher is perhaps the most important part of the process of turning an idea for a book into the reality of a published text, which is why, in what follows, there is so much emphasis on the writing of proposals.

Stages in publishing a book

It is hard to delineate precisely the process of getting a book into print because there will be many variations, depending on authors, publishers and the topic the book covers. However, most academic authors will go through a series of stages that overlap substantially with those we describe on page 165.

Stages in publishing a book

- STAGE 1: Forming a convincing shape
- STAGE 2: Deciding on a publisher
- STAGE 3: Proposing to a publisher
- STAGE 4: The review process
- STAGE 5: Signing a contract
- STAGE 6: Developing the text through successive drafts
- STAGE 7: Submitting your manuscript to the publisher
- STAGE 8: Responding to copy editor's queries and suggestions
- STAGE 9: Correcting proofs and providing an index

Stage 1: Forming a convincing shape

Creativity is a strange thing, whether it manifests itself in a new recipe by a top chef, a work of art, or an idea for an academic book. It is rarely a simple once and for ever matter. Fully fledged ideas for recipes, works of art and even academic books, do not usually leap uninvited and with no prompting, into the consciousness of those who bring them to fruition. Ideas for academic books are usually triggered by some stimulus or set of stimuli, such as something you have read or seen, something a colleague or a student says, or perhaps by the responses you receive after making a presentation at a conference. Or you may just be looking over your published journal articles and realize that, put together and developed with reference to related publications, they would make a useful book.

Once you are convinced that the idea you are toying with really is the basis of a book that you want to nurture into existence, the first step is to form it into a convincing shape – one in which a publisher might have some interest. This may take many months, during which you sketch successive versions of a plan. It may involve a great deal of discussion with friends, colleagues and family, as a result of which it will develop, and may even metamorphose into a radically different book. In a way this is the most exciting stage for an author or editor. It is certainly the stage in writing or editing a book where it is possible to be most adventurous and free – where your wishes and ambitions predominate, free from the constraints of trying to make your ideas fit into a publisher's current catalogue or publishing plans.

The next thing you have to do is to convince a publishing house that they should publish it. To do this you will have to write a book proposal. But before doing so you should reflect carefully about which publisher you should approach, out of the large number available.

Stage 2: Deciding on a publisher

The decision about which publisher to approach might seem easy, because there is a clear 'market leader' in your academic area. However, before making your decision you should talk to anyone you know who has published books, about their experience of the publishers with whom they have worked, especially if they have published with a company in which you are interested. It is also worth taking a stroll through the internet or, what is probably better, a couple of bookshops, to become as familiar as possible with books by companies that are publishing in your area of interest. The ideal publisher is one that has published other books that overlap to some extent with your intended focus, because this means that they have an interest in selling books to the particular audience at which you are aiming.

Questions to ask about potential publishers

- Do they publish books in your academic area?
- Do they have any other titles in your specialized area?
- Do they have any series of books into which your book might fit?
- Are they well thought of by academics?
- Are their books well presented – both inside and out?
- Do their books look serious?
- How well do they market their books?
- Are their books visible when you walk into bookshops?
- Do their books appear regularly at the major conferences in your academic or professional area?

Bear in mind both that it can take quite a long time for a proposal to be considered and for a contract to be offered, and that most publishers reject many more proposals than they commission. And so, although you may aspire to publishing with one of the more prestigious publishing companies in your area of interest, you might want to consider whether it would be prudent to go directly to another, less well-known company with your proposal, especially if it is your first book. If you do so, remember that this does not prevent you going to a more prestigious company in the future. If, on the other hand, you are lucky enough to land a contract with one of the major publishers in your academic area with your first book, you may want to stay with them for some time. Familiarity is a good thing, because it can make the process of obtaining further contracts easier, if a commissioning editor knows that you are capable of delivering the goods. However, there is nothing wrong with changing publishing stables, depending on your topic and on the type of book you are planning. Indeed, given that different publishers specialize in different subjects and kinds of books, it will often make a great deal of sense to do so. Choosing a publisher is a little like choosing which restaurant to eat in; some are good for some things and some for others; none is good for everything. Of course, unlike restaurants, publishers will quickly tell you if they do not handle the kind of book you have in mind and will often be very happy to suggest other publishers who might

Stage 3: Proposing to a publisher

Having decided on the publisher, you next have to construct the proposal by which you will try to persuade them that your book is for them. It is vital that you begin this process conscious of the fact that although it might seem obvious to you that the world needs your book, this does not mean that a commissioning editor is going to take on the task of publishing it. It is your job to persuade her.

Book proposals are curious documents. Partly they are aimed at providing information about the book and why it should be published. But partly they are about seduction, about drawing a publisher into a relationship with you, out of which your book will be born. That is why, in writing your proposal, you must not only be informative, but also persuasive. It is why you must seek to persuade not only through rational argument but by making your book sound interesting, even exciting. The book you want to write might be really important; it might fill a real niche in the market; tens of thousands of people might be ready to buy it; but unless you can interest a commissioning editor in it, it is not going to get into print.

There is no point in approaching a publisher until you have a good idea of the content of the book you want to propose. In addition, you should have a picture in mind of how it will be structured, and the order in which ideas will be presented. Many academic books fall naturally into a dozen or so chapters, which cluster together into larger parts consisting of several chapters on cognate themes, whereas others work best if they are split into three or four large 'parts', each comprising a number of sections that flow into one another so much that they are not really separate chapters. You have to decide which structure will best allow you to tell the story or stories you want to tell, to put forward the theories you want to present and discuss, or to make the case for the view of the world you want to support.

Where the book you are planning is an edited one, there are also decisions to be made about structure – for example, about whether to organize the chapters in clusters with related topics, or to organize them in some other way. If your book concerns some aspect of professional practice and its relationship to theory, you might wish to begin with more theoretical chapters and end with discussions of situations in which theory can be found underpinning practice. The possibilities are endless: organized around historical sequence or from general to particular issues, from established positions to speculation. The important point is that the stronger the central theme and structure, the clearer your storyline, the more readily will the publisher (and eventual reader) grasp what your book is about.

Commissioning editors

Most publishing companies divide up editorial work in such a way that editors develop specialist expertise, which means that there will probably be a commissioning editor who handles books in your discipline, and perhaps even in the particular part of your discipline to which your proposal relates. When you have decided which publisher to approach, you should take the trouble to identify this person, most probably by consulting the publisher's website or a catalogue of books in your area, or by approaching the publisher's representative at a conference, who may even be a commissioning editor. Since it will be helpful to fit your proposal to their requirements as far as possible, you should write them a brief letter saying who you are and a little about your proposed book, and asking whether they have a standard format for proposals. You might even consider telephoning to ask about this, since many editors will be happy to give a few minutes of their time to a conversation about your proposal, in which they will share such information. This can give you the opportunity to float your ideas by them in a brief way, thus whetting their appetite for your proposal.

No matter how thrilled you are about your idea for a book, you should not expect a commissioning editor to fall over herself in her excitement about the possibility of getting her hands on your proposal. However, if it is at least feasible that your project will come within her range of interests, you can expect her to advise you about how to construct your proposal, either by offering some informal guidance in a letter or by sending you a copy of whatever guidance they provide for authors about how to submit a book proposal. This may well be part of a booklet outlining their guidelines or instructions for authors in relation to all parts of the publishing process, including the preparation of manuscripts. Alternatively, you may be able to access such information via their website.

As well as helping you to structure your proposal, a publisher's guidelines for authors will usually include detailed instructions about how manuscripts should be presented – about, for example, page layout, line spacing, the use of abbreviations, and the use of numerals within the text. They will probably also refer to spelling, where you may well be required to use American spellings rather than English ones. In addition, some publishers will provide you with detailed advice about other aspects of the writing process, including the development of the text, how to get permission to use others' work, information on the production process, and a glossary of publishing terms.

What should be included in a proposal?

Although there are a number of possible variations, most publishers will ask for much the same information, including some or all of the following:

- Title
- Length
- Author(s) or editor(s)
- Timescale
- Rationale
- Outline and overview of contents
- Sample chapters (in draft form)
- Readership
- Competing titles
- Referees

Some publishers will provide a form that you can use to submit your proposal. You might find this too constraining, but even if you decide not to use it, you should try to address all of the issues it raises.

Get the title right

The title you propose for your book is important because it will allow the commissioning editor to form an immediate impression both about whether it might fit into her list and about whether it might be financially viable. Bear in mind that the title you submit may not be the one with which you end up, since it will be negotiable for a long time after you obtain a contract. However, it should represent a serious attempt to sum up your book's main thrust in a way that will attract readers.

It may be worth offering more than one possible title. For example, an author who has recently completed a PhD about the conceptual and ethical issues that arise from the debate about when human beings become people, might offer the following titles, all of which in some way give a picture of what his book will be about:

1 *Conceptual and ethical issues that arise from the debate about when, in the life of a pre-embryo, embryo, fetus, neonate and toddler, a human being becomes a person*

2 *Are all human beings, persons? Some conceptual and ethical issues*

3 *Human being and personhood: one and the same?*

4 *The importance of being a person*

Which of these possible titles do you think is most interesting? Which do you imagine is closest to the title of the thesis on which it is based? Which is most likely to attract readers?

Devising a title for your book

A proposed title should:

- Accurately reflect the content of your book
- Be likely to grab the attention of potential readers
- Not be so clever it deceives potential buyers

Length of text
You should give an estimate of the length of the text you expect to write, including contents list, references, index and any appendices. It will be useful to give this with a margin of error, for example 60,000–65,000 words (although US publishers seem to prefer an estimated number of pages). The length of a book might have an influence over whether an agreement to publish can be obtained. You may well believe that it is important for your life's work to be published as one vast tome that covers all relevant aspects of your topic; unfortunately, publishers are more likely to be interested in an averagely long, and hence averagely priced, 70,000–80,000 word book that is easy to produce and market, and that they have good reason to believe will sell to enough people to make it a worthwhile investment. As a guide, most run-of-the-mill academic texts tend to be between 70,000 and 85,000 words, and publishers will rarely want to go much above this because doing so affects their production costs.

Authors or editors
You should give your full name, title, institution and contact details and the name, title and institution of any co-author (or co-editor, in the case of an edited book). In a separate document you should also provide a brief CV of each author or editor – no more than a page, emphasizing aspects that are relevant to the proposed book.

Timescale
You should give as honest an estimate as you can of the time it will take to deliver the manuscript, from the date you sign a contract. In the rosy enthusiasm that usually accompanies the conception of a new project it is quite likely that your first estimate will be somewhat optimistic. Our advice would be to double this estimate, because then you will be more likely to

submit before the deadline, which is a much better position to be in than struggling to meet a deadline that was never really tenable in the first place. Commissioning editors, by and large, would prefer this to having to enter into cajoling, jollying along, and even – in most cases after severe provocation – into threatening to withdraw the contract, as you fail to meet not only the first deadline but a number of deadlines, and sometimes a number of 'final' deadlines.

Rationale

If you are going to persuade a publisher to commission your book, you must present them with a reasoned account of why it is worth publishing, or even better, of why it is necessary. Has there been a recent growth of interest in the topic or topics you address? Has little been published about it in the past? Or has what has been published failed to do justice to those aspects on which you will focus? Do you think your book is needed because of the number of times you are asked for advice on the topic? Say so. If your book is a textbook, or fills a need for a sensible and rigorous account of an area that is missed by other books, are there some new courses for which it will become the obvious text of choice? Perhaps you are the director of such a course, or perhaps, better still, you are a member of a network of people who teach such courses. If you can cite direct evidence about the numbers of students who are likely to buy your book, then do so. For example, if you wanted to write a book intended for the UK market, about the philosophy and practice of the forest schools and nurseries that are common in Denmark, you might want to cite evidence about the burgeoning development of early years courses across the UK, as well as evidence about the growth of interest in outdoor education among early years educators.

In writing the rationale for your book you should try to make your case strongly, but without going over the top. For example, phrases like, 'The time is right for X (insert the title of your book)' might be useful. Using the proposed name of your book is a good thing to do, because it can help to lull your chosen editor into thinking that it is already a real thing, and not just an idea in someone's head. (Bear in mind, however, that commissioning editors are aware of the tricks that authors get up to in trying to persuade them that they should give them contracts.)

Where your book is an edited one, your rationale should include a discussion of the reasons that an edited book is more appropriate than an authored one. For example, you may think an edited book is the only possible way to cover a rapidly developing field, because no one has, or could have, the expertise to write authoritatively about the whole range of research and thinking. On the other hand, your reason for deciding on an edited book might be that you have spotted the emergence of a new area of academic activity and want to begin mapping it out by gathering together contributions by some of the people whose work is helping to create it. These are good reasons for editing rather than authoring academic books, as would be the fact that you wanted to produce a course reader aimed at giving a large student audience easy access to high quality writing by some of the major authors working in an area. Be aware, however, that in many academic areas, edited books tend to be less popular than books with a single author, although publishers do differ in their views on this.

Outline and overview of contents

You have to persuade the publisher, not only that your topic is one that people will want to read about, but also that you will produce a book that they will want to read. In order to do this you will have to offer an interesting and persuasive sketch of the territory you intend to cover, and of the way in which you intend to do so. You should give an overview of the contents of the book and a list of chapters and/or parts. In addition to this, some publishers will ask you to provide, for each chapter, as many subheadings as possible. This can prove difficult, because it presumes not only that you know pretty much what the book will contain, but that you have already worked out the best way to present it, which is unlikely. A much easier way of conveying a sense of what your book will be about is to offer a short account of the content of each chapter. These should not be long – one or, at most, two paragraphs each – but they should say enough to allow the reviewers who will appraise your proposal to assess whether it is coherent and seems to cover the field that you set out to address. Try to give chapters, and/or parts, titles that are both informative and interesting.

Where you are proposing an edited book, as well as giving an overview of the book as a whole, you should aim in your outline to provide the publishers with as full a list of contributors as possible, along with an outline of each chapter. It will be helpful if your overview makes some links between the individual contributions, demonstrating how they complement and strengthen one another. In selecting potential contributors, it is worth bearing in mind that it will help your case significantly if you manage to include one or two well-known figures in your field. In general, too, because of the vast size of the US market and curious insularity of many US academics, a few US contributors are always welcomed by publishers.

Sample chapters (in draft form)

In addition to an outline of the content of your proposed book, many publishers will ask you to submit a draft chapter or two. They may take some things on trust from an author that they have reason to believe will come up with the goods – usually one who has published in the past. However, if you are unknown to them, or if you are a novice author, you may not be able to avoid submitting samples, and perhaps doing a tap dance too. Nonetheless, our advice would be not to submit any sample chapters unless you are specifically asked to do so. A single chapter is never easy to produce in isolation. However, since one of the main reasons that publishers ask to see draft chapters is that they want to have some evidence that you can write in an appropriate style, it will often be worthwhile sending them something that you have already written, and preferably published, on a similar topic.

Readership
You should describe, as honestly as you can, the groups that you expect to read your book. For example, in the proposal he submitted for a forthcoming book, Gavin described his anticipated readership like this:

> *Plagiarism: What it is, why it is important, and how to avoid it,* is aimed at ᴄᴜsᴛᴏᴍᴇʀs ᴏf ᴍᴏɴᴇʏ ᴄᴏᴘɪᴇs, ᴘʀɪᴍᴀʀɪʟʏ ɪɴ ʜɪɢʜᴇʀ ᴇᴅᴜᴄᴀᴛɪᴏɴ, ᴛʜᴏᴜɢʜ ɪᴛ ᴡɪʟʟ also be of interest to students in FE, the sixth form of schools and on postgraduate programmes, especially in the case of students who are returning to study after some time in employment. Sixth form teachers, as well as lecturers on access courses, foundation and undergraduate degree programmes will also find it of interest.

It will be helpful if you can say which group you expect to represent the principal readership, and which you merely hope for. If you know of networks, associations or courses with large numbers of people who are likely to buy your book, say so; and if you can give numbers of students for courses that might adopt your book as a set text, do so. If you think that your book will attract an international readership, you should say so, but you should also say why you believe this. Remember that the publisher will think about how they can market the book, so any large organizations or big conferences that would contain people interested in your topic should be mentioned. Whatever you do, don't fib – they will know if you are flannelling them.

Competing texts
Here you should give a brief, but informed, view about texts that might be thought of, by a publisher, as competing with your proposed book. Don't allow yourself to develop the view that if there are other books out there then the publisher will not think it worthwhile to commission your book. Certainly do not deliberately try to conceal from the publisher your awareness of competing texts just because you are nervous about the possibility that this will put them off publishing your book. The fact that there are already books available on a topic will often be viewed positively, because it demonstrates that there is a market for the book you are proposing. However, you should indicate what makes your book different from and, hopefully, better than those that you identify as the opposition. What does it do that they do not? What does it do better than them? What makes it unique among all the titles that overlap with it to some extent? If you were asked to suggest three unique features of your book, what would they be?

Referees

Finally, you may want to suggest some people whom the publishers could invite to review your proposal. Many publishers will ask you to provide the names of three or four people who could be asked to give an opinion of your proposal, and in particular about whether your book is likely to find a readership. It is probably best to offer the names of people you admire, who have the expertise necessary to give a balanced view based on their experience and knowledge of the territory your book covers. There is nothing wrong with using friends for this purpose, but you should only do so if they have relevant expertise and can be relied upon to give a candid opinion. Of course you want them to recommend that the book be published; but you want them to do so on its merits, and not because they are your friends. You also want to benefit from their comments, which the publisher will pass on to you, which often prove to be very useful when you begin to work on the text.

Additional information

We have taken rather a broad view of the information you should include in your proposal. This is the kind of information that most publishers will find useful. In practice, individual publishers may request specific information that will be helpful to them because of the nature of the books they publish. For example, some will ask for information about any artwork that you intend to use in your text, including diagrams, tables and graphs, and how much space you expect them to take up, whereas others will ask you to describe the style in which you will write and the way you will organize your material. And in the case of a textbook, they may want to know about pedagogical features that you intend to use, including chapter summaries; exercises or tasks to allow students to practise skills or test their recall; and web links.

Stage 4: The review process

If, after reading your proposal, the commissioning editor decides that it has some merit, she will typically seek advice about it from two or more reviewers with relevant expertise. Such reviewers may include authors who have already published with them, as well as any you suggested in your proposal. After it has entered the black box that is the reviewing process you will probably find yourself fretting about what is happening to it for several weeks or even months.

The role of reviewers is similar to the role played by those who review articles for journals, though there are some differences. One of these is that while no payment is made to academics who review articles for journals, those who review book proposals for publishers typically receive either a small honorarium for the work they do – sometimes enough for a modest lunch for two or a couple of CDs – or some books from the publisher's catalogue. More importantly, a commissioning editor will also be interested in whether the reviewers believe that your book is likely to sell. In other words, she will have commercial concerns as well as intellectual ones. She may even ask the reviewer how many copies of your book are likely to be sold.

If, on the basis of the reviews she receives, and her calculations about the costs of production and likely sales, the commissioning editor thinks your book is likely to enhance her company's catalogue and, hopefully, its income, she will present it to her editorial board, or to a 'new book proposals meeting' where the decision will be made whether to issue you with a contract for your book. Although the process from submission to receiving this decision may take as little as a few weeks (or with e-mail we have had book proposals accepted within an hour), six months is more likely, and if you are unlucky and have made a very poor choice of publisher, it could even take a whole year before you receive a final response. If you are extremely unlucky, after a year of encouraging noises from a commissioning editor the response you receive will be a negative one. If, on the other hand, you have found an appropriate publisher you will eventually receive a contract outlining the legal agreement into which you will have to enter with the publisher if you want to proceed.

Stage 5: Signing a contract

When your commissioning editor has successfully persuaded her editorial board that your book is a viable proposition, she will send you two signed copies of a contract. Provided that you agree to the terms it outlines, you should sign both, file one away carefully as your own record, and return the other. In signing it you will be agreeing to produce a manuscript of a specified length with an agreed title, by a certain date. The publisher will be agreeing, in general, to publish that manuscript, provided that it is delivered on time and is of good enough quality. In the case of edited books there will often be a separate, but much simpler contractual agreement between each contributor and the publisher, referring to the fact that, on publication, the contributor will receive a free copy of the book, as well as, possibly, a small fee.

Along with your contract, or some time shortly afterwards, you will be sent an 'authors' questionnaire', asking for information that will be used in developing the marketing strategy for your book. This will include details of any conferences you know of at which the book might be advertised and of journals to which you would wish review copies to be sent, as well as a list of people you would like to receive free copies, who will usually be academics who might be in a position to promote your book in their institutions or on their courses.

For many academic authors, especially those who have not published books before, the receipt of a signed contract generates a mixture of feelings: elation that the nascent idea for the book has been recognized by someone who will commit money to help it see the light of day; disquiet that now the book really will have to be written, with all the pressure that entails. After all, once you have signed a contract, it is no longer just an interesting idea, but a potential commodity that people will be asked to pay for, and that you have agreed to produce.

What does a contract contain?

Book contracts are substantial legal documents that contain many clauses about the benefits that will come to you in return for giving the publisher the right to publish your manuscript, and about your responsibilities as an author or editor. It would be inappropriate to take up too much space discussing their intricacies here. However, there are certain common elements that you should be aware of, and pay close attention to, before you sign. Before doing so, you might also want to seek help from someone who understands contract law or who is an experienced author, or, if it is a book that may sell tens of thousands of copies, from a literary agent, as we discussed in Chapter 8.

Contracted benefits
The description of the benefits you will receive as author or editor will include a statement of the number of free copies that you will be sent when your book is published, and of your entitlement to discount on purchases of copies of your book and others in your publisher's catalogue (usually 25–30 per cent). Typically you will receive ten or twelve free copies, which will be equally divided between contributors in the case of books of which you are a co-author or co-editor. In addition, in the case of an edited book, an additional copy will usually be allocated for the author(s) of each chapter, which the publisher will distribute. Perhaps more importantly, there will also be a statement about the payments that will be made to you as author or editor.

Some publishers will be prepared to pay an advance, either at the stage at which you sign contracts, or on receipt of your manuscript, or both. Such advances are then deducted from royalties after the book is published. Next there will be a description of the payments you will receive for each copy of the book that is sold at home and abroad, of payments you will receive should the book be translated into another language or languages, or if, for example, it should be serialized in a newspaper or magazine (you should be so lucky). Royalty rates vary greatly and are often different for hardback and paperback copies. If you are unlucky, you may be offered 5 per cent, and if you are extremely lucky (or, more likely, well known and therefore in a position to attract a larger readership) you may be offered as much as 15 per cent. Most likely, though you will be offered somewhere between 7.5 and 10 per cent of the price the publisher is paid for the book by the retail outlet. This is known as the 'nett price'. David remembers in the early days of his publishing career that he got 10 per cent of the 'list price', that is, of the cover price of the book in the bookshop. But that is extremely rare these days. Sometimes royalty rates rise after a certain number of copies have been sold, and some publishers will be open to a bit of bartering about what the rate should be, though depending on how you are getting on with the commissioning editor, it could be unwise to make your negotiations too tough.

Contractual responsibilities

The description of your responsibilities as author or editor will include clauses relating to the preparation of the text, the form in which you will submit it and so on, including your responsibility to warrant that you really do have the right to publish it as it stands. Apart from the question of whether you have ownership of the major part of the text or, in the case of an edited book, an agreement with the individual authors that you may publish their texts, this means that you will be responsible for gaining permission to reproduce copyright material, including text, pictures, diagrams and so forth from other published sources. This can be a burdensome process and may also involve some cost, though most publishers will be willing to negotiate about charges for reproducing text from books they have published if they think that it serves their commercial purposes to do so. As well as undertaking to ensure that you have the right to publish the entire text of the book, by signing the contract you will be giving your guarantee that it contains nothing that will cause legal problems – because, for example, of offence to others.

Stage 6: Developing the text through successive drafts

Successful academic books have to be authoritative, which means that they must sound as if the author knows what he is talking about. More than that, however, successful academic books have to be interesting: like novels, they have to draw in their readership and make them want to read. An academic book might be jam-packed with information about the best research on a topic, but be so badly written that that no one will want to put in the effort to read it. Successful academic books also have to be structured in such a way that they convey their meanings as easily as possible. In order to achieve this, it is part of your responsibility as an author to ensure that the headings and sub-headings you use facilitate your readers' understanding of what you have to say. This is an important part of the process of preparing your text, and one that you should always bear in mind as you draft and redraft.

Creating the text of an authored book

Every academic author has a different creative process, some of which we discussed in Chapter 5. However, it is worth saying a few things here about the kinds of ways in which some academic authors that we know, including ourselves, approach the process of developing text from the embryonic form at the centre of a proposal to a publisher into the full text that is submitted for publication.

There is more than one way to approach the task of turning the embryo into a finished text. Some authors begin by writing the introduction, or even the preface, and then, if their book is organized as a series of more or less discrete chapters, they write each chapter in turn till they get to the end of a first draft. Then they gradually read and redraft chapters in the same order until they are satisfied. By contrast, others find it helpful to begin with the chapter that interests them most, or with a chapter or section of text that they intend to base on an article they have already published, or some teaching material they have produced, changing that into a form that is suitable for a book, picking off the other chapters in turn, when they feel ready to do so.

Whatever their general approach, many authors end up working on text for more than one chapter at a time, as ideas for material emerge if they come across relevant information. This can get very confusing unless you keep careful track of your ideas. So, it is a good idea to begin the process of writing a book by creating a new word-processing file for each major section of text – each chapter or each part – as well as catch-all files for unplaced 'thoughts' or 'findings'. Although, at first, it might be rather unsettling to find yourself thinking about several areas of your project at a time, it is a good sign because it means that you are working on the book as a whole, even as you focus attention on particular areas.

It is important to maintain impetus when you are writing a book. One way of avoiding coming to a stop as you run out of steam is to take a break by visiting another section of text. Whether you take a holiday from the problem for a few minutes or for a few days, switching tracks and undertaking some work on another section for a while can help you to avoid losing momentum. Indeed, as you progress with your writing, you may find that you even develop a preference for working on several chapters at once, moving between them as you feel inspired to do so. One advantage of this is that working on chapters in parallel rather than in series can make it more likely that you will be able to reread what you have written with fresh eyes, noticing places where it would benefit from being extended, or recast. So, try if you can (some people cannot) to give yourself permission to work on several aspects or areas of your text at the same time, because the best way to deal with ideas or work you want to include, that emerge as you are writing, is usually to record them in an ongoing draft.

You will probably find at times that some text on which you are working might fit in better elsewhere. When you do, you should take the opportunity to explore the alternatives in order to decide which will best allow the flow of your ideas and the development of your argument. You may find it useful to make notes about what you are doing, or to create a new file into which you copy the relevant sections for the purpose of trying out alternative versions. This way you preserve your original work as it was, until you have decided how best to say what you want to say.

You may also want to maintain a record of ideas that come to mind as you are writing but which have not yet told you where they belong. It is also a good idea to maintain a separate record of 'things to do'; this might include references you have to check; ideas you want to think about further; diagrams you want to play with; paragraphs you want to develop; sections of your text that you have to write; or any other task from which you want to hide, for the moment. It is also worth establishing a box file in which you gather together annotated copies of relevant literature to which you will want to refer at some point. In doing so you should make sure that you maintain full bibliographical records of the sources from which you gleaned them.

Developing the text of an edited book: the editor's role

Editors vary in the extent to which they act in a 'hands on' way, becoming involved in the development of individual chapters. If you are planning an edited book, you should therefore ask yourself the question, 'What kind of editor do I want to be?'

If you want to edit a really strong book it is essential to make sure that you identify individuals who will treat the project seriously and who really are in a position to make a strong contribution. Beware of the dangers of inviting well-known contributors for whom your project may be a low priority, and who might cause you trouble by acting the prima donna as you try to meet deadlines, or by just recycling for you material everyone has seen before.

Having selected your team, you have to decide whether simply to let them get on with it, trusting in both their judgement and their commitment to producing a good product, or to walk with them along the path from a chapter outline to a completed text that makes a significant contribution to the book as a whole. Whatever you decide, it is best to be absolutely clear at the beginning of the project what you expect of your contributors. If all you are interested in receiving from them is a product that they consider finished, provided you get it by an agreed date, tell them so. If, on the other hand, what you want of them is willingness to work with you in ensuring that their chapter adds to the overall coherence of the book, you should tell them this at the outset. In order to do so, you might also want to let them know that you will keep them informed about what other contributors are saying in their chapters, sending them copies as necessary, to allow them to make appropriate cross-references. You should also be clear about whether you expect to work with them on successive drafts, offering advice about further development.

While it might be thought that inexperienced authors are more likely to appreciate support in their writing than experienced authors, we have found that the reverse is often true. Fledgling authors, we find, are more likely to take offence at having errors pointed out and to find it more difficult to accept advice, than authors with strong records of publication. Early in his career as an editor of academic books, Gavin well remembers receiving a delightful letter from a very senior, influential academic, Rom Harré, in which Gavin and his co-editor were thanked in the most gracious way for their help in making his contribution to the book clearer. His letter arrived on the same day as an irate letter from an inexperienced contributor to the same book, expressing disbelief in the fact that he was being told that some aspects of his text were less clear than they might be.

Most importantly, perhaps, if you intend to take it upon yourself to decide what the final version of your contributors' texts should look like, by 'correcting' it, you should let them know this. Many authors would baulk at the idea that another person should make such decisions on their behalf, though strangely enough, some editors seem to think it is perfectly acceptable to rework other people's text. In our view this is bad manners. Some contributors will be grateful if they know what you are doing, but it will not endear you to others.

Stage 7: Submitting your manuscript to the publisher

When you think that your text is more or less complete you should read it carefully, making sure that it has as few mistakes in punctuation, spelling and grammar as possible. You should also run your text past a spellchecker, while remaining aware of the cautionary note about such devices that we shared in Chapter 4.

Once you are satisfied that your text is as good as you can make it, you should go through it carefully ensuring that it meets the requirements for manuscripts laid down by your publisher, before submitting it to your commissioning editor. Nowadays many publishers will want you to submit your manuscript both electronically (on disk, CD-ROM or, increasingly, as an e-mail attachment) and on paper (usually two copies), although this is one area where the technology is changing as we speak.

Be aware that no matter what your text looks like when you submit it, your publisher will want to modify it to accord with their house style, and so there is usually little point in trying to make your manuscript look pretty just for the sake of it. The crucial point is to let them have as clear and clean a piece of work as possible in order to maximize your chances both of its being accepted and of your saving time, effort and angst in revising what the publisher proposes to print.

Most publishers will lay down strict expectations about how they want your text to look when they receive it from you. There is considerable variety in the level of detail that is included in publishers' guidance or instructions for authors. While some will require little more than that you should provide a double-spaced manuscript, others will specify the font size and width of margins that you should use, the quality of paper on which you should print your manuscript, and go into some detail about, for example, how you should indicate levels of subheading, whether and how you should use abbreviations, how to indicate foreign words, and whether you should use roman numerals for numbered lists

Most publishers will want you to use as simple a layout for your text as possible, ensuring that you are consistent in the spaces you leave between paragraphs and after subheadings, and in the ways you deal with quoted

Pre-submission checklist for authors and editors

- Is your manuscript double-spaced (not right justified, i.e. 'ragged right')?
- Are the pages numbered?
- Does your manuscript have generous margins all round?
- Have you included a complete and accurate list of contents as you would wish them to appear in the book?
- Have you clearly indicated the level of all headings and subheadings?
- Have you provided all necessary artwork, including figures and tables, along with captions?
- Have you included a title page showing the book's full title?
- Have you included full bibliographical references for all sources, and made sure that all sources cited in the text appear in the reference list and vice versa?
- Have you obtained all necessary permissions to reproduce previously published material, including text and artwork? Are you sending a copy with your manuscript?
- Have you ensured that any acknowledgements to previously published work are correct and complete?
- If your book is an edited one, have you provided a list of contributors, with brief biographical details?
- Have you prepared two identical copies of your manuscript and an identical disk copy?
- Have you ensured that the electronic copy you have retained for your records is identical to the copies you are submitting?
- Are you sure that the disk copy and both hard copies of your manuscript are identical?

material; usually you will be asked to separate quotations of more than 40 or fifty words from the rest of the text, indenting them from the left margin. One common requirement is that you should leave the text unjustified on the right side of the page, although this is not as widespread as it was a couple of years ago. This makes their job easier when it comes to translating your text into the software they use for the production of the text in proof form.

As part of the package of advice that is included in the guidance they provide authors, your publisher may have provided a checklist to use in ensuring that, once submitted, your manuscript will have the smoothest journey possible through the publication process. Before submitting your manuscript, the last thing you should do is to check it against this list. It will probably contain most of the items listed in the box on page 181, and perhaps several more.

Stage 8: Responding to copy editor's queries and suggestions

Some time after submitting your manuscript to your publisher (probably between three and six months), it will be returned to you by a copy editor who will have gone through your manuscript with a fine-toothed comb. His role is to help you to ensure, as far as he can, that your text makes sense and does not contain significant errors in grammar, punctuation or spelling. He will also have considered whether it is as well structured as it might be, checking, for example, that headings and subheadings are consistent and helpful. Of course, there is some room for disagreement about all of these things.

Publishers employ copy editors because they want to ensure that the books they publish not only have some literary merit but are also free from mistakes. No doubt you want to do that too, and so you should welcome the fact that the publisher is willing to part with money to hire a copy editor to help you, even if their main intention in doing so is to avoid the possibility of looking incompetent if they publish a book full of glaring errors. Sometimes, unfortunately, a copy editor will spot 'mistakes' where you believe there are none – because, for example, he has strongly held beliefs about some aspects of punctuation that contradict your own. In such circumstances it is very easy to become upset by what copy editors do, but by and large it is best to try to stay calm and to look for a way through that does not involve irate phone calls and e-mails. While politely pointing out what they have done, it is usually helpful in such circumstances if you try to persuade yourself to live with at least some of the copy editor's decisions, even if you disagree with them. Unfortunately, however, rather than mere disagreements between you, you may well discover that the copy editor has been inconsistent in some of the changes he suggests. For example, you might meet, as we have, with a copy editor who objects to a form of punctuation that you favour, and assiduously changes it for page after page at the beginning of your book, but then just as assiduously begins to insert it later in the text, in places where you would not have used it.

You might even be unfortunate enough to come across a copy editor who tries to tell you how to write your text. We have come across exactly this problem. For example, Gavin and his friend Denis Rowley once had such a bad time with a copy editor over her view of the style in which they had written a book that there was, for a time, a distinct possibility that the book would not happen. Certainly it could not have been published in the state into which it had been rendered by the copy editor's interference. The worst aspect of this situation was that rather than returning the 'marked up' manuscript with suggestions in order to allow for negotiation about any contested points, the copy editor in question had suggested going directly to proofs, because there were so few such points and they were so trivial, as not to be worth discussing. In reality, it turned out that her copy editing was in many places a rewriting of the text, rendering it into a much more academic style than the storytelling way in which it had been conceived and written. She had assumed that the book had been written in the narrative style because the authors were incapable of adopting a more formal, pseudo-academic prose style of the kind that she then tried to impose. In this instance, the publisher tried at first to stand firm, refusing to change the book back to the style the authors had chosen to adopt, because it seemed appropriate. However, after considerable discussion, the publisher's representative conceded and the book reverted to its original style, despite the fact that this involved considerable new typesetting.

If you are editing a book, the comments you receive from copy editors may relate not only to those parts of the book that you have written yourself, but also to those written by other contributors. In some cases the contributors will receive their own copy editing comments directly. You need to decide how much to involve the contributors and how much responsibility to take yourself. Your decision about this will depend on your relationships with the contributors, the nature of the book and the time available, but the more you allow individual contributors to respond to comments about their work the happier they are likely to be unless the modifications are so minimal that they find it annoying to have to approve them.

Stage 9: Correcting proofs and providing an index

The final stage in preparing your text will come some months later, perhaps as many as six or eight, when you are asked to check the 'page proofs' of your book. These will be sent to you by your publisher, once they have achieved a version that is as close to what they wish to print as possible. Proofs represent the first attempt to set out your book in the way it will appear in the finished product, including all the elements of layout – headings, fonts, tables, diagrams and so on. At this stage you have two main tasks to undertake, whether you are the author or the editor of the book: correcting the proofs and providing an index.

Your tasks as a proofreader

The first and probably the most important task is to make sure that the text as it appears in the proofs is an accurate representation of the text that was agreed between you and the copy editor, incorporating all the changes you negotiated. The second task when you are proofreading is to look critically at the general appearance of the text to see whether it has been set out in a way that helps readers to grasp your meaning. It is not, at this stage, usually possible to make any significant changes to the text, though changing the odd word here and there might be permitted – if, for example, you suddenly spot an error that neither you nor the copy editor picked up earlier. However, it will often be possible to have some influence over the general appearance of the pages if decisions that have been made about the run-on of text across pages make for ugliness or awkward textual jumps. For example, if a page break means that a list utilizing bullet points was introduced by a colon at the bottom of a page, while the bulleted list appeared at the top of the next page, a simple layout change would make this both visually more pleasing and easier to follow.

Proofs may be sent to you in two forms – either as paper copies, or in the form of a computer file that cannot be directly edited. Increasingly this is in the form of a pdf file produced using Adobe Acrobat software. This software allows the creation of files that have an embedded control so that only the originator of the file can modify it, which means that when you receive it from the publisher you cannot start fiddling with it. In either case, the publisher will want you to read the proofs carefully, and to indicate any corrections you would like to see, on a printed copy, often using a special system of notation (see box below).

Examples of proofreading notation

No.	Instruction	Textual mark	Marginal mark	Notes
B5	Wrong font. Replace by character(s) of correct font	Circle character(s) to be changed	⊗	P Use to indicate wrong typeface or size
B6	Change damaged character(s) or remove extraneous marks	Circle character(s) to be changed or mark(s) to be removed	✕	P
B7	Set in or change to italic	_____ under character(s) to be set or changed	↙	M P Where space does not permit textual marks, or for clarity, circle the affected area instead

It is important to realize that at this stage in the process, publishers are looking for corrections to the work they have done in typesetting, rather than corrections to what you have written. Generally speaking they will, however, accommodate some changes to what you wrote, if it makes a significant difference to how your text communicates what you wanted to say; but they will be unhappy if you try to make anything that could be considered a major change, and may make a charge against your future royalties if you try to insist that they do so.

Creating an index

The stage at which you are asked to correct proofs is also the one at which you will be given the opportunity to create an index for your book. Though you may have begun preparatory work for your index much earlier by compiling a list of key concepts that you want to include, this is the first stage at which you will have the opportunity to give page numbers to entries that match up as nearly as possible with the page numbers that will appear in the published version. You may be able to make a start on an index by drawing the words from the index to a book that covers a similar topic. Essentially the creation of an index involves the attempt to become intimately familiar with the conceptual and intellectual landscape your book covers, in a way that is akin to the world of a map-maker, by reading through your text over and over again.

Constructing an index

Constructing an index involves several steps:

1   Read through the book several times rather quickly – scanning each page in turn, listing the important words and concepts that appear on each page.

2   Having created a list of important words and concepts, go back through the book several times, as far as possible noting every significant occurrence of each listed item.

3   Ensure that where an idea appears twice in different forms, the page numbers agree – for example, if you had 'language, plain' and 'plain language', or 'Jackson, the cat' and 'cat, Jackson the'.

In constructing your index, you will probably have some difficulty in deciding which concepts are the most important, especially if some appear so frequently that it seems that almost every page will be listed. You might also find it hard to decide whether to list every appearance of a word or concept, or only those where something significant is said. Our view is that since the point of an index is to facilitate readers in using your book, it is best only to include significant uses of the selected concepts.

Some authors relinquish responsibility for the creation of the index, allowing the publisher to arrange for someone else to prepare the index for them, at a cost that will be deducted from their royalties (usually a few hundred pounds). Gavin's view is that since the index is an integral part of the book, it is best created by the authors, if it is at all possible for them to do so. David believes there is a real professional skill in producing an index and has always got the publisher to do so (except for once when he employed his daughter). You can make your own choice.

The journey from idea to index can be a rollercoaster with excitements and despair dotted along the way. It helps to have some sort of road for this journey, or, to change the metaphor, a clear idea of the stages the developing book will go through. Figure 13.1 is a simplified summary of this life history.

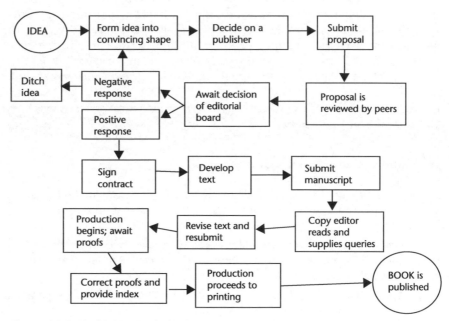

Figure 13.1 The life history of a book

14   Changing media

Consistency and change • The way ahead • The
importance of quality • Dumbing down and the
mass media

Consistency and change

The changes in the publishing world and the technologies that support getting
into print have been enormous even during the (rather long) period that we
have been writing this book. There also seems to be no let up in the pace of
change. It might therefore seem foolhardy to make any predictions about
how the future of academic publishing will unfold. However, as social scientists, perhaps we might be permitted a little reflection on some of the inherent
stabilities in becoming an author and some thoughts on what the future is
most likely to hold.

The book as the primary vehicle for the mass distribution of the printed
word is well over five hundred years old, and despite frequent claims that it is
dying, there is ample evidence that the opposite is true. Indeed, despite the
recent popularity of the idea that the communication of ideas in printed form
is in terminal decline, the uses of print are, if anything, increasing. Not only
that, but the number of paper-based academic book titles published each year

does not seem to be declining and the number of new journals started each year certainly outweighs the number that cease publication. We are therefore confident that the written word will continue to be a dominant form for scholarly and professional communication long into the future.

The rise in computer-based technology – especially the internet and World Wide Web – has meant an explosion of new ways of communicating ideas that would once have been printed and circulated on paper. Publishing in this way is much faster than it was possible to publish using paper-based technology. For example, you can now get the latest sports reports 'texted' to you over a mobile phone; you can buy books in electronic form over the internet; you can send large chunks of text around the world at close to the speed of light (if the system is working!), and you can publish your meandering thoughts on the World Wide Web in the form of a 'blog' that is instantly available to millions of people. The ready availability of new technologies, combined with the pressures on education and scholarship, has resulted in these active and interactive forms of communication becoming a more significant part of research and training in our universities. But neither these changes nor any of the other linked developments decreases our use of the written word. Rather, they extend the uses of print by setting it in another medium.

Late twentieth and early twenty-first century technologies have not undermined the centrality of print in academic communication; they have merely assimilated it. Print allows the presentation of rich ideas in a form that can capture all the subtleties an author wishes to communicate if she is skilled enough as a writer, and allows careful study of those ideas over and over again. Not only that, but print, whether it is in paper or electronic form, can survive long after its author, allowing future generations easy access to ideas, even if they need further contextual information to grasp nuances of intended meaning.

The medium in which print is presented and stored has some practical significance, in that the requirements for the long-term health of a cellulose-based material, be it papyrus or paper, are quite different from, for example, those for a silicon-derived medium such as a computer chip. It can also make some difference to the relationship between the reader and the material with which he is working. Think, for example, how different is reading a first draft of something you have written on screen, from reading it on paper. However, the medium in which the ideas an author has rendered into print are stored does not profoundly change the fundamental relationship between the author and the reader.

The way ahead

The changes that are occurring in publication in the computer age may be loosely characterized as 'democratization'. Many aspects of the publishing process, which in the past would have required specialist skills that were the monopoly of particular trades, are now open to anyone who can master the computer software – from the ability to create professional-level illustrations, through to the ability to publish material directly to a mass market. In the past, publishing your own book, like issuing your own musical recording, or creating your own photographic illustrations, required considerable financial outlay and a great deal of hands-on technical knowledge. Today, we can sit in front of computers at opposite ends of the planet and discuss which font to use for our draft manuscript. These new illustrations for example – and at the touch of a button we can change the appearance of its pages.

More importantly, using the right software it is possible to produce pages ready for printing and binding that are every bit as good as those produced by commercial publishers. And the whole process can be achieved without the intrusion of any publisher, printer, typographic artist or typesetter. This is very different from the somewhat amateurish 'camera-ready' texts that were sometimes produced, even in the relatively recent past. The ready availability of more sophisticated publishing software by which professional-quality copy can be produced now makes it possible for anyone to publish their own paper-based materials, while the internet makes it possible for university departments, and for individuals, to publish electronically or to market home-grown paper-based materials. It also makes it a relatively simple business for academics to publish books in a downloadable form.

Nowadays you can use the internet to access almost anything, including the published daily diaries of people anywhere in the world, and newspapers produced by local groups on other continents. More relevantly, given our focus in this book, you can read the lecture notes of many university teachers across many countries on their open websites. Considered from the point of view of those whose motivation is simply to find a way of making what they think available to a mass audience, this ready availability of the means of publishing 'academic material' for all, can seem like a heaven-sent gift. However, it is the source of real problems. For one thing it assumes that since people will read and study anything that is available without concern for its quality, it is worth making almost anything available to them. As a result of the growth of independent publishing, one vision of the way ahead for academic publishing foresees the gradual demise of formal, professional outlets publishing in either paper or electronic forms. In this vision, becoming an academic author would merely involve mastering the appropriate computer-based technologies and developing the will to publish on the World Wide Web. Without doubt this practice is developing fast.

A rather different vision is of a future in which the internet moves out of its initial anarchic stage and slowly gets absorbed into the systems that have controlled the quality of publications since the earliest days of the printed word. In this vision, open publications will continue unmanaged on the internet as now, so that there is huge increase in the amount of rubbish that is available in electronic form. However, people who have a regard for the truth and for high intellectual and professional standards, including the academics, will be increasingly vocal about the need for quality assurance processes of the kind that is currently provided by experienced editors and reviewers. In the academic community, the flourishing of peer-reviewed internet journals that function very much like paper-based ones is one indication of the shape of things to come.

Increasingly, as readers, we will download material for ourselves and carry it about in electronic formats. There may be more illustrations, including full-colour photographs, within the printed material than in the past, but what we read will still be remarkably close in form to the books that Gutenberg and Caxton first produced half a millennium ago. As computer-based print becomes more important for academics, more and more scholarly material will become available both formally, through reviewed journals, and informally, via university websites on which research groups and individuals may publish their work. Against this increased freedom and access to vast quantities of material there will be an even greater need to make choices and to search for material of value rather than just taking what happens to be available. It will thus be important that reliable selection processes are used to guarantee the quality of material that is published on such sites.

What this means is that many of the issues we have been discussing throughout earlier chapters will remain important beyond the foreseeable future. There will be changes in emphasis from what was regarded as appropriate for academic writing in the past, and text will be published via an increasing array of media. Yet all these changes are literally superficial, about how the material looks and the surfaces on which the words are presented, not about the underlying process of communicating through text and illustrations. Despite changes in the forms in which text will be accessed and presented there will still be a central need for authors to be able to communicate with their readers. Skills in organizing text in a coherent, logical and convincing manner will still be paramount to publishing work of quality. Indeed, against the backdrop of the plethora of textual material available, mastery of writing and strong validation of your trustworthiness as a scholar are likely to be even more important if you are to be not only heard, but heeded.

The importance of quality

Technological developments are increasing the standards expected of any published product. This means that just as academic authors in the past few years have had to be able to use, at least at the elementary level, the wonders of the word-processor, in the future they will have to go further and master their evolving add-ons. They will need to understand the sorts of subtleties that came in the past with secretarial training such as the organization of complex tables, columns, exotic fonts and formatting instructions. One pitfall will be that just as Jane Austen may have got distracted by deciding which quill pen to select before she started writing, so future authors will be able to delay the moment before they fill the blank page by pondering which of the formats on offer they should select or whether they should just go with the default provided.

Notwithstanding the many complications that the new opportunities provide, the easy availability of these increased skills is already being reflected by much of my own intellectual culture being produced to a very high presentational standard. You can find beautifully produced websites, or be given copies of elegantly laid-out reports that contain complete dross. In the past, publishers and printers were less likely to invest in poor work. This meant the effort put into the production of the text did reflect, at least to a limited degree, the inherent quality of the material. Nowadays many academics can produce stylish-looking, apparently polished publications. So even if your work is of outstanding intellectual significance, unless it is able to vie for attention in how it is presented with comparatively mediocre material, it may not get the notice it deserves.

One important development that computers facilitate is the inclusion of illustrations of many different forms, whether it is graphs or tables, drawings or photographs, charts or flow diagrams. It therefore seems likely that all forms of visual representation will be more widely employed as people gain real control of graphics software, digital photography and the various drawing and data visualization packages that are increasingly available. The integration of text and visualizations requires skills that have not been so prevalent in the past. So although the written word will still be supreme, scholars in the future will use the opportunities provided by the new, ever easier to use software, to illustrate their words in many different ways.

As Marshall McLuhan so famously indicated in the 1960s by his oft quoted slogan 'The Medium is the Message', the way in which media are used is becoming ever more part of how the quality of work is evaluated. McLuhan (1964) was drawing attention to the evolving broadcast media, but his arguments apply just as readily to the internet and the developments in multimedia presentations. It is already the case that many reports are produced not as conventional written documents, but as PowerPoint, interactive graphic displays. How long will it be before we expect any argument to be supported by a musical soundtrack, or by moving cartoon images?

In an age where the easiest way for me to find out about McLuhan, even if just to check the spelling of his surname, is by using an internet search engine, and this takes us to 83,400 locations, which the search engine boasts took only 0.22 seconds, then the choice of which of those sites I may follow up is bound to be influenced by how easy it is to access any site and how easy it is to read and make sense of the material when I get to that site. The ease of access does not, of course, necessarily guarantee the intellectual probity or trustworthiness of the source. But with such a plethora of material available there will be a tendency for some to equate slick use of the medium with scholarship. In our opinion, anyone who ignores this tendency runs the risk of being trampled in the rush to the latest glitzy website, or full-colour, photograph-filled report. The battle for attention from potential readers only increases with the growth in availability of written material.

Dumbing down and the mass media

A rather more optimistic possibility of the consequences of the democratization of publishing is that a wider variety of people will be reading and becoming authors than was the case in even the recent past. This will mean that more people of less knowledge and ability will seek and access published material. There is considerable anecdotal evidence that 'research' on the web is certainly now a hobby for lots of relatively uneducated people. The ease of access via the internet to books and reports on everything from how to find your ancestors to developments in zoology, by way of gardening and cooking recipes and so very much more, must mean that people are exploring ideas and seeking information in a way that they never would have if it had required a trip to a somewhat imposing and hushed library or the actual purchase of a book. For scholars and other professionals this provides an increased opportunity to reach out to groups that would not in the past have thought of reading their material – but only if authors are prepared to write in ways that this different readership can understand.

One example of this, of which David has direct experience, is the way in which his university website (www.i-psy.com), which was originally set up for communication with colleagues researching in related areas, is now being used by sixth-formers, journalists and many other groups without detailed specialist knowledge. There is no requirement from those non-specialist groups that the website should be especially simplified for them, but if, in effect, they are looking over his shoulder, then there is an implicit pressure to present the material in a way that allows them to make sense of what they read. This pressure is different from writing for one's peers because so much less can be assumed of their background knowledge or intellectual skills.

Certainly many research groups and universities around the world are now including such considerations in how they organize and present the material they publish on their websites. As a consequence, there may be a temptation just to oversimplify and even distort material so that it will be attractive to a mass audience. But it is not essential to make material less intelligent just because it may be read by a less well-informed and less sophisticated readership. As ever, the choice will have to be made between intellectually demanding material that reaches a limited audience who are sophisticated in a given area, or more generally accessible writing that does not assume very much about the background of the readership, with the various possibilities between the two ends of this continuum. As an author, this is a choice you have to make all the time, but as the options increase so will the challenge of which option to select. A few academics do manage to write for a wide spectrum of readers, either in one extremely well-written document or in a variety of different documents written in different ways for different people, but most stick to what they know and feel able to do. Which of the many options you choose to follow in any piece of academic writing for publication will depend on your

Postscript: Becoming an academic author

Membership of any profession carries with it a responsibility to contribute to that profession's development. That is why we believe that integral to the role of every professional is the duty to share their experience and their thinking with colleagues, thus adding to the running stream of knowledge and understanding that helps to maintain professional health and growth. One way in which they can do this is by writing about their work. Despite this, we recognize that even in universities, where along with research, publication is held to be so important, some people never publish, and many publish a lot less than they could. One possible explanation for this state of affairs relates to the fact that most academics are inadequately prepared for this aspect of academic life.

For most university teachers and researchers, undertaking a postgraduate research degree was the apprenticeship by which they prepared for their academic career. Given this, and given that publication is such a central plank of academic life, the fact that few postgraduates finish their studies ready to make published contributions to their field of enquiry is a clear indication of failure in the training they have received. After all, if a plumber or surgeon was incapable of carrying out surgery – whether on a hot water system or a human body – we would seriously question whether her training had been appropriate.

Admitting this failure in the ways we train tomorrow's university teachers and researchers, and other academically focused professionals would, we suggest, inevitably lead to serious rethinking of the requirements of most postgraduate degrees, to ensure that they included training in all aspects of writing for publication. It might also lead to rethinking of the extent to which a monolithic thesis written for no other purpose than to be examined, is the most cost effective and beneficial way of testing whether postgraduate candidates have attained the appropriate academic level. Such rethinking might lead, for example, to consideration being given to the possibility that a better test might be to require doctoral students to present their research and original thinking in the form of published work, whether as a book or as a series of articles. Such a route has always been available in many universities and the DSc – the highest degree – is normally only available by submitting published works for examination. The increasing recognition of the value of the route to PhD via publication may well be an indication that the university community as a whole is moving towards this view.

As a postgraduate you are expected to absorb the skills you need in order to communicate with other academics, at your supervisors' knee, often with very little direct help to develop as a writer, other than odd remarks on successive drafts of a thesis, and with little help in coming to understand the mysteries of academic and professional publishing. The result is that those who successfully complete research degrees often have only a rudimentary understanding of the requirements of writing for publication. Something similar is true of professionals in, say, medicine and clinical or educational psychology, who may have to publish in academic and professional journals in order to gain career advancement, but who will rarely have been taught anything about the processes of either writing or publishing, which they seem to have to absorb from their seniors as if by osmosis.

Most academic and professional authors are bad at sharing their experience and accumulated wisdom with one another, and as a result, most academics will have to struggle to find their way in the world of publishing, without support, unless they are wise enough – and courageous enough – to elicit help from trustworthy colleagues. Often the first time that fledgling authors will benefit from the hands-on, 'let's have a look at what you've written' kind of assistance from which all authors could benefit, is when they receive their first set of detailed comments from journal referees who have reviewed an article.

Most academics fall short of perfection in their writing habits, and in the ways they approach the tasks involved in getting published. However, provided that they find the time to write, ensure that what they write is as clear as it can be, and make wise decisions about where and when to publish it, success as an academic author is open to all. Of course, luck plays a part here, as it does in all aspects of professional development. Meeting an influential and supportive senior colleague at the right point in your career can have a profound effect, and can make the difference between rapid development towards glittering success as an author and a life in which publication plays no part.

Regardless of whether you have supportive senior colleagues who will do what they can to assist you, we hope that the advice we have offered throughout *Becoming an Author* will help you to establish a successful career as an academic author. We want to end by summarizing some of this advice in the form of ten fundamental principles or commandments for authors.

Ten commandments for successful academic authors

1. Do not wait for the mood or time to be right for you to write

Write whenever there is time, but make time to write, no matter how short. Do not assume that colleagues who publish prolifically necessarily have fewer teaching and administrative duties than you. Make the most of whatever time you have, or can make, for writing – be it a sabbatical year (unlikely) or five minutes between lectures and meetings. If you hold it (and many people do), give up the untenable belief that in order to get down to writing you need to have lots of free time – say a free week every so often, or even a free day once a fortnight. You don't, and waiting until you have this much free time might mean you never get started.

2. Be clear about your central storyline

Whenever you write, think of your text as a story. Aim to engage and motivate your readers. What are the main episodes in your narrative? What is the best sequence in which to present them if your readers are to follow the plot? What did you do? Why did you do it? What was the result? Who, or what, is the hero in your story? Who, or what, the villain?

If you have any doubt about whether your story is clearly told, do not submit your text for publication. Make sure, before you submit your work to a journal or publishing house, that your arguments and ideas are as well stated as possible, and hence that your academic story is as clear, coherent and as interesting as you can make it.

3. Write 'one page at a time'

Doing so will help you to avoid becoming daunted by the apparent scale of your project. That page might contain the headings and subheadings that lay out the topics you are considering; it might hold your detailed notes for one section; or it might be a single page of text. Often the problem with writing one component is not that material itself, but how it fits into the larger picture. Curiously, focusing on one page at a time, rather than trying to think through what will be happening five pages on, is the best way of ensuring that you maintain a grasp of the whole of your text. As you write each page, you should keep asking yourself, 'Where does this fit into the bigger picture?', 'How can I write this page so that it connects to the rest of my text, and hence has maximum impact?'

4. Choose your words carefully and structure them well

Words are the tools by which you convey your meanings. Choose words that do the job of communicating clearly, not words that make you sound clever. Always remember that even if you have all the right words, if you fail to get them in the right order, no one will know what you are talking about, and all your efforts will have been wasted. Take care over structure – at the level of the sentence, the paragraph, the section. This applies to titles, headings and subheadings as much as it does to the body of text.

5. Take account of your audience

Successful authors write in a way that allows them to make a helpful relationship with their readers – one that will motivate their readers to work at understanding the text. Academics may aim to communicate simply and directly with their readers; or they may set out to frustrate them by withholding information that might render reading easier. Sometimes they might challenge them by presenting issues, dilemmas and puzzles. Whatever they do, however, successful authors will always remain aware of their audience, thinking of their needs, their experience and their motivation.

6. Aim to be your own most critical reader; act on advice you receive

One way of becoming clear about what you want to say, and perhaps even about what you think, is to write about it. Rereading what you have written can help you to attain clarity about what you think, and about what you want to say. Learn to read your work as if it was written by someone else; that way you will find it easier to decide how best to develop and improve it. This is easier if you leave some time between writing and rereading your text in order to develop it further, but you should try to reread whenever you can bring yourself to do so.

As often as you can, invite others to read and comment on your work. But only invite people that you can trust to be truthful, even if that means taking the risk that they might offend you. Always take their comments seriously, especially if they are having trouble following your line of argument. If they tell you that they cannot understand what you have written, put aside the assumption that they must be stupid or deranged; and do not fall out with them. By all means try to find out exactly what they are having difficulty with, but do so in order to work out how you can improve your text, not with the intention of proving that the problem in understanding lies with them.

Avoid inviting sycophants to comment on your work. They will not help you to write better, only to feel better.

7. Never submit a draft

It is likely that a draft will fail to get past the review process, in which case, not only will you have lost time on the publication merry-go-round, but you may also have got yourself noted as someone whose submits half-baked work that is not worthy of close reading. Worse than that, though, it might just slip through the editorial net and get into print with the result that you spend the rest of your academic career trying to live it down. Publication lasts. Do not publish in your youth what you may regret in your old age.

8. Choose your publishing outlet as you would a new car

Think of how it will suit your purposes. Will it be as responsive as you would wish? Will it do the job you want it to do? Carry out a benefit analysis. What do you stand to gain from publishing here rather than elsewhere, and at what cost to you in terms, for example, of time and perhaps compromise in what you want to say, or how you would ideally wish to say it? Has your choice of an outlet been influenced merely by the need to get from A to B in your career? Or has it been influenced by issues of self-presentation and status? Do you feel comfortable with your chosen outlet and think it suits your personality?

Remember that, just as most people expect and look for different things in the cars they drive at different periods in their life, so the expectations you have in terms of what you expect and hope to get from a publisher or academic journal will change as you progress on your academic career. For example, at the beginning of their publishing careers many authors will be happy to get a book into print with any publisher, but later they will probably prefer to publish with one of the market leaders in their field.

9. Remain aware of your ethical responsibilities as an author

Ethical issues surround academic publishing – from the wrong that one person does to others by plagiarizing their ideas, to the wrong that a publisher can do to an author by publishing a text that is not as strong as it might be, just because it is likely to make money. As well as responsibilities to their publishers, authors have responsibilities to anyone who has shared information that they use in their published writing. It may sound pompous to say so, but academic authors also have a responsibility to posterity. The only point of publishing as a scholar is to contribute to society, by setting down one's experiences, findings, ideas and arguments in a more or less permanent form. That is what distinguishes scholarly writing from many other forms of published output, including journalism, which often has an ephemeral quality. And it is why it is unethical to use the medium of academic publication in the knowledge that what you write is trivial and frivolous. Be a responsible and honourable author.

10. Keep umbrage at bay: be prepared for the long haul

Do not take umbrage and give up – either when journal reviewers misunderstand you, or when publishers turn down your book proposals. The publishing world is awash with accounts of significant work that was initially rejected. Do not be offended by such rejections, and do not let them put you off. Remember that most people who publish as academics experience rejection repeatedly, even those who seem to be most successful. Try instead to grow as a result of each knock back, by understanding the reasons for rejection, even if they seem silly. The Talmud contains a salutary, often quoted comment that could easily have been written for our purposes here. The rabbi asks: 'How will you recognize that a man is wise?' The answer is: 'Because he can learn even from fools.'

In *Becoming an Author* we set out to offer aspiring academic and professional authors some help on the journey to print. In discussing the development of academic style, we suggested that at the beginning of a career as a scholarly author it is a good idea to examine closely how others write, in order to determine what style and format are acceptable within your academic peer group. You might want to change the world, beginning with the discipline in which you are working, but in order to do so you first have to get a foot in the door. And so, at least at the beginning of your publishing career, you probably need to conform with the academic club that you aspire to join, and the easiest way to do that is to learn their rules and their preferences and act as if you are one of them. Once you have mastered their way of doing things, and established your acceptability, it is easier to push back the boundaries, in terms of both what and how you write. The important point is that any challenges that you make should still be related to the context that your readers understand. The breadth of academic and scientific audiences is so great that this is much less of a limitation than you may think. If you wish to challenge the fundamentals of any discipline, you will always find an audience, provided that you express yourself in ways to which that audience can relate.

Relating to your audience does not mean, though, that you will never challenge the weaknesses in the work of others just because they have authority. Nor does it mean that you will unquestioningly follow fashion without ever pricking the bubble of pomposity. We have also been at pains to show you that hiding the faults in your own work by florid writing will only provide short-lived success, if any at all. All authorship is a contribution to knowledge. In contributing it is inevitable that you will challenge what has gone before at least to some small degree. You will need the contained arrogance of all academic and professional authors. This is the belief that you are indeed helping to reveal and grasp the truth. You should therefore take heed of what Roger Bacon wrote over eight hundred years ago.

There are four chief obstacles in grasping truth, which hinder every man, however learned, and scarcely allow any one to win a clear title to learning, namely, submission to faulty and unworthy authority, influence of custom, popular prejudice, and concealment of our own ignorance accompanied by an ostentatious display of our knowledge.

(Roger Bacon, *Opus Majus*, 1266–67)

Bibliography and references

The following lists publications cited in the text and some useful resources indicated by an asterisk.

*American Psychological Association (2001) *Publication Manual of the American Psychological Association*, 5th edn. Washington, DC: American Psychological Association. (Also available are Mastering APA Style: Instructor's Resource Guide, Student's Workbook and Training Guide, and APA Style Helper 3.0fi on CD-ROM.)

Andreski, S. (1972) *Social Sciences as Sorcery*. London: Andre Deutsch.

Bender, M. (1974) Psychology: industry and/or scientific craft? *Bulletin of the British Psychological Society*, 27: 107–15.

Bold, C. (ed.) (2004) *Supporting Learning and Teaching*. London: David Fulton.

Bouckaert, B. and De Geest, G. (eds) (2000) *Encyclopedia of Law and Economics*. Cheltenham: Edward Elgar.

Bruner, K.F. (1942) Of psychological writing: being some valedictory remarks on style, *Journal of Abnormal and Social Psychology*, 37: 52–70.

*Butcher, J. (2002) *Copy-Editing: The Cambridge Handbook for Editors, Authors and Publishers*, 3rd edn. Cambridge: Cambridge University Press.

Byatt, A.S. (1990) *Possession*. London: Chatto & Windus.

Calvino, I. (1997) *Invisible Cities*, translated from the Italian by W. Weaver. London: Vintage.

Canter, D. (1995) *Criminal Shadows: Inside the Mind of the Serial Killer*. London: HarperCollins.

Chadwick, R. (ed.) (1997) *Encyclopaedia of Applied Ethics*. San Diego: Academic Press.

*Citation Indexing information is available through http://www.isinet.com/cit/

Curtis, P. (2004) Research funding system 'needs radical overhaul', MPs told, *The Guardian*, 19 May.

Darwin, C. (1859) *On the Origin of Species*. London: John Murray.

David, E. (1951) *French Country Cooking*. Harmondsworth: Penguin.

Dawkins, R. (1989) *The Selfish Gene*. Oxford: Oxford University Press.

*Day, A. (1996) *How To Get Research Published in Journals*. Aldershot: Gower.

de Cameron, N.S. (1989) Embryos again, *Ethics and Medicine*, 5(2): 17.

Dickson, E.J., Reader, C., Sweet, M., Walsh, J. and Wilson, M. (2004) Dawn of a new word order, *The Independent Review*, 4 November, pp. 2–3.

*Dummett, M. (1993) *Grammar and Style*. London: Duckworth.

Fairbairn, G.J. (1991) Enforced death: enforced life, *Journal of Medical Ethics*, 17(3): 144–50.

Fairbairn, G. (1995) *Contemplating Suicide: The Language and Ethics of Self Harm*. London: ⅼⅼⅼⅼⅼⅼⅼⅼⅼⅼ

*Fairbairn, G. and Fairbairn, S. (2001) *Reading at University: A Guide for Researchers*. Buckingham: Open University Press.

*Fairbairn, G. and Fairbairn, S. (2004) *Writing your Abstract: A Guide for Would-be Conference Presenters*. Salisbury: APS Books.

*Fairbairn, G. and Winch, C. (1996) *Reading, Writing and Reasoning: A Guide for Students*, 2nd edn. Buckingham: Open University Press.

Fortey, R. (1998) *Life: An Unauthorised Biography*. London: Flamingo Books.

Gratzer, W. (2000) *The Undergrowth of Science*. Oxford: Oxford University Press.

Greenfield, S. (2002) *The Private Life of the Brain*. Harmondsworth: Penguin.

Halliday, M.A.K. (1990) *Spoken and Written Language*. Oxford: Oxford University Press.

Harré, R. (1994) Some narrative conventions of scientific discourse, in C. Nash (ed.) *Narrative in Culture*. London: Routledge, pp. 81–101.

Hill, S. and Provost, F. (2004) The myth of the double-blind review? Author identification using only citations, *SIGGKDD Explorations*, 5(2): 179–84.

Hojat, M., Gonnella, L. and Caelleigh, A.S. (2003) Impartial judgment by the 'gatekeepers' of science: fallibility and accountability in the peer review process, *Advances in Health Sciences Education*, 8(1): 75–96.

Huff, D. (1954) *How to Lie with Statistics*. New York: W.W. Norton.

Huff, D. (1993) *How to Lie with Statistics*, with illustrations by Irving Geiss. New York: W.W. Norton.

Jones, G.E. (1995) *How to Lie with Charts*. San Francisco: Sybex.

Jones, S. (1999) *Almost Like a Whale: The Origin of Species updated*. New York: Doubleday.

*Lamott, A. (1995) *Bird by Bird: Some Instructions on Writing and Life*. New York: Anchor Books.

McLuhan, M. (1964) *Understanding Media: The Extensions of Man*. New York: McGraw-Hill.

*McInerney, D.M. (2001) *Publishing Your Psychology Research: A Guide to Writing for Journals in Psychology and Related Fields*. London: Sage.

*Nicol, A.A.M. and Pexman, P.M. (2003) *Displaying Your Findings: A Practical Guide for Creating Figures, Posters and Presentations*. New York: American Psychological Association.

Opthof, T., Coronel, R. and Janse, M.J. (2002) The significance of the peer review process against the background of bias: priority ratings of reviewers and editors and the prediction of citation, the role of geographical bias, *Cardiovascular Research*, 56: 339–46.

*Parody, A. (2004) *Eats, Shites and Leaves: Crap English and How To Use It*. London: Michael O'Mara Books.

*Partridge, E. (1991) *A Dictionary of Clichés*, 5th edn. London: Routledge.

Pax, S. (2004) *The Baghdad Blog*. London: Guardian Books.

*Peters, A.D. (1996) *How to Get Research Published in Journals*. Aldershot: Gower.

Peters, D.P. and Ceci, S.J. (1982) Peer-review practice of psychological journals: the fate of submitted articles, submitted again, *Behaviour and Brain Science*, 5: 1877–80.

Rawls, J. (1971) *A Theory of Justice*. Oxford: Oxford University Press.

Rees, M.J. (1999) *Just Six Numbers*. London: Wiedenfeld & Nicolson.

Russo, W. (1980) *A New Approach: Composing Music*. Chicago: University of Chicago Press.

*Sternberg R.J. (ed.) (2000) *Guide to Publishing in Psychology Journals*. Cambridge: Cambridge University Press.

Toulmin, S. (1958) *The Uses of Argument*. Cambridge: Cambridge University Press.

*Trask, R.L. (1997) *Penguin Guide to Publication*, Harmondsworth: Penguin.

*Tufte, E.R. (1983) *The Visual Display of Quantitative Information*. Cheshire, Conn.: Graphics Press.

*Tufte, E.R. (1990) *Envisioning Information*. Cheshire, Conn.: Graphics Press.

*Tufte, E.R. (1997) *Visual Explanations*. Cheshire, Conn.: Graphics Press.

*University of Texas, at http://www.lib.utexas.edu/subject/ss/publishing.html (a very good website dealing with citations and publishing resources).

*Wang, A.Y. (1989) *Author's Guide to Journals in the Behavioral Sciences*. London: Lawrence Erlbaum.

*Wellington, J. (2003) *Getting Published: A Guide for Lecturers and Researchers*. London: Routledge/Falmer.

*_Writers' and Artists' Yearbook 2005_. Foreword by Maeve Binchy. London: A & C Black.

Index

Related books from Open University Press
Purchase from www.openup.co.uk or order through your local bookseller

WRITING FOR ACADEMIC JOURNALS

Rowena Murray

Whether writing the first draft or the final draft, this book enables and inspires academics in developing their own writing strategies and goals.

Lorna Gillies, University of Leicester

Our experience is that Rowena's practical approach works for busy academic staff. Not only does it enable them to increase their publication output and meet deadlines, but it boosts enthusiasm for writing and stimulates creative thinking.

Kate Morss, Queen Margaret University College, Edinburgh

This approach provides scientists with a systematic step-by-step method of producing a paper for publication. The approach streamlines the process and provides strategies for overcoming barriers. Feedback from the professions using the approach was excellent.

Dr Mary Newton, Greater Glasgow Primary Care NHS Trust

This book unpacks the process of writing academic papers. It tells readers what good papers look like, and explains how they come to be written.

Busy academics must develop productive writing practices quickly. No one has time for trial and error. To pass external tests of research output we must write to a high standard while juggling other professional tasks. This may mean changing writing behaviours.

Writing for Academic Journals draws on current research and theory to provide new knowledge on writing across the disciplines. Drawing on her extensive experience of running writing workshops and working closely with academics on developing writing, Rowena Murray offers a host of practical tried and tested strategies for good academic writing.

This jargon free, user-friendly, practical and motivational book is essential for the desk of every academic, postgraduate student and researcher for whom publication is an indicator of the quality of their work and their ability.

Contents

256pp   0 335 21392 8 (Paperback)   0 335 21393 6 (Hardback)